THE NOVELS OF

# IVAN TURGENEV

# THE NOVELS OF
# IVAN TURGENEV

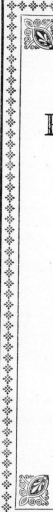

IVAN TURGENEV

★

# FATHERS AND CHILDREN

★

*Translated
from the Russian by*
CONSTANCE GARNETT

WILLIAM HEINEMANN LTD
MELBOURNE    LONDON    TORONTO

*First Published 1895*
*Reprinted 1899, 1901, 1903, 1905,*
*1906 (twice), 1910, 1913, 1915, 1916,*
*1917, 1919, 1920 (twice), 1951*

PRINTED IN GREAT BRITAIN
AT THE WINDMILL PRESS
KINGSWOOD, SURREY

# INTRODUCTION

WHILE *On the Eve* signalises the end of the Crimea epoch and the break-up of the crushing, overwhelming régime of Nicolas, *Fathers and Children* is a forecast of the new Liberal movement, which arose in the Russia of the sixties, and an analysis of the formidable type appearing on the political horizon—the Nihilist.

Turgenev was the first man to detect the existence of this new type, the Nihilist. His own account of his discovery gives us such an interesting glimpse of his method in creative work that we transcribe a passage from his paper on *Fathers and Children,* written at Baden in 1869:—

'It was in the month of August 1860, when I was taking sea baths at Ventnor, in the Isle of Wight, that the first idea of *Fathers and Children* came into my head; that novel, thanks to which the favourable opinion of the younger generation about me has come to an end. Many times I have heard and read in critical journals that I have only been elaborating an idea of my own. . . . For my part, I ought to confess that I never attempted to create a type without having, not an idea, but a living person, in whom the various elements were harmonised together, to work from. I have always needed some groundwork on which I could tread firmly. This was the case with *Fathers and Children*. At the foundation of the principal figure, Bazarov, was the personality of a young provincial doctor. He died not long before 1860. In that remarkable man was incarnated to my ideas the just rising element, which, still chaotic, afterwards received the title of Nihilism. The impression produced by this individual was very strong. At first I could not clearly define him to myself. But I strained my eyes and ears, watching everything surrounding me, anxious to trust simply in my own sensations. What confounded me was that I had met not a single idea or hint of what seemed appearing to me on all sides. And the doubt involuntarily suggested itself. . . .'

*Fathers and Children* was published in the spring of 1862 in Katkoff's paper, *The Russian Messenger,* the organ of 'the Younger Generation', and the stormy controversy that the novel immediately provoked was so bitter, deep, and lasting that the episode forms one of the most interesting chapters in literary history. Rarely has so great an artist so thoroughly drawn public attention to a scrutiny of the new ideas rising in its midst; rarely has so great an artist come into such violent collision with his own party thereby; never perhaps has there been so striking an illustration of the incapacity of the public, swayed by party passion, to understand a pure work of art. The effect of the publication was widespread excitement in both political camps. Everybody was, at the time, on the alert to see what would be the next move on the political board. The recent Emancipation of the Serfs was looked upon by young Russia as only a prelude to many democratic measures, while the Reactionists professed to see in that measure the ruin of the country and the beginning of the end. The fast increasing antipathy between the Old Order and the New, like a fire, required only a puff of wind to set it ablaze. And Bazarov's character and aims came as a godsend to the Reactionists, who hailed in it the portrait of the insidious revolutionary Ideas current in young Russia; and they hastened to crowd round Turgenev, ironically congratulating the former champion of Liberalism on his penetration and honesty in unmasking the Nihilist. But we will quote Turgenev's own words: —

'I will not enlarge on the effect produced by this novel. I will only say that everywhere the word Nihilist was caught up by a thousand tongues, and that on the day of the conflagration of the Apraksinsky shops, when I arrived in St. Petersburg, the first exclamation with which I was greeted was,

''Just see what your Nihilists are doing!'' . . . I experienced
a coldness approaching to indignation from people near and
sympathetic to me. I received congratulations, almost caresses,
from people of the opposite camp, from enemies. This confused me, wounded me; but my conscience did not reproach
me. I knew very well I had carried out honestly the type I
had sketched, carried it out not only without prejudice, but
positively with sympathy. . . . While some attack me for out-
raging the Younger Generation, and promise me, with a laugh
of contempt, to burn my photograph, others, on the contrary,
with indignation, reproach me for my servile cringing to the
younger generation. . . . ''You are grovelling at the feet of
Bazarov. You pretend to find fault with him, and you are
licking the dust at his feet,'' says one correspondent. Another
critic represented M. Katkoff and me as two conspirators,
''plotting in the solitude of our chamber our traps and slanders
against the forces of young Russia''. An effective picture! . . .
My critics called my work a pamphlet, and referred to my
wounded and irritated vanity. . . . But a shadow lay on my
name. I don't deceive myself. I know that shadow will
remain.'

Politics is a game where the mistakes and admissions of
your adversary are your own good character in Public
Opinion—a definition which goes far to account for the easy
predominance of the political sharper—and so Turgenev, the
great artist, he who, in creating Bazarov for an ungrateful
public, to use his own words, *simply did not know how to
work otherwise,* found to his cost. The Younger Generation,
irritated by the public capital made out of Bazarov and his
Nihilism by 'the Fathers', flew into the other extreme, and
refused to see in Bazarov anything other than a *caricature* of
itself. It denied Bazarov was of its number, or represented
its views in any way; and to this day surviving Nihilists will
demonstrate warmly that the creation of his sombre figure is
'a mistake from beginning to end.' The reason for this whole-
sale rejection of Bazarov is easy to account for; and Turgenev,
whose clear-sightedness about his works was unaffected either
by vanity, diffidence, or the ignorant onslaughts of the whole

tribe of minor critics, penetrates at once to the heart of the matter: —

'The whole ground of the misunderstanding lay in the fact that the type of Bazarov had not time to pass through the usual phases. At the very moment of his appearance the author attacked him. It was a new method as well as a new type I introduced—that of Realising instead of Idealising. . . . The reader is easily thrown into perplexity when the author does not show clear sympathy or antipathy to his own child. The reader readily gets angry. . . . After all, books exist to entertain.'

An excellent piece of analysis and a quiet piece of irony this! The character of Bazarov was in fact such an epitome of the depths of a great movement that the mass of common-place educated minds, the future tools of the movement, looked on it with alarm, dislike, and dread. The average man will only recognise his own qualities in his fellows, and endow a man with his own littlenesses. So Bazarov's depth excited the superficiality of the eternally omnipresent average mind. The Idealists in the Younger Generation were morally grieved to see that Bazarov was not wholly inspired by their dreams; he went deeper, and the average man received a shock of surprise that hurt his vanity. So the hue and cry was raised around Turgenev, and raised only too well. Bazarov is the most dominating of Turgenev's creations, yet it brought upon him secret distrust and calumny, undermined his influence with those he was with at heart, and went far to damage his position as the leading novelist of his day. The lesson is significant. No generation ever understands itself; its members welcome eagerly their portraits drawn by their friends, and the caricatures drawn of their adversaries; but to the new type no mercy is shown, and everybody hastens to misunderstand, to abuse, to destroy.

So widely indeed was Bazarov misunderstood that Turgenev once asserted, 'At this very moment there are only two people who have understood my intentions—Dostoievsky and Botkin.'

And Dostoievsky was of the opposite camp—a Slavophil.

## II

What, then, is Bazarov?

Time after time Turgenev took the opportunity, now in an article, now in a private or a public letter, to repel the attacks made upon his favourite character. Thus in a letter to a Russian lady,[1] he says—

'What, you too say that in drawing Bazarov I wished to make a caricature of the young generation. You repeat this— pardon my plain speaking—idiotic reproach. Bazarov, my favourite child, cn whose account I quarrelled with Katkoff; Bazarov, on whom I lavished all the colours at my disposal; Bazarov, this man of intellect, this hero, a caricature! But I see it is useless for me to protest.'

And in a letter addressed to the Russian students at Heidelberg, he reiterates:—

'*Flatter comme un caniche,* I did not wish; although in this way I could no doubt have all the young men at once at my side; but I was unwilling to buy popularity by concessions of this kind. It is better to lose the campaign (and I believe I have lost it) than win by this subterfuge. I dreamed of a sombre, savage, and great figure, only half emerged from barbarism, strong, *méchant,* and honest, and nevertheless doomed to perish because it is always in advance of the future. I dreamed of a strange parallel to Pugatchev. And my young contemporaries shake their heads and tell me,, "*Vous êtes foutu,* old fellow. You have insulted us. Your Arkady is far better. It's a pity you haven't worked him out a little more." There is nothing left for me but, in the words of the gipsy song, "to take off my hat with a very low bow".'

[1] *Souvenirs sur Tourguéneff,* 1887.

What, then, is Bazarov?

Various writers have agreed in seeing in him only 'criticism, pitiless, barren, and overwhelming analysis, and the spirit of absolute negation,' but this is an error. Representing the creed which has produced the militant type of Revolutionist in every capital of Europe, *he is the bare mind of Science first applied to Politics*. His own immediate origin is German Science interpreted by that spirit of logical intensity, Russian fanaticism, or devotion to the Idea, which is perhaps the distinguishing genius of the Slav. But he represents the roots of the modern Revolutionary movements in thought as well as in politics, rather than the branches springing from those roots. Inasmuch as the early work of the pure scientific spirit, knowing itself to be fettered by the superstitions, the confusions, the sentimentalities of the Past, was necessarily destructive, Bazarov's primary duty was to Destroy. In his essence, however, he stands for *the sceptical conscience of modern Science*. His watchword is *Reality*, and not Negation, as everybody in pious horror hastened to assert. Turgenev, whose first and last advice to young writers was, 'You need truth, remorseless truth, as regards your own sensations,' was indeed moved to declare, 'Except Bazarov's views on Art, I share almost all his convictions.' The crude materialism of the sixties was not the basis of the scientific spirit, it was merely its passing expression; and the early Nihilists who denounced Art, the Family, and Social Institutions were simply freeing themselves from traditions preparatory to a struggle that was inevitable. Again, though Bazarov is a Democrat, perhaps his kinship with the people is best proved by the contempt he feels for them. He stands forward essentially as an Individual, with the 'isms' that can aid him, mere tools in his hand; Socialist, Communist, or Individualist, in his necessary phases he fought this century against the tyranny of centralised Governments, and next century he will be fighting against the stupid tyranny of the Mass. Looking at Bazarov, however, as a type that has played its part and vanished with its generation, as a man he is a new departure in history. His appearance marks the dividing line between two religions, that of the Past—Faith, and that growing religion of to-day—Science. His is the duty of breaking away from all things that men called Sacred, and his savage egoism is essential to that duty. He is subject to neither Custom nor Law. He is his own law, and is occupied simply with the fact he is studying. He has thrown aside the ties of love and duty that cripple the advance of the strongest men. He typifies Mind grappling with Nature, seeking out her inexorable laws, Mind in pure devotion to the What Is, in startling contrast to the minds that follow their self-created kingdom of What Appears, and Ought to Be. He is therefore a foe to the poetry and art that help to increase Nature's glamour over man by alluring him to yield to her; for Bazarov's great aim is to see Nature at work behind the countless veils of illusions and ideals, and all the special functions of belief which she develops in the minds of the masses to get them unquestioning to do her bidding. Finally, Bazarov, in whom the comfortable compromising English mind sees only a man of bad form, bad taste, bad manners, and overwhelming conceit—finally, Bazarov stands for Humanity awakened from century-old superstitions, and the long dragging oppressive dream of tradition. Naked he stands under a deaf, indifferent sky, but he feels and knows that he has the strong brown earth beneath his feet.

This type, though it has developed into a network of special branches to-day, it is not difficult for us to trace as it has appeared and disappeared in the stormy periods of the last thirty years. Probably the genius and energy of the type was chiefly devoted to positive Science, and not to Politics; but it is sufficient to glance at the Revolutionary History, in theory and action, of the Continent to see that every movement was inspired by the ideas of the Bazarovs, though led by a variety of leaders. Just as the popular movements for Liberty fifty years earlier found sentimental and *romantic* expression in Byronism, so the popular movements of our time have been realistic in idea, and have looked to Science for their justification. Proudhon, Bakunin, Karl Marx, the Internationals, the Russian Terrorists, the Communists, all have a certain relation to Bazarov, but his nearest kinsmen in these and other movements we believe have worked, and have remained, obscure. It was a stroke of genius on Turgenev's part to make Bazarov die on the threshold unrecognised. He is Aggression, destroyed in his destroying. And there are many reasons in life for the Bazarovs remaining obscure. For one thing, their few disciples, the Arkadys, do not understand them; for another, the whole swarm of little interested persons who make up a movement are more or less engaged in personal interests, and they rarely take for a leader a man who works for his own set of Truths, scornful of all cliques, penalties, and rewards. Necessarily, too, the Bazarovs work alone, and are given the most dangerous tasks to accomplish unaided. Further, they are men whose brutal and breaking force attracts ten men where it repels a thousand. The average man is too afraid of Bazarov to come into contact with him. Again, the Bazarovs, as Iconoclasts, are always unpopular in their own circles. Yesterday in political life they were suppressed or exiled, and even in science they were the men who were supplanted before their real claim was recognised, and to-day when order reigns for a time, the academic circles and the popular critics will demonstrate that Bazarov's existence was a mistake, and the crowd could have got on much better without him.

The Crowd, the ungrateful Crowd, though for it Bazarov has wrested much from effete or corrupt hands, and has fought and weakened despotic and bureaucratic power, what has its opinion or memory to do with his brave heroic figure? Yes, heroic, as Turgenev, in indignation with Bazarov's shallow accusers, was betrayed into defining his own creation, Bazarov, whose very atmosphere is difficulty and danger, who cannot move without hostility, carrying as he does destruction to the old worn-out truths, contemptuous of censure, still more contemptuous of praise, he goes his way against wind and tide. Brave man, given up to his cause, whatever it be, it is his joy to *stand alone*, watching the crowd as it races wherever reward is and danger is not. It is Bazarov's life to despise honours, success, opinion, and to let nothing, not love itself, come between him and his inevitable course, and, when death comes, to turn his face to the wall, while in the street below he can hear the voices of men cheering the popular hero who has last arrived. The Crowd! Bazarov is the antithesis of the cowardice of the Crowd. That is the secret why we love him.

III

As a piece of art *Fathers and Children* is the most powerful of all Turgenev's works. The figure of Bazarov is not only the political centre of the book, against which the other characters show up in their respective significance, but a figure in which the eternal tragedy of man's impotence and insignificance is realised in scenes of a most ironical human drama. How admirably this figure dominates everything and everybody. Everything falls away before this man's biting sincerity. In turn the figure-heads of Culture and Birth, Nikolai and Pavel representing the Past; Arkady the sentimentalist representing the Present; the father and mother representing the ties of family that hinder a man's life-work; Madame Odintsov embodying the fascination of a beautiful woman—all fall into their respective places. But the particular power of *Fathers and Children,* of epic force almost, arises from the way in which Turgenev makes us feel the individual human tragedy of Bazarov in relation to the perpetual tragedy everywhere in indifferent Nature. In *On the Eve,* Turgenev cast his figures against a poetic background by creating an atmosphere of War and Patriotism. But in *Fathers and Children* this poetic background is Nature herself, Nature who sows, with the same fling of her hand, life and death springing each from each, in the same rhythmical cast of fate. And with Nature for the background, there comes the

xiii

wonderful sense conveyed to the reader throughout the novel, of the generations with their fresh vigorous blood passing away quickly, a sense of the coming generations, whose works, too, will be hurried away into the background, a sense of the silence of Earth while her children disappear into the shadows, and are whelmed in turn by the inexorable night. While everything in the novel is expressed in the realistic terms of daily commonplace life, the characters appear now close to us as companions, and now they seem like distant figures walking under an immense sky; and the effect of Turgenev's simply and subtly drawn landscapes is to give us a glimpse of men and women in their actual relation to their mother earth and the sky over their heads. This effect is rarely conveyed in the modern Western novel, which deals so much with purely indoor life; but the Russian novelist gained artistic force for his tragedies by the vague sense ever present with him of the enormous distances of the vast steppes, bearing on their bosom the peasants' lives, which serve as a sombre background to the life of the isolated individual figures with which he is dealing. Turgenev has availed himself of this hidden note of tragedy, and with the greatest art he has made Bazarov, with all his ambition opening out before him, and his triumph awaited, the eternal type of man's conquering egoism conquered by the pin-prick of Death. Bazarov, who looks neither to the right hand nor the left, who delays no longer in his life-work of throwing off the mind-forged manacles; Bazarov, who trusts not to Nature, but would track the course of her most obscure laws; Bazarov, in his keen pursuit of knowledge, is laid low by the weapon he has selected to wield. His own tool, the dissecting knife, brings death to him, and his body is stretched beside the peasant who had gone before. Of the death-scene, the great culmination of this great novel, it is impossible to speak without emotion. The voice of the reader, whosoever he be, must break when he comes to those passages of infinite pathos where the father, Vassily Ivano-vitch, is seen peeping from behind the door at his dying son, where he cries, 'Still living, my Yevgeny is still living, and now he will be saved. Wife, wife!' and where, when death has come, he cries, 'I said I should rebel. I rebel, I rebel!' What art, what genius, we can only repeat, our spirit humbled to the dust by the exquisite solemnity of that undying simple scene of the old parents at the grave, the scene where Turgenev epitomises in one stroke the infinite aspiration, the eternal insignificance of the life of man.

Let us end here with a repetition of a simple passage that, echoing through the pages of *Fathers and Children,* must find an echo in the hearts of Turgenev's readers: ' "To the memory of Bazarov," Katya whispered in her husband's ear, . . . but Arkady did not venture to propose the toast aloud.' We, at all events, can drink the toast to-day as a poor tribute in recompense for those days when Turgenev in life proposed it, and his comrades looked on him with distrust, with coldness, and with anger.

EDWARD GARNETT

*June* 1895

# THE NAMES OF THE CHARACTERS IN THE BOOK

NIKOLÁI PETRÓVITCH KIRSÁNOV.

PÁVEL PETRÓVITCH KIRSÁNOV.

ARKÁDY (ARKÁSHA) NIKOLÁ-EVITCH (*or* NIKOLÁITCH).

YEVGÉNY (ÉNYUSHA) VASSÍL-YEVITCH (*or* VASSÍLYITCH) BAZÁROV.

VASSÍLY IVÁNOVITCH (*or* IVÁNITCH).

ARÍNA VLÁSYEVNA.

FEDÓS-YA (FÉNITCHKA) NIKOLÁ-EVNA.

ÁNNA SÉRG-YEVNA ODÍNTSOV.

KÁTYA SÉRG-YEVNA.

PORFÍRY PLATÓNITCH.

MATVY IL-YITCH KOLYÁZIN.

EVDÓKS-YA (*or* AVDÓTYA) NIKÍTISHNA KÚKSHIN.

VÍKTOR SÍTNIKOV.

PIOTR (*pron. P-yotr*).

PROKÓFITCH.

DUN-YÁSHA.

MÍT-YA.

TIMÓFEITCH.

---

In transcribing the Russian names into English—
   *a* has the sound of *a* in *father*.
   *e*    ,,    ,,    *a* in *pane*.
   *i*    ,,    ,,    *ee*.
   *u*    ,,    ,,    *oo*.
   *y* is always consonantal except when it is the last letter of the word.
   *g* is always hard.

# 1

'WELL, Piotr, not in sight yet?' was the question asked on May the 20th, 1859, by a gentleman of a little over forty, in a dusty coat and checked trousers, who came out without his hat on to the low steps of the posting station at S——. He was addressing his servant, a chubby young fellow, with whitish down on his chin, and little, lack-lustre eyes.

The servant, in whom everything—the turquoise ring in his ear, the streaky hair plastered with grease, and the civility of his movements—indicated a man of the new, improved generation, glanced with an air of indulgence along the road, and made answer:

'No, sir; not in sight.'

'Not in sight?' repeated his master.

'No, sir,' responded the man a second time.

His master sighed, and sat down on a little bench. We will introduce him to the reader while he sits, his feet tucked under him, gazing thoughtfully round.

His name was Nikolai Petrovitch Kirsanov. He had, twelve miles from the posting station, a fine property of two hundred souls, or, as he expressed it—since he had arranged the division of his land with the peasants, and started 'a farm'— of nearly five thousand acres. His father, a general in the army, who served in 1812, a coarse, half-educated, but not ill-natured man, a typical Russian, had been in harness all his life, first in command of a brigade, and then of a division, and lived constantly in the provinces, where, by virtue of his rank, he played a fairly important part. Nikolai Petrovitch was born in the south of Russia like his elder brother, Pavel, of whom more hereafter. He was educated at home till he was fourteen, surrounded by cheap tutors, free-and-easy but toadying adjutants, and all the usual regimental and staff set. His mother, one of the Kolyazin family, as a girl called Agathe, but as a general's wife Agathokleya Kuzminishna Kirsanov, was one of those military ladies who take their full share of the duties and dignities of office. She wore gorgeous caps and rustling silk dresses; in church she was the first to advance to the cross; she talked a great deal in a loud voice, let her children kiss her hand in the morning, and gave them her blessing at night—in fact, she got everything out of life she could. Nikolai Petrovitch, as a general's son—though so far from being distinguished by courage that he even deserved to be called 'a funk'—was intended, like his brother Pavel, to enter the army; but he broke his leg on the very day when the news of his commission came, and, after being two months in bed, retained a slight limp to the end of his days. His father gave him up as a bad job, and let him go into the civil service. He took him to Petersburg directly he was eighteen, and placed him in the university. His brother happened about the same time to be made an officer in the Guards. The young men started living together in one set of rooms, under the remote supervision of a cousin on their mother's side, Ilya Kolyazin, an official of high rank. Their father returned to his division and his wife, and only rarely sent his sons large sheets of grey paper, scrawled over in a bold clerkly hand. At the bottom of these sheets stood in letters, enclosed carefully in scroll-work, the words, 'Piotr Kirsanov, General-Major'. In 1835 Nikolai Petrovitch left the university, a graduate, and in the same year General Kirsanov was put on to the retired list after an unsuccessful review, and came to Petersburg with his wife to live. He was about to take a house in the Tavrichesky Gardens, and had joined the English club, but he died suddenly of an apoplectic fit. Agathokleya Kuzminishna soon followed him; she could not accustom herself to a dull life in the capital; she was consumed by the ennui of existence away from the regiment. Meanwhile Nikolai Petrovitch had already, in his parents' lifetime and to their no slight chagrin, had time to fall in love with the daughter of his landlord, a petty official, Prepolovensky. She was a pretty and, as it is called, 'advanced' girl; she used to read the serious articles in the 'Science' column of the journals. He married her directly the term of mourning was over; and leaving the civil service in which his father had by favour procured him a post, was perfectly blissful with his Masha, first in a country villa near the Lyesny Institute, afterwards in town in a pretty little flat with a clean staircase and a draughty drawing-room, and then in the country, where he settled finally, and where in a short time a son, Arkady, was born to him. The young couple lived very happily and peacefully; they were scarcely ever apart; they read together, sang and played duets together on the piano; she tended her flowers and looked after the poultry-yard; he sometimes went hunting, and busied himself with the estate, while Arkady grew and grew in the same happy and peaceful way. Ten years passed like a dream. In 1847 Kirsanov's wife died. He almost succumbed to this blow; in a few weeks his hair was grey; he was getting ready to go abroad, if possible to distract his mind . . . but then came the year 1848. He returned unwillingly to the country, and, after a rather prolonged period of inactivity, began to take an interest in improvements in the management of his land. In 1855 he brought his son to the university; he spent three winters with him in Petersburg, hardly going out anywhere, and trying to make acquaintance with Arkady's young companions. The last winter he had not been able to go, and here we have seen him in the May of 1859, already quite grey, stoutish, and rather bent, waiting for his son, who had just taken his degree, as once he had taken it himself.

The servant, from a feeling of propriety, and perhaps, too, not anxious to remain under the master's eye, had gone to the gate, and was smoking a pipe. Nikolai Petrovitch bent his head, and began staring at the crumbling steps; a big mottled fowl walked sedately towards him, treading firmly with its great yellow legs; a muddy cat gave him an unfriendly look, twisting herself coyly round the railing. The sun

3

was scorching; from the half-dark passage of the posting station came an odour of hot rye-bread. Nikolai Petrovitch fell to dreaming. 'My son . . . a graduate . . . Arkasha . . .' were the ideas that continually came round again and again in his head; he tried to think of something else, and again the same thoughts returned. He remembered his dead wife. . . . 'She did not live to see it!' he murmured sadly. A plump, dark-blue pigeon flew into the road, and hurriedly went to drink in a puddle near the well. Nikolai Petrovitch began looking at it, but his ear had already caught the sound of approaching wheels.

'It sounds as if they're coming, sir,' announced the servant, popping in from the gateway.

Nikolai Petrovitch jumped up, and bent his eyes on the road. A carriage appeared with three posting-horses harnessed abreast; in the carriage he caught a glimpse of the blue band of a student's cap, the familiar outline of a dear face.

'Arkasha! Arkasha!' cried Kirsanov, and he ran waving his hands. . . . A few instants later, his lips were pressed to the beardless, dusty, sunburnt cheek of the youthful graduate.

## 2

'LET me shake myself first, daddy,' said Arkady, in a voice tired from travelling, but boyish and clear as a bell, as he gaily responded to his father's caresses; 'I am covering you with dust.'

'Never mind, never mind,' repeated Nikolai Petrovitch, smiling tenderly, and twice he struck the collar of his son's cloak and his own greatcoat with his hand. 'Let me have a look at you; let me have a look at you,' he added, moving back from him, but immediately he went with hurried steps towards the yard of the station, calling, 'This way, this way; and horses at once.'

Nikolai Petrovitch seemed far more excited than his son; he seemed a little confused, a little timid. Arkady stopped him.

'Daddy,' he said, 'let me introduce you to my great friend, Bazarov, about whom I have so often written to you. He has been so good as to promise to stay with us.'

Nikolai Petrovitch went back quickly, and going up to a tall man in a long, loose, rough coat with tassels, who had only just got out of the carriage, he warmly pressed the ungloved red hand, which the latter did not at once hold out to him.

'I am heartily glad,' he began, 'and very grateful for your kind intention of visiting us. . . . Let me know your name, and your father's.'

'Yevgeny Vassilyev,' answered Bazarov, in a lazy but manly voice; and turning back the collar of his rough coat, he showed Nikolai Petrovitch his whole face. It was long and lean, with a broad forehead, a nose flat at the base and sharper at the end, large greenish eyes, and drooping whiskers of a sandy colour; it was lighted up by a tranquil smile, and showed self-confidence and intelligence.

'I hope, dear Yevgeny Vassilyitch, you won't be dull with us,' continued Nikolai Petrovitch.

Bazarov's thin lips moved just perceptibly, though he made no reply, but merely took off his cap. His long, thick hair did not hide the prominent bumps on his head.

'Then, Arkady,' Nikolai Petrovitch began again, turning to his son, 'shall the horses be put to at once? or would you like to rest?'

'We will rest at home, daddy; tell them to harness the horses.'

'At once, at once,' his father assented. 'Hey, Piotr, do you hear? Get things ready, my good boy; look sharp.'

Piotr, who as a modernised servant had not kissed the young master's hand, but only bowed to him from a distance, again vanished through the gateway.

'I came here with the carriage, but there are three horses

for your coach too,' said Nikolai Petrovitch fussily, while Arkady drank some water from an iron dipper brought him by the woman in charge of the station, and Bazarov began smoking a pipe and went up to the driver, who was taking out the horses; 'there are only two seats in the carriage, and I don't know how your friend' . . .

'He will go in the coach,' interposed Arkady in an undertone. 'You must not stand on ceremony with him, please. He's a splendid fellow, so simple—you will see.'

Nikolai Petrovitch's coachman brought the horses round.

'Come, hurry up, bushy beard!' said Bazarov, addressing the driver.

'Do you hear, Mityuha,' put in another driver, standing by with his hands thrust behind him into the opening of his sheepskin coat, 'what the gentleman called you? It's a bushy beard you are too.'

Mityuha only gave a jog to his hat and pulled the reins off the heated shaft-horse.

'Look sharp, look sharp, lads, lend a hand,' cried Nikolai Petrovitch; 'there'll be something to drink our health with!'

In a few minutes the horses were harnessed; the father and son were installed in the carriage; Piotr climbed up on to the box; Bazarov jumped into the coach and nestled his head down into the leather cushion; and both the vehicles rolled away.

FATHERS AND CHILDREN

3

'So here you are, a graduate at last, and come home again,' said Nikolai Petrovitch, touching Arkady now on the shoulder, now on the knee. 'At last!'

'And how is uncle? quite well?' asked Arkady, who, in

spite of the genuine, almost childish delight filling his heart, wanted as soon as possible to turn the conversation from the emotional into a commonplace channel.

'Quite well. He was thinking of coming with me to meet you, but for some reason or other he gave up the idea.'

'And how long have you been waiting for me?' inquired Arkady.

'Oh, about five hours.'

'Dear old dad!'

Arkady turned round quickly to his father, and gave him a sounding kiss on the cheek. Nikolai Petrovitch gave vent to a low chuckle.

'I have got such a capital horse for you!' he began. 'You will see. And your room has been fresh papered.'

'And is there a room for Bazarov?'

'We will find one for him too.'

'Please, dad, make much of him. I can't tell you how I prize his friendship.'

'Have you made friends with him lately?'

'Yes, quite lately.'

'Ah, that's how it is I did not see him last winter. What does he study?'

'His chief subject is natural science. But he knows everything. Next year he wants to take his doctor's degree.'

'Ah! he's in the medical faculty,' observed Nikolai Petrovitch, and he was silent for a little. 'Piotr,' he went on, stretching out his hand, 'aren't those our peasants driving along?'

Piotr looked where his master was pointing. Some carts harnessed with unbridled horses were moving rapidly along a narrow by-road. In each cart there were one or two peasants in sheepskin coats, unbuttoned.

'Yes, sir,' replied Piotr.

'Where are they going—to the town?'

'To the town, I suppose. To the gin-shop,' he added contemptuously, turning slightly towards the coachman, as though he would appeal to him. But the latter did not stir a muscle;

he was a man of the old stamp, and did not share the modern views of the younger generation.

'I have had a lot of bother with the peasants this year,' pursued Nikolai Petrovitch, turning to his son. 'They won't pay their rent. What is one to do?'

'But do you like your hired labourers?'

'Yes,' said Nikolai Petrovitch between his teeth. 'They're being set against me, that's the mischief; and they won't do their best. They spoil the tools. But they have tilled the land pretty fairly. When things have settled down a bit, it will be all right. Do you take an interest in farming now?'

'You've no shade; that's a pity,' remarked Arkady, without answering the last question.

'I have had a great awning put up on the north side over the balcony,' observed Nikolai Petrovitch; 'now we can have dinner even in the open air.'

'It'll be rather too like a summer villa. . . . Still, that's all nonsense. What air though here! How delicious it smells! Really I fancy there's nowhere such fragrance in the world as in the meadows here! And the sky too.'

Arkady suddenly stopped short, cast a stealthy look behind him, and said no more.

'Of course,' observed Nikolai Petrovitch, 'you were born here, and so everything is bound to strike you in a special——'

'Come, dad, that makes no difference where a man is born.'

'Still——'

'No; it makes absolutely no difference.'

Nikolai Petrovitch gave a sidelong glance at his son, and the carriage went on half a mile farther before the conversation was renewed between them.

'I don't recollect whether I wrote to you,' began Nikolai Petrovitch, 'your old nurse, Yegorovna, is dead.'

'Really? Poor thing! Is Prokofitch still living?'

'Yes, and not a bit changed. As grumbling as ever. In fact, you won't find many changes at Maryino.'

'Have you still the same bailiff?'

'Well, to be sure, there is a change here. I decided not to keep about me any freed serfs who have been house servants, or, at least, not to entrust them with duties of any responsibility.' (Arkady glanced towards Piotr.) *'Il est libre, en effet,'* observed Nikolai Petrovitch in an undertone; 'but, you see, he's only a valet. Now I have a bailiff, a townsman; he seems a practical fellow. I pay him two hundred and fifty roubles a year. But,' added Nikolai Petrovitch, rubbing his forehead and eyebrows with his hand, which was always an indication with him of inward embarrassment, 'I told you just now that you would not find changes at Maryino. . . . That's not quite correct. I think it my duty to prepare you, though . . .'

He hesitated for an instant, and then went on in French.

'A severe moralist would regard my openness as improper; but, in the first place, it can't be concealed, and secondly, you are aware I have always had peculiar ideas as regards the relation of father and son. Though, of course, you would be right in blaming me. At my age. . . . In short . . . that . . . that girl, about whom you have probably heard already . . .'

'Fenitchka?' asked Arkady easily.

Nikolai Petrovitch blushed. 'Don't mention her name aloud, please. . . . Well . . . she is living with me now. I have installed her in the house . . . there were two little rooms there. But that can all be changed.'

'Goodness, daddy, what for?'

'Your friend is going to stay with us . . . it would be awkward . . .'

'Please, don't be uneasy on Bazarov's account. He's above all that.'

'Well, but you too,' added Nikolai Petrovitch. 'The little lodge is so horrid—that's the worst of it.'

'Goodness, dad,' interposed Arkady, 'it's as if you were apologising; I wonder you're not ashamed.'

'Of course, I ought to be ashamed,' answered Nikolai Petrovitch, flushing more and more.

9

'Nonsense, dad, nonsense; please don't!' Arkady smiled affectionately. 'What a thing to apologise for!' he thought to himself, and his heart was filled with a feeling of condescending tenderness for his kind, soft-hearted father, mixed with a sense of secret superiority. 'Please, stop,' he repeated once more, instinctively revelling in a consciousness of his own advanced and emancipated condition.

Nikolai Petrovitch glanced at him from under the fingers of the hand with which he was still rubbing his forehead, and there was a pang in his heart. . . . But at once he blamed himself for it.

'Here are our meadows at last,' he said after a long silence.

'And that in front is our forest, isn't it?' asked Arkady.

'Yes. Only I have sold the timber. This year they will cut it down.'

'Why did you sell it?'

'The money was needed; besides, that land is to go to the peasants.'

'Who don't pay you their rent?'

'That's their affair; besides, they will pay it some day.'

'I am sorry about the forest,' observed Arkady, and he began to look about him.

The country through which they were driving could not be called picturesque. Fields upon fields stretched all along to the very horizon, now sloping gently upwards, then dropping down again; in some places woods were to be seen, and winding ravines, planted with low, scanty bushes, recalling vividly the representation of them on the old-fashioned maps of the times of Catherine. They came upon little streams too with hollow banks; and tiny lakes with narrow dykes; and little villages, with low hovels under dark and often tumble-down roofs, and slanting barns with walls woven of brushwood and gaping doorways beside neglected threshing-floors; and churches, some brick-built, with stucco peeling off in patches, others wooden, with crosses fallen askew, and overgrown graveyards. Slowly Arkady's heart sank. To complete the picture, the peasants they met were all in tatters

and on the sorriest little nags; the willows, with their trunks
stripped of bark, and broken branches, stood like ragged
beggars along the roadside; cows, lean and shaggy and looking
pinched up by hunger, were greedily tearing at the grass along
the ditches. They looked as though they had just been
snatched out of the murderous clutches of some threatening
monster; and the piteous state of the weak, starved beasts
in the midst of the lovely spring day called up, like a white
phantom, the endless, comfortless winter with its storms, and
frosts, and snows. . . . 'No,' thought Arkady, 'this is not
a rich country; it does not impress one by plenty or industry;
it can't, it can't go on like this, reforms are absolutely
necessary . . . but how is one to carry them out, how is one
to begin?'

Such were Arkady's reflections; . . . but even as he
reflected, the spring regained its sway. All around was golden
green, all—trees, bushes, grass—shone and stirred gently in
wide waves under the soft breath of the warm wind; from
all sides flooded the endless trilling music of the larks; the
peewits were calling as they hovered over the low-lying
meadows, or noiselessly ran over the tussocks of grass; the
rooks strutted among the half-grown short spring-corn, standing out black against its tender green; they disappeared in
the already whitening rye, only from time to time their heads
peeped out amid its grey waves. Arkady gazed and gazed,
and his reflections grew slowly fainter and passed away. . . .
He flung off his cloak and turned to his father, with a face
so bright and boyish, that the later gave him another hug.

'We're not far off now,' remarked Nikolai Petrovitch; 'we
have only to get up this hill, and the house will be in sight.
We shall get on together splendidly, Arkasha; you shall help
me in farming the estate, if only it isn't a bore to you. We
must draw close to one another now, and learn to know each
other thoroughly, mustn't we!'

'Of course,' said Arkady; 'but what an exquisite day it is
to-day!'

'To welcome you, my dear boy. Yes, it's spring in its full

loveliness. Though I agree with Pushkin—do you remember in Yevgeny Onyegin—

> 'To me how sad thy coming is,
> Spring, spring, sweet time of love!
> What . . .'

'Arkady!' called Bazarov's voice from the coach, 'send me a match; I've nothing to light my pipe with.'

Nikolai Petrovitch stopped, while Arkady, who had begun listening to him with some surprise, though with sympathy too, made haste to pull a silver match-box out of his pocket, and sent it to Bazarov by Piotr.

'Will you have a cigar?' shouted Bazarov again.

'Thanks,' answered Arkady.

Piotr returned to the carriage, and handed him with the match-box a thick black cigar, which Arkady began to smoke promptly, diffusing about him such a strong and pungent odour of cheap tobacco that Nikolai Petrovitch, who had never been a smoker from his youth up, was forced to turn away his head, as imperceptibly as he could for fear of wounding his son.

A quarter of an hour later, the two carriages drew up before the steps of a new wooden house, painted grey, with a red iron roof. This was Maryino, also known as New-Wick, or, as the peasants had nicknamed it, Poverty Farm.

FATHERS AND CHILDREN

4

No crowd of house-serfs ran out on to the steps to meet the gentlemen; a little girl of twelve years old made her appearance alone. After her there came out of the house a young lad, very like Piotr, dressed in a coat of grey livery, with white armorial buttons, the servant of Pavel Petrovitch

Kirsanov. Without speaking, he opened the door of the carriage and unbuttoned the apron of the coach. Nikolai Petrovitch with his son and Bazarov walked through a dark and almost empty hall, from behind the door of which they caught a glimpse of a young woman's face, into a drawing-room furnished in the most modern style.

'Here we are at home,' said Nikolai Petrovitch, taking off his cap, and shaking back his hair. 'That's the great thing; now we must have supper and rest.'

'A meal would not come amiss, certainly,' observed Bazarov, stretching, and he dropped on to a sofa.

'Yes, yes, let us have supper, supper directly.' Nikolai Petrovitch with no apparent reason stamped his foot. 'And here just at the right moment comes Prokofitch.'

A man about sixty entered, white-haired, thin, and swarthy, in a cinnamon-coloured dress-coat with brass buttons, and a pink neckerchief. He smirked, went up to kiss Arkady's hand, and bowing to the guest retreated to the door, and put his hands behind him.

'Here he is, Prokofitch,' began Nikolai Petrovitch; 'he's come back to us at last. . . . Well, how do you think him looking?'

'As well as could be,' said the old man, and was grinning again, but he quickly knitted his bushy brows. 'You wish supper to be served?' he said impressively.

'Yes, yes, please. But won't you like to go to your room first, Yevgeny Vassilyitch?'

'No, thanks; I don't care about it. Only give orders for my little box to be taken there, and this garment, too,' he added, taking off his frieze overcoat.

'Certainly. Prokofitch, take the gentleman's coat.' (Prokofitch, with an air of perplexity, picked up Bazarov's 'garment' in both hands, and holding it high above his head, retreated on tiptoe.) 'And you, Arkady, are you going to your room for a minute?'

'Yes, I must wash,' answered Arkady, and was just moving towards the door, but at that instant there came into the drawing-room a man of medium height, dressed in a dark English suit, a fashionable low cravat, and kid shoes, Pavel Petrovitch Kirsanov. He looked about forty-five: his close-cropped, grey hair shone with a dark lustre, like new silver; his face, yellow but free from wrinkles, was exceptionally regular and pure in line, as though carved by a light and delicate chisel, and showed traces of remarkable beauty; specially fine were his clear, black, almond-shaped eyes. The whole person of Arkady's uncle, with its aristocratic elegance, had preserved the gracefulness of youth and that air of striving upwards, away from earth, which for the most part is lost after the twenties are past.

Pavel Petrovitch took out of his trouser pocket his exquisite hand with its long tapering pink nails, a hand which seemed still more exquisite from the snowy whiteness of the cuff, buttoned with a single, big opal, and gave it to his nephew. After a preliminary handshake in the European style, he kissed him thrice after the Russian fashion, that is to say, he touched his cheek three times with his perfumed moustaches, and said, 'Welcome.'

Nikolai Petrovitch presented him to Bazarov; Pavel Petrovitch greeted him with a slight inclination of his supple figure, and a slight smile, but he did not give him his hand, and even put it back in his pocket.

'I had begun to think you were not coming to-day,' he began in a musical voice, with a genial swing and shrug of the shoulders, as he showed his splendid white teeth. 'Did anything happen on the road?'

'Nothing happened,' answered Arkady; 'we were rather slow. But we're as hungry as wolves now. Hurry up Prokofitch, dad; and I'll be back directly.'

'Stay, I'm coming with you,' cried Bazarov, pulling himself up suddenly from the sofa. Both the young men went out.

'Who is he?' asked Pavel Petrovitch.

'A friend of Arkasha's; according to him, a very clever fellow.'

'Is he going to stay with us?'

'Yes.'

'That unkempt creature?'

'Why, yes.'

Pavel Petrovitch drummed with his finger-tips on the table. 'I fancy Arkady *s'est dégourdi*,' he remarked. 'I'm glad he has come back.'

At supper there was little conversation. Bazarov especially said nothing, but he ate a great deal. Nikolai Petrovitch related various incidents in what he called his career as a farmer, talked about the impending government measures, about committees, deputations, the necessity of introducing machinery, etc. Pavel Petrovitch paced slowly up and down the dining-room (he never ate supper), sometimes sipping at a wineglass of red wine, and less often uttering some remark or rather exclamation, of the nature of 'Ah! aha! hm!' Arkady told some news from Petersburg, but he was conscious of a little awkwardness, that awkwardness which usually overtakes a youth when he has just ceased to be a child, and has come back to a place where they are accustomed to regard him and treat him as a child. He made his sentences quite unnecessarily long, avoided the word 'daddy', and even sometimes replaced it by the word 'father', mumbled, it is true, between his teeth; with an exaggerated carelessness he poured into his glass far more wine than he really wanted, and drank it all off. Prokofitch did not take his eyes off him, and kept chewing his lips. After supper they all separated at once.

'Your uncle's a queer fish,' Bazarov said to Arkady, as he sat in his dressing-gown by his bedside, smoking a short pipe. 'Only fancy such style in the country! His nails, his nails—you ought to send them to an exhibition!'

'Why, of course, you don't know,' replied Arkady. 'He was a great swell in his own day, you know. I will tell you his story one day. He was very handsome, you know, used to turn all the women's heads.'

'Oh, that's it, is it? So he keeps it up in memory of the past. It's a pity there's no one for him to fascinate here though. I kept staring at his exquisite collars. They're like marble, and his chin's shaved simply to perfection. Come, Arkady Nikolaitch, isn't that ridiculous?'

'Perhaps it is; but he's a splendid man, really.'

'An antique survival! But your father's a capital fellow. He wastes his time reading poetry, and doesn't know much about farming, but he's a good-hearted fellow.'

'My father's a man in a thousand.'

'Did you notice how shy and nervous he is?'

Arkady shook his head as though he himself were not shy and nervous.

'It's something astonishing,' pursued Bazarov, 'these old idealists, they develop their nervous systems till they break down . . . so balance is lost. But good-night. In my room there's an English washstand, but the door won't fasten. Anyway that ought to be encouraged—an English washstand stands for progress!'

Bazarov went away, and a sense of great happiness came over Arkady. Sweet it is to fall asleep in one's own home, in the familiar bed, under the quilt worked by loving hands, perhaps a dear nurse's hands, those kind, tender, untiring hands. Arkady remembered Yegorovna, and sighed and wished her peace in heaven. . . . For himself he made no prayer.

Both he and Bazarov were soon asleep, but others in the house were awake long after. His son's return had agitated Nikolai Petrovitch. He lay down in bed, but did not put out the candles and, his head propped on his hand, he fell into long reveries. His brother was sitting long after midnight in his study, in a wide armchair before the fireplace, on which there smouldered some faintly glowing embers. Pavel Petrovitch was not undressed, only some red Chinese slippers had replaced the kid shoes on his feet. He held in his hand the last number of *Galignani,* but he was not reading; he gazed fixedly into the grate, where a bluish flame flickered, dying down, then flaring up again. . . . God knows where his thoughts were rambling, but they were not rambling in the past only; the expression of his face was concentrated and surly, which is not the way when a man is absorbed solely in recollections. In a small back room there sat, on a large chest, a young woman in a blue dressing-jacket with a white kerchief thrown over her dark hair, Fenitchka. She was half listening, half dozing, and often looked across towards the open door, through which a child's cradle was visible and the regular breathing of a sleeping baby could be heard.

FATHERS AND CHILDREN

## 5

THE next morning Bazarov woke up earlier than anyone and went out of the house. 'Oh, my!' he thought, looking about him, 'the little place isn't much to boast of!' When Nikolai Petrovitch had divided the land with his peasants, he had had to build his new manor-house on four acres of perfectly flat and barren land. He had built a house, offices, and farm buildings, laid out a garden, dug a pond, and sunk two wells; but the young trees had not done well, very little water had collected in the pond, and that in the wells tasted brackish. Only one arbour of lilac and acacia had grown fairly well; they sometimes had tea and dinner in it. In a few minutes Bazarov had traversed all the little paths of the garden; he went into the cattle-yard and the stable, routed out two farm-boys, with whom he made friends at once, and set off with them to a small swamp about a mile from the house to look for frogs.

'What do you want frogs for, sir?' one of the boys asked him.

'I'll tell you what for,' answered Bazarov, who possessed the special faculty of inspiring confidence in people of a lower class, though he never tried to win them, and behaved very casually with them; 'I shall cut the frog open, and see what's going on in his inside, and then, as you and I are much the same as frogs, only that we walk on legs, I shall know what's going on inside us too.'

'And what do you want to know that for?'

'So as not to make a mistake, if you're taken ill, and I have to cure you.'

'Are you a doctor then?'

'Yes.'

'Vaska, do you hear, the gentleman says you and I are the same as frogs; that's funny!'

'I'm afraid of frogs,' observed Vaska, a boy of seven, with a head as white as flax, and bare feet, dressed in a grey smock with a stand-up collar.

'What is there to be afraid of? Do they bite?'

'There, paddle into the water, philosophers,' said Bazarov.

Meanwhile Nikolai Petrovitch too had waked up, and gone in to see Arkady, whom he found dressed. The father and son went out on to the terrace under the shelter of the awning; near the balustrade, on the table, among great bunches of lilac, the samovar was already boiling. A little girl came up, the same who had been the first to meet them at the steps on their arrival the evening before. In a shrill voice she said:

'Fedosya Nikolaevna is not quite well, she cannot come; she gave orders to ask you, will you please to pour out tea yourself, or should she send Dunyasha?'

'I will pour out myself, myself,' interposed Nikolai Petrovitch hurriedly. 'Arkady, how do you take your tea, with cream, or with lemon?'

'With cream,' answered Arkady; and after a brief silence, he uttered interrogatively, 'Daddy?'

Nikolai Petrovitch in confusion looked at his son.

'Well?' he said.

Arkady dropped his eyes.

'Forgive me, dad, if my question seems unsuitable to you,' he began, 'but you yourself, by your openness yesterday, encourage me to be open . . . you will not be angry . . . ?'

'Go on.'

'You give me confidence to ask you. . . . Isn't the reason, Fen . . . isn't the reason she will not come here to pour out tea, because I'm here?'

Nikolai Petrovitch turned slightly away.

'Perhaps,' he said at last, 'she supposes . . . she is ashamed.'

Arkady turned a rapid glance on his father.

'She has no need to be ashamed. In the first place, you are aware of my views' (it was very sweet to Arkady to utter that word); 'and secondly, could I be willing to hamper your life, your habits in the least thing? Besides, I am sure you could not make a bad choice; if you have allowed her to live under the same roof with you, she must be worthy of it; in any case, a son cannot judge his father—least of all, I, and least of all such a father who, like you, has never hampered my liberty in anything.'

Arkady's voice had been shaky at the beginning; he felt himself magnanimous, though at the same time he realised he was delivering something of the nature of a lecture to his father; but the sound of one's own voice has a powerful effect on any man, and Arkady brought out his last words resolutely, even with emphasis.

'Thanks, Arkasha,' said Nikolai Petrovitch thickly, and his fingers again strayed over his eyebrows and forehead. 'Your suppositions are just, in fact. Of course, if this girl had not deserved . . . It is not a frivolous caprice. It's not easy for me to talk to you about this; but you will understand that it is difficult for her to come here, in your presence, especially the first day of your return.'

'In that case, I will go to her,' cried Arkady, with a fresh rush of magnanimous feeling, and he jumped up from his seat. 'I will explain to her that she has no need to be ashamed before me.'

Nikolai Petrovitch too got up.

'Arkady,' he began, 'be so good . . . how can . . . there . . . I have not told you yet . . .'

But Arkady did not listen to him, and ran off the terrace. Nikolai Petrovitch looked after him, and sank into his chair overcome by confusion. His heart began to throb. Did he at that moment realise the inevitable strangeness of the future relations between him and his son? Was he conscious that Arkady would perhaps have shown him more respect if he had never touched on this subject at all? Did he reproach himself for weakness?—it is hard to say; all these feelings were within him, but in the state of sensations—and vague sensations—while the flush did not leave his face, and his heart throbbed.

There was the sound of hurrying footsteps, and Arkady came on to the terrace. 'We have made friends!' he cried, with an expression of a kind of affectionate and good-natured triumph on his face. 'Fedosya Nikolaevna is not quite well to-day really, and she will come a little later. But why didn't you tell me I had a brother? I should have kissed him last night, as I have kissed him just now.'

Nikolai Petrovitch tried to articulate something, tried to get up and open his arms. Arkady flung himself on his neck.

'What's this? embracing again?' sounded the voice of Pavel Petrovitch behind them.

Father and son were equally rejoiced at his appearance at that instant; there are positions, genuinely affecting, from which one longs to escape as soon as possible.

'Why should you be surprised at that?' said Nikolai Petrovitch gaily. 'Think what ages I have been waiting for Arkasha. I've not had time to get a good look at him since yesterday.'

'I'm not at all surprised,' observed Pavel Petrovitch; 'I feel not indisposed to be embracing him myself.'

Arkady went up to his uncle, and again felt his cheeks caressed by his perfumed moustache. Pavel Petrovitch sat down to the table. He wore an elegant morning suit in the English style, and a gay little fez on his head. This fez and the carelessly tied little cravat carried a suggestion of the freedom of country life, but the stiff collars of his shirt—not white, it is true, but striped, as is correct in morning dress —stood up as inexorably as ever against his well-shaved chin.

'Where's your new friend?' he asked Arkady.

'He's not in the house; he usually gets up early and goes off somewhere. The great thing is, we mustn't pay any attention to him; he doesn't like ceremony.'

'Yes, that's obvious.' Pavel Petrovitch began deliberately spreading butter on his bread. 'Is he going to stay long with us?'

'Perhaps. He came here on the way to his father's.'

'And where does his father live?'

'In our province, sixty-four miles from here. He has a small property there. He was formerly an army doctor.'

'Tut, tut, tut! To be sure, I kept asking myself, "Where have I heard that name, Bazarov?" Nikolai, do you remember, in our father's division there was a surgeon named Bazarov?'

'I believe there was.'

'Yes, yes, to be sure. So that surgeon was his father. Hm!' Pavel Petrovitch pulled his moustaches. 'Well, and what is Mr. Bazarov himself?' he asked, deliberately.

'What is Bazarov?' Arkady smiled. 'Would you like me, uncle, to tell you what he really is?'

'If you will be so good, nephew.'

'He's a nihilist.'

'Eh?' inquired Nikolai Petrovitch, while Pavel Petrovitch lifted a knife in the air with a small piece of butter on its tip, and remained motionless.

'He's a nihilist,' repeated Arkady.

'A nihilist,' said Nikolai Petrovitch. 'That's from the Latin, *nihil, nothing,* as far as I can judge; the word must mean a man who . . . who accepts nothing?'

'Say, "who respects nothing," ' put in Pavel Petrovitch, and he set to work on the butter again.

'Who regards everything from the critical point of view,' observed Arkady.

'Isn't that just the same thing?' inquired Pavel Petrovitch.

'No, it's not the same thing. A nihilist is a man who does not bow down before any authority, who does not take any principle on faith, whatever reverence that principle may be enshrined in.'

'Well, and is that good?' interrupted Pavel Petrovitch.

'That depends, uncle. Some people it will do good to, but some people will suffer for it.'

'Indeed. Well, I see it's not in our line. We are old-fashioned people; we imagine that without principles, taken as you say on faith, there's no taking a step, no breathing. *Vous avez changé tout cela.* God give you good health and the rank of a general, while we will be content to look on and admire, worthy . . . what was it?'

'Nihilists,' Arkady said, speaking very distinctly.

'Yes. There used to be Hegelists, and now there are nihilists. We shall see how you will exist in void, in vacuum; and now ring, please, brother Nikolai Petrovitch; it's time I had my cocoa.'

Nikolai Petrovitch rang the bell and called 'Dunyasha!' But instead of Dunyasha, Fenitchka herself came on to the terrace. She was a young woman about three-and-twenty, with a white soft skin, dark hair and eyes, red, childishly-pouting lips, and little delicate hands. She wore a neat print dress; a new blue kerchief lay lightly on her plump shoulders. She carried a large cup of cocoa, and setting it down before Pavel Petrovitch, she was overwhelmed with confusion; the hot blood rushed in a wave of crimson over the delicate skin of her pretty face. She dropped her eyes, and stood at the table, leaning a little on the very tips of her fingers. It seemed as though she were ashamed of having come in, and at the same time felt that she had a right to come.

Pavel Petrovitch knitted his brows severely, while Nikolai Petrovitch looked embarrassed.

'Good morning, Fenitchka,' he muttered through his teeth.

'Good morning,' she replied in a voice not loud but resonant, and with a sidelong glance at Arkady, who gave her a friendly smile, she went gently away. She walked with a slightly rolling gait, but even that suited her.

For some minutes silence reigned on the terrace. Pavel

22

Petrovitch sipped his cocoa; suddenly he raised his head. 'Here is Sir Nihilist coming towards us,' he said in an undertone.

Bazarov was in fact approaching through the garden, stepping over the flower-beds. His linen coat and trousers were besmeared with mud; clinging marsh weed was twined round the crown of his old round hat; in his right hand he held a small bag; in the bag something alive was moving. He quickly drew near the terrace, and said with a nod, 'Good morning, gentlemen; sorry I was late for tea; I'll be back directly; I must just put these captives away.'

'What have you there—leeches?' asked Pavel Petrovitch.

'No, frogs.'

'Do you eat them—or keep them?'

'For experiment,' said Bazarov indifferently, and he went off into the house.

'So he's going to cut them up,' observed Pavel Petrovitch. 'He has no faith in principles, but he has faith in frogs.'

Arkady looked compassionately at his uncle; Nikolai Petrovitch shrugged his shoulders stealthily. Pavel Petrovitch himself felt that his epigram was unsuccessful, and began to talk about husbandry and the new bailiff, who had come to him the evening before to complain that a labourer, Foma, 'was deboshed', and quite unmanageable. 'He's such an Æsop,' he said among other things; 'in all places he has protested himself a worthless fellow; he's not a man to keep his place; he'll walk off in a huff like a fool.'

FATHERS AND CHILDREN

# 6

BAZAROV came back, sat down to the table, and began hastily drinking tea. The two brothers looked at him in silence, while Arkady stealthily watched first his father and then his uncle.

'Did you walk far from here?' Nikolai Petrovitch asked at last.

'Where you've a little swamp near the aspen wood. I started some half-dozen snipe; you might slaughter them, Arkady.'

'Aren't you a sportsman then?'

'No.'

'Is your special study physics?' Pavel Petrovitch in his turn inquired.

'Physics, yes; and natural science in general.'

'They say the Teutons of late have had great success in that line.'

'Yes; the Germans are our teachers in it,' Bazarov answered carelessly.

The word Teutons, instead of Germans, Pavel Petrovitch had used with ironical intention; none noticed it, however.

'Have you such a high opinion of the Germans?' said Pavel Petrovitch, with exaggerated courtesy. He was beginning to feel a secret irritation. His aristocratic nature was revolted by Bazarov's absolute nonchalance. This surgeon's son was not only not overawed, he even gave abrupt and indifferent answers, and in the tone of his voice there was something churlish, almost insolent.

'The scientific men there are a clever lot.'

'Ah, ah. To be sure, of Russian scientific men you have not such a flattering opinion, I dare say?'

'That's very likely.'

'That's very praiseworthy self-abnegation,' Pavel Petrovitch declared, drawing himself up, and throwing his head back. 'But how is this? Arkady Nikolaitch was telling us just now that you accept no authorities. Don't you believe in *them?*'

'And how am I accepting them? And what am I to believe in? They tell me the truth, I agree, that's all.'

'And do all Germans tell the truth?' said Pavel Petrovitch, and his face assumed an expression as unsympathetic, as remote, as if he had withdrawn to some cloudy height.

24

'Not all,' replied Bazarov, with a short yawn. He obviously did not care to continue the discussion.

Pavel Petrovitch glanced at Arkady, as though he would say to him, 'Your friend's polite, I must say.' 'For my own part,' he began again, not without some effort, 'I am so unregenerate as not to like Germans. Russian Germans I am not speaking of now; we all know what sort of creatures they are. But even German Germans are not to my liking. In former days there were some here and there; they had— well, Schiller, to be sure, Goethe . . . my brother—he takes a particularly favourable view of them. . . . But now they have all turned chemists and materialists . . .'

'A good chemist is twenty times as useful as any poet,' broke in Bazarov.

'Oh, indeed,' commented Pavel Petrovitch, and, as though falling asleep, he faintly raised his eyebrows. 'You don't acknowledge art then, I suppose?'

'The art of making money or of advertising pills!' cried Bazarov, with a contemptuous laugh.

'Ah, ah. You are pleased to jest, I see. You reject all that, no doubt? Granted. Then you believe in science only?'

'I have already explained to you that I don't believe in anything; and what is science—science in the abstract? There are sciences, as there are trades and crafts; but abstract science doesn't exist at all.'

'Very good. Well, and in regard to the other traditions accepted in human conduct, do you maintain the same negative attitude?'

'What's this, an examination?' asked Bazarov.

Pavel Petrovitch turned slightly pale. . . . Nikolai Petrovitch thought it his duty to interpose in the conversation.

'We will converse on this subject with you more in detail some day, dear Yevgeny Vassilyitch; we will hear your views, and express our own. For my part, I am heartily glad you are studying the natural sciences. I have heard that Liebig has made some wonderful discoveries in the amelioration of soils. You can be of assistance to me in my agricultural

25

labours; you can give me some useful advice.'

'I am at your service, Nikolai Petrovitch; but Liebig's miles over our heads! One has first to learn the a b c, and then begin to read, and we haven't set eyes on the alphabet yet.'

'You are certainly a nihilist, I see that,' thought Nikolai Petrovitch. 'Still, you will allow me to apply to you on occasion,' he added aloud. 'And now I fancy, brother, it's time for us to be going to have a talk with the bailiff.'

Pavel Petrovitch got up from his seat.

'Yes,' he said, without looking at anyone; 'it's a misfortune to live five years in the country like this, far from mighty intellects! You turn into a fool directly. You may try not to forget what you've been taught, but—in a snap!—they'll prove all that's rubbish, and tell you that sensible men have nothing more to do with such foolishness, and that you, if you please, are an antiquated old fogey. What's to be done? Young people, of course, are cleverer than we are!'

Pavel Petrovitch turned slowly on his heels, and slowly walked away; Nikolai Petrovitch went after him.

'Is he always like that?' Bazarov coolly inquired of Arkady, directly the door had closed behind the two brothers.

'I must say, Yevgeny, you weren't nice to him,' remarked Arkady. 'You have hurt his feelings.'

'Well, am I going to consider them, these provincial aristocrats! Why, it's all vanity, dandy habits, fatuity. He should have continued his career in Petersburg, if that's his bent. But there, enough of him! I've found a rather rare species of a water-beetle, *Dytiscus marginatus;* do you know it? I will show you.'

'I promised to tell you his story,' began Arkady.

'The story of the beetle?'

'Come, don't, Yevgeny. The story of my uncle. You will see he's not the sort of man you fancy. He deserves pity rather than ridicule.'

'I don't dispute it; but why are you worrying over him?'

'One ought to be just, Yevgeny.'

'How does that follow?'

'No; listen . . .'

And Arkady told him his uncle's story. The reader will find it in the following chapter.

FATHERS AND CHILDREN

# 7

PAVEL PETROVITCH KIRSANOV was educated first at home, like his younger brother, and afterwards in the Corps of Pages. From childhood he was distinguished by remarkable beauty; moreover he was self-confident, somewhat ironical, and had a rather biting humour; he could not fail to please. He began to be seen everywhere, directly he had received his commission as an officer. He was much admired in society, and he indulged every whim, even every caprice and every folly, and gave himself airs, but that too was attractive in him. Women went out of their senses over him; men called him a coxcomb, and were secretly jealous of him. He lived, as has been related already, in the same apartments as his brother, whom he loved sincerely, though he was not at all like him. Nikolai Petrovitch was a little lame, he had small, pleasing features of a rather melancholy cast, small, black eyes, and thin, soft hair; he liked being lazy, but he also liked reading, and was timid in society. Pavel Petrovitch did not spend a single evening at home, prided himself on his ease and audacity (he was just bringing gymnastics into fashion among young men in society), and had read in all some five or six French books. At twenty-eight he was already a captain; a brilliant career awaited him. Suddenly everything was changed.

At that time, there was sometimes seen in Petersburg society a woman who has even yet not been forgotten, Princess R——. She had a well-educated, well-bred, but rather stupid husband, and no children. She used suddenly to go abroad, and suddenly to return to Russia, and led an eccentric life in general. She had the reputation of being a frivolous coquette, abandoned herself eagerly to every sort of pleasure, danced to exhaustion, laughed and jested with young men, whom she received in the dim light of her drawing-room before dinner; while at night she wept and prayed, found no peace in anything, and often paced her room till morning, wringing her hands in anguish, or sat, pale and chill, over a psalter. Day came, and she was transformed again into a grand lady; again she went out, laughed, chattered, and simply flung herself headlong into anything which could afford her the slightest distraction. She was marvellously well-proportioned, her hair coloured like gold and heavy as gold hung below her knees, but no one would have called her a beauty; in her whole face the only good point was her eyes, and even her eyes were not good—they were grey, and not large—but their glance was swift and deep, unconcerned to the point of audacity, and thoughtful to the point of melancholy—an enigmatic glance. There was a light of something extraordinary in them, even while her tongue was lisping the emptiest of inanities. She dressed with elaborate care. Pavel Petrovitch met her at a ball, danced a mazurka with her, in the course of which she did not utter a single rational word, and fell passionately in love with her. Being accustomed to make conquests, in this instance, too, he soon attained his object, but his easy success did not damp his ardour. On the contrary, he was in still more torturing, still closer bondage to this woman, in whom, even at the very moment when she surrendered herself utterly, there seemed always something still mysterious and unattainable, to which none could penetrate. What was hidden in that soul—God knows! It seemed as though she were in the power of mysterious forces, incomprehensible even to herself; they seemed to play on her at will; her intellect was not powerful enough to master their caprices. Her whole behaviour presented a series of inconsistencies; the only letters which could have awakened her husband's just suspicions she wrote to a man who was almost a stranger to her, whilst

28

her love had always an element of melancholy; with a man she had chosen as a lover, she ceased to laugh and to jest, she listened to him, and gazed at him with a look of bewilderment. Sometimes, for the most part suddenly, this bewilderment passed into chill horror; her face took a wild, death-like expression; she locked herself up in her bedroom, and her maid, putting her ear to the keyhole, could hear her smothered sobs. More than once, as he went home after a tender interview, Kirsanov felt within him that heart-rending, bitter vexation which follows on a total failure.

'What more do I want?' he asked himself, while his heart was heavy. He once gave her a ring with a sphinx engraved on the stone.

'What's that?' she asked; 'a sphinx?'

'Yes,' he answered, 'and that sphinx is you.'

'I?' she queried, slowly raising her enigmatical glance upon him. 'Do you know that's awfully flattering?' she added with a meaningless smile, while her eyes still kept the same strange look.

Pavel Petrovitch suffered even while Princess R—— loved him; but when she grew cold to him, and that happened rather quickly, he almost went out of his mind. He was on the rack, and he was jealous; he gave her no peace, followed her about everywhere; she grew sick of his pursuit of her, and she went abroad. He resigned his commission in spite of the entreaties of his friends and the exhortations of his superiors, and followed the princess; four years he spent in foreign countries, at one time pursuing her, at another time intentionally losing sight of her. He was ashamed of himself, he was disgusted with his own lack of spirit . . . but nothing availed. Her image, that incomprehensible, almost meaningless, but bewitching image, was deeply rooted in his heart. At Baden he once more regained his old footing with her; it seemed as though she had never loved him so passionately . . . but in a month it was all at an end: the flame flickered up for the last time and went out for ever. Foreseeing inevitable separation, he wanted at least to remain her friend, as though friendship with such a woman was possible. . . . She secretly left Baden, and from that time steadily avoided Kirsanov. He returned to Russia, and tried to live his former life again; but he could not get back into the old groove. He wandered from place to place like a man possessed; he still went into society; he still retained the habits of a man of the world; he could boast of two or three fresh conquests; but he no longer expected anything much of himself or of others, and he undertook nothing. He grew old and grey; spending all his evenings at the club, jaundiced and bored, and arguing in bachelor society became a necessity for him— a bad sign, as we all know. Marriage, of course, he did not even think of. Ten years passed in this way; they passed by colourless and fruitless—and quickly, fearfully quickly. Nowhere does time fly past as in Russia; in prison they say it flies even faster. One day at dinner at the club, Pavel Petrovitch heard of the death of the Princess R——. She had died at Paris in a state bordering on insanity. He got up from the table, and a long time he paced about the rooms of the club, or stood stock-still near the card-players, but he did not go home earlier than usual. Some time later he received a packet addressed to him; in it was the ring he had given the princess. She had drawn lines in the shape of a cross over the sphinx and sent him word that the solution of the enigma—was the cross.

This happened at the beginning of the year 1848, at the very time when Nikolai Petrovitch came to Petersburg, after the loss of his wife. Pavel Petrovitch had scarcely seen his brother since the latter had settled in the country; the marriage of Nikolai Petrovitch had coincided with the very first days of Pavel Petrovitch's acquaintance with the princess. When he came back from abroad, he had gone to him with the intention of staying a couple of months with him, in sympathetic enjoyment of his happiness, but he had only succeeded in standing a week of it. The difference in the positions of the two brothers was too great. In 1848, this difference had grown less; Nikolai Petrovitch had lost his wife,

Pavel Petrovitch had lost his memories; after the death of the princess he tried not to think of her. But to Nikolai there remained the sense of a well-spent life, his son was growing up under his eyes; Pavel, on the contrary, a solitary bachelor, was entering upon the indefinite twilight period of regrets that are akin to hopes, and hopes that are akin to regrets, when youth is over, while old age has not yet come.

This time was harder for Pavel Petrovitch than for another man; in losing his past, he lost everything.

'I will not invite you to Maryino now,' Nikolai Petrovitch said to him one day (he had called his property by that name in honour of his wife); 'you were dull there in my dear wife's time, and now I think you would be bored to death.'

'I was stupid and fidgety then,' answered Pavel Petrovitch; 'since then I have grown quieter, if not wiser. On the contrary, now, if you will let me, I am ready to settle with you for good.'

For all answer Nikolai Petrovitch embraced him; but a year and a half passed after this conversation before Pavel Petrovitch made up his mind to carry out his intention. When he was once settled in the country, however, he did not leave it, even during the three winters which Nikolai Petrovitch spent in Petersburg with his son. He began to read, chiefly English; he arranged his whole life, roughly speaking, in the English style, rarely saw the neighbours, and only went out to the election of marshals, where he was generally silent, only occasionally annoying and alarming landowners of the old school by his liberal sallies, and not associating with the representatives of the younger generation. Both the latter and the former considered him 'stuck up'; and both parties respected him for his fine aristocratic manners; for his reputation for successes in love; for the fact that he was very well dressed and always stayed in the best room in the best hotel; for the fact that he generally dined well, and had once even dined with Wellington at Louis Philippe's table; for the fact that he always took everywhere with him a real silver dressing-case and a portable bath; for the fact that he always smelt of some exceptionally 'good form' scent; for the fact that he played whist in masterly fashion, and always lost; and lastly, they respected him also for his incorruptible honesty. Ladies considered him enchantingly romantic, but he did not cultivate ladies' acquaintance. . . .

'So you see, Yevgeny,' observed Arkady, as he finished his story, 'how unjustly you judge of my uncle! To say nothing of his having more than once helped my father out of difficulties, given him all his money—the property, perhaps you don't know, wasn't divided—he's glad to help anyone, among other things he always sticks up for the peasants; it's true, when he talks to them he frowns and sniffs eau-de-Cologne.' . . .

'His nerves, no doubt,' put in Bazarov.

'Perhaps! but his heart is very good. And he's far from being stupid. What useful advice he has given me especially . . . especially in regard to relations with women.'

'Aha! a scalded dog fears cold water, we know that!'

'In short,' continued Arkady, 'he's profoundly unhappy, believe me; it's a sin to despise him.'

'And who does despise him?' retorted Bazarov. 'Still, I must say that a fellow who stakes his whole life on one card— a woman's love—and when that card fails, turns sour, and lets himself go till he's fit for nothing, is not a man, but a male. You say he's unhappy; you ought to know best; to be sure, he's not got rid of all his fads. I'm convinced that he solemnly imagines himself a superior creature because he reads that wretched *Galignani,* and once a month saves a peasant from a flogging.'

'But remember his education, the age in which he grew up,' observed Arkady.

'Education?' broke in Bazarov. 'Every man must educate himself, just as I've done, for instance. . . . And as for the age, why should I depend on it? Let it rather depend on me. No, my dear fellow, that's all shallowness, want of backbone! And what stuff it all is, about these mysterious relations between a man and woman! We physiologists know what these relations are. You study the anatomy of the eye; where does the enigmatical glance you talk about come in there? That's all romantic, nonsensical, æsthetic rot. We had much better go and look at the beetle.'

And the two friends went off to Bazarov's room, which was already pervaded by a sort of medico-surgical odour, mingled with the smell of cheap tobacco.

# 8

PAVEL PETROVITCH did not long remain present at his brother's interview with his bailiff, a tall, thin man with a sweet consumptive voice and knavish eyes, who to all Nikolai Petrovitch's remarks answered, 'Certainly, sir,' and tried to make the peasants out to be thieves and drunkards. The estate had only recently been put on to the new reformed system, and the new mechanism worked, creaking like an ungreased wheel, warping and cracking like home-made furniture of unseasoned wood. Nikolai Petrovitch did not lose heart, but often he sighed and was gloomy; he felt that the thing could not go on without money, and his money was almost all spent. Arkady had spoken the truth Pavel Petrovitch had more than once helped his brother; more than once, seeing him struggling and cudgelling his brains, at a loss which way to turn, Pavel Petrovitch moved deliberately to the window and, with his hands thrust into his pockets, muttered between his teeth, *'mais je puis vous donner de l'argent,'* and gave him money; but to-day he had none himself, and he preferred to go away. The petty details of agricultural management worried him; besides, it constantly struck him that Nikolai Petrovitch, for all his zeal and industry, did not set about things in the right way, though he would not have been able to point out precisely where Nikolai Petrovitch's mistake lay.

D

'My brother's not practical enough,' he reasoned to himself; 'they impose upon him.' Nikolai Petrovitch, on the other hand, had the highest opinion of Pavel Petrovitch's practical ability, and always asked his advice. 'I'm a soft, weak fellow, I've spent my life in the wilds,' he used to say; 'while you haven't seen so much of the world for nothing, you see through people; you have an eagle eye.' In answer to which Pavel Petrovitch only turned away, but did not contradict his brother.

Leaving Nikolai Petrovitch in his study, he walked along the corridor which separated the front part of the house from the back; when he had reached a low door, he stopped in hesitation, then pulling his moustaches, he knocked at it.

'Who's there? Come in,' sounded Fenitchka's voice.

'It's I,' said Pavel Petrovitch, and he opened the door.

Fenitchka jumped up from the chair on which she was sitting with her baby, and giving him into the arms of a girl, who at once carried him out of the room, she put straight her kerchief hastily.

'Pardon me, if I disturb you,' began Pavel Petrovitch, not looking at her; 'I only wanted to ask you . . . they are sending into the town to-day, I think . . . please let them buy me some green tea.'

'Certainly,' answered Fenitchka; 'how much do you desire them to buy?'

'Oh, half a pound will be enough, I imagine. You have made a change here, I see,' he added, with a rapid glance round him, which glided over Fenitchka's face too. 'The curtains here,' he explained, seeing she did not understand him.

'Oh, yes, the curtains; Nikolai Petrovitch was so good as to make me a present of them; but they have been put up a long while now.'

'Yes, and it's a long while since I have been to see you. Now it is very nice here.'

'Thanks to Nikolai Petrovitch's kindness,' murmured Fenitchka.

'You are more comfortable here than in the little lodge

you used to have?' inquired Pavel Petrovitch urbanely, but without the slightest smile.

'Certainly, it's more comfortable.'

'Who has been put in your place now?'

'The laundry-maids are there now.'

'Ah!'

Pavel Petrovitch was silent. 'Now he is going,' thought Fenitchka; but he did not go, and she stood before him motionless.

'What did you send your little one away for?' said Pavel Petrovitch at last. 'I love children; let me see him.'

Fenitchka blushed all over with confusion and delight. She was afraid of Pavel Petrovitch; he had scarcely ever spoken to her.

'Dunyasha,' she called, 'will you bring Mitya, please.' (Fenitchka did not treat anyone in the house familiarly.) 'But wait a minute; he must have a frock on,' Fenitchka was going towards the door.

'That doesn't matter,' remarked Pavel Petrovitch.

'I will be back directly,' answered Fenitchka, and she went out quickly.

Pavel Petrovitch was left alone, and he looked round this time with special attention. The small low-pitched room in which he found himself was very clean and snug. It smelt of the freshly painted floor and of camomile. Along the walls stood chairs with lyre-shaped backs, bought by the late general on his campaign in Poland; in one corner was a little bedstead under a muslin canopy beside an iron-clamped chest with a convex lid. In the opposite corner a little lamp was burning before a big dark picture of St. Nikolai the wonder-worker; a tiny porcelain egg hung by a red ribbon from the protruding gold halo down to the saint's breast; by the windows greenish glass jars of last year's jam carefully tied down could be seen; on their paper covers Fenitchka herself had written in big letters 'Gooseberry'; Nikolai Petrovitch was particularly fond of that preserve. On a long cord from the ceiling a cage hung with a short-tailed siskin in it;

35

he was constantly chirping and hopping about, the cage was constantly shaking and swinging, while hempseeds fell with a light tap on to the floor. On the wall just above a small chest-of-drawers hung some rather bad photographs of Nikolai Petrovitch in various attitudes, taken by an itinerant photographer; there too hung a photograph of Fenitchka herself, which was an absolute failure; it was an eyeless face wearing a forced smile, in a dingy frame, nothing more could be made out; while above Fenitchka, General Yermolov, in a Circassian cloak, scowled menacingly upon the Caucasian mountains in the distance, from beneath a little silk shoe for pins which fell right on to his brows.

Five minutes passed; bustling and whispering could be heard in the next room. Pavel Petrovitch took up from the chest-of-drawers a greasy book, an odd volume of Masalsky's *Musketeer,* and turned over a few pages. . . . The door opened, and Fenitchka came in with Mitya in her arms. She had put on him a little red smock with embroidery on the collar, had combed his hair and washed his face; he was breathing heavily, his whole body was working, and his little hands waving in the air, as is the way with all healthy babies; but his smart smock obviously impressed him, an expression of delight was reflected in every part of his little fat person. Fenitchka had put her own hair too in order, and had arranged her kerchief; but she might well have remained as she was. And really is there anything in the world more captivating than a beautiful young mother with a healthy baby in her arms?

'What a chubby fellow!' said Pavel Petrovitch graciously, and he tickled Mitya's little double chin with the tapering nail of his forefinger. The baby stared at the siskin and chuckled.

'That's uncle,' said Fenitchka, bending her face down to him and slightly rocking him, while Dunyasha quietly set in the window a smouldering perfumed stick, putting a half-penny under it.

'How many months old is he?' asked Pavel Petrovitch.

'Six months; it will soon be seven, on the eleventh.'

'Isn't it eight, Fedosya Nikolaevna?' put in Dunyasha, with some timidity.

'No, seven; what an idea!' The baby chuckled again, stared at the chest, and suddenly caught hold of his mother's nose and mouth with all his five little fingers. 'Saucy mite,' said Fenitchka, not drawing her face away.

'He's like my brother,' observed Pavel Petrovitch.

'Who else should he be like?' thought Fenitchka.

'Yes,' continued Pavel Petrovitch, as though speaking to himself; 'there's an unmistakable likeness.' He looked attentively, almost mournfully at Fenitchka.

'That's uncle,' she repeated, in a whisper this time.

'Ah! Pavel! so you're here!' was heard suddenly the voice of Nikolai Petrovitch.

Pavel Petrovitch turned hurriedly round, frowning; but his brother looked at him with such delight, such gratitude, that he could not help responding to his smile.

'You've a splendid little cherub,' he said, looking at his watch. 'I came in here to speak about some tea.'

And, assuming an expression of indifference, Pavel Petrovitch at once went out of the room.

'Did he come of himself?' Nikolai Petrovitch asked Fenitchka.

'Yes; he knocked and came in.'

'Well, and has Arkasha been in to see you again?'

'No. Hadn't I better move into the lodge, Nikolai Petrovitch?'

'Why so?'

'I wonder whether it wouldn't be best just for the first.'

'N . . . no,' Nikolai Petrovitch brought out hesitatingly, rubbing his forehead. 'We ought to have done it before. . . . How are you, fatty?' he said, suddenly brightening, and going up to the baby, he kissed him on the cheek; then he bent a little and pressed his lips to Fenitchka's hand, which lay white as milk upon Mitya's little red smock.

'Nikolai Petrovitch! what are you doing?' she whispered, dropping her eyes, then slowly raised them. Very charming

37

was the expression of her eyes when she peeped, as it were, from under her lids, and smiled tenderly and a little foolishly.

Nikolai Petrovitch had made Fenitchka's acquaintance in the following manner. He had once happened three years before to stay a night at an inn in a remote district town. He was agreeably struck by the cleanness of the room assigned to him, the freshness of the bed-linen. Surely the woman of the house must be a German? was the idea that occurred to him; but she proved to be a Russian, a woman of about fifty, neatly dressed, of a good-looking, sensible countenance and discreet speech. He entered into conversation with her at tea; he liked her very much. Nikolai Petrovitch had at that time only just moved into his new home and, not wishing to keep serfs in the house, he was on the look-out for wage-servants; the woman of the inn on her side complained of the small number of visitors to the town, and the hard times; he proposed to her to come into his house in the capacity of housekeeper; she consented. Her husband had long been dead, leaving her an only daughter, Fenitchka. Within a fortnight Arina Savishna (that was the new housekeeper's name) arrived with her daughter at Maryino and installed herself in the little lodge. Nikolai Petrovitch's choice proved a successful one. Arina brought order into the household. As for Fenitchka, who was at that time seventeen, no one spoke of her, and scarcely anyone saw her; she lived quietly and sedately, and only on Sundays Nikolai Petrovitch noticed in the church somewhere in a side place the delicate profile of her white face. More than a year passed thus.

One morning, Arina came into his study and, bowing low as usual, she asked him if he could do anything for her daughter, who had got a spark from the stove in her eye. Nikolai Petrovitch, like all stay-at-home people, had studied doctoring and even compiled a homœopathic guide. He at once told Arina to bring the patient to him. Fenitchka was much frightened when she heard the master had sent for her; however, she followed her mother. Nikolai Petrovitch led her to the window and took her head in his two hands. After

38

thoroughly examining her red and swollen eye, he prescribed a fomentation, which he made up himself at once, and tearing his handkerchief in pieces, he showed her how it ought to be applied. Fenitchka listened to all he had to say, and then was going. 'Kiss the master's hand, silly girl,' said Arina. Nikolai Petrovitch did not give her his hand, and in confusion himself kissed her bent head on the parting of her hair. Fenitchka's eye was soon well again, but the impression she had made on Nikolai Petrovitch did not pass away so quickly. He was for ever haunted by that pure, delicate, timidly raised face; he felt on the palms of his hands that soft hair, and saw those innocent, slightly parted lips, through which pearly teeth gleamed with moist brilliance in the sunshine. He began to watch her with great attention in church, and tried to get into conversation with her. At first she was shy of him, and one day meeting him at the approach of evening in a narrow footpath through a field of rye, she ran into the tall thick rye, overgrown with cornflowers and wormwood, so as not to meet him face to face. He caught sight of her little head through a golden network of ears of rye, from which she was peeping out like a little animal, and called affectionately to her—

'Good-evening, Fenitchka! I don't bite.'

'Good-evening,' she whispered, not coming out of her ambush.

By degrees she began to be more at home with him, but was still shy in his presence, when suddenly her mother, Arina, died of cholera. What was to become of Fenitchka? She inherited from her mother a love for order, regularity, and respectability; but she was so young, so alone. Nikolai Petrovitch was himself so good and considerate. . . . It's needless to relate the rest . . .

'So my brother came in to see you?' Nikolai Petrovitch questioned her. 'He knocked and came in?'

'Yes.'

'Well, that's a good thing. Let me give Mitya a swing.'

And Nikolai Petrovitch began tossing him almost up to the

ceiling, to the huge delight of the baby, and to the considerable uneasiness of the mother, who every time he flew up stretched her arms up towards his little bare legs.

Pavel Petrovitch went back to his artistic study, with its walls covered with handsome bluish-grey hangings, with weapons hanging upon a variegated Persian rug nailed to the wall; with walnut furniture, upholstered in dark green velveteen, with a *renaissance* bookcase of old black oak, with bronze statuettes on the magnificent writing-table, with an open hearth. He threw himself on the sofa, clasped his hands behind his head, and remained without moving, looking with a face almost of despair at the ceiling. Whether he wanted to hide from the very walls that which was reflected in his face, or for some other reason, he got up, drew the heavy window curtains, and again threw himself on the sofa.

# 9

ON the same day Bazarov made acquaintance with Fenitchka. He was walking with Arkady in the garden, and explaining to him why some of the trees, especially the oaks, had not done well.

'You ought to have planted silver poplars here by preference, and spruce firs, and perhaps limes, giving them some loam. The arbour there has done well,' he added, 'because it's acacia and lilac; they're accommodating good fellows, those trees, they don't want much care. But there's someone in here.'

In the arbour was sitting Fenitchka, with Dunyasha and Mitya. Bazarov stood still, while Arkady nodded to Fenitchka like an old friend.

'Who's that?' Bazarov asked him directly they had passed by. 'What a pretty girl!'

'Whom are you speaking of?'

'You know; only one of them was pretty.'

Arkady, not without embarrassment, explained to him briefly who Fenitchka was.

'Aha!' commented Bazarov; 'your father's got good taste, one can see. I like him, your father, ay, ay! He's a jolly fellow. We must make friends though,' he added, and turned back towards the arbour.

'Yevgeny!' Arkady cried after him in dismay; 'mind what you are about, for mercy's sake.'

'Don't worry yourself,' said Bazarov; 'I know how to behave myself—I'm not a booby.'

Going up to Fenitchka, he took off his cap.

'Allow me to introduce myself,' he began, with a polite bow. 'I'm a harmless person, and a friend of Arkady Nikolaevitch's.'

Fenitchka got up from the garden seat and looked at him without speaking.

'What a splendid baby!' continued Bazarov; 'don't be uneasy, my praises have never brought ill-luck yet. Why is it his cheeks are so flushed? Is he cutting his teeth?'

'Yes,' said Fenitchka; 'he has cut four teeth already, and now the gums are swollen again.'

'Show me, and don't be afraid, I'm a doctor.'

Bazarov took the baby up in his arms, and to the great astonishment both of Fenitchka and Dunyasha the child made no resistance, and was not frightened.

'I see, I see . . . It's nothing, everything's as it should be; he will have a good set of teeth. If anything goes wrong, tell me. And are you quite well yourself?'

'Quite, thank God.'

'Thank God, indeed—that's the great thing. And you?' he added, turning to Dunyasha.

Dunyasha, a girl very prim in the master's house and a romp outside the gates, only giggled in answer.

'Well, that's all right. Here's your gallant fellow.'

Fenitchka received the baby in her arms.

'How good he was with you!' she commented in an under-tone.

'Children are always good with me,' answered Bazarov; 'I have a way with them.'

'Children know who loves them,' remarked Dunyasha.

'Yes, they certainly do,' Fenitchka said. 'Why, Mitya will not go to some people for anything.'

'Will he come to me?' asked Arkady, who, after standing in the distance for some time, had gone up to the arbour.

He tried to entice Mitya to come to him, but Mitya threw his head back and screamed, to Fenitchka's great confusion.

'Another day, when he's had time to get used to me,' said Arkady indulgently, and the two friends walked away.

'What's her name?' asked Bazarov.

'Fenitchka . . . Fedosya,' answered Arkady.

'And her father's name? One must know that too.'

'Nikolaevna.'

'*Bene.* What I like in her is that she's not too embarrassed. Some people, I suppose, would think ill of her for it. What nonsense! What is there to embarrass her? She's a mother—she's all right.'

'She's all right,' observed Arkady—'but my father.'

'And he's right too,' put in Bazarov.

'Well, no, I don't think so.'

'I suppose an extra heir's not to your liking?'

'I wonder you're not ashamed to attribute such ideas to me!' retorted Arkady hotly; 'I don't consider my father wrong from that point of view; I think he ought to marry her.'

'Hoity-toity!' responded Bazarov tranquilly. 'What magnanimous fellows we are! You still attach significance to marriage; I did not expect that of you.'

The friends walked a few paces in silence.

'I have looked at all your father's establishment,' Bazarov began again. 'The cattle are inferior, the horses are broken down; the buildings aren't up to much, and the workmen look

42

confirmed loafers; while the superintendent is either a fool or a knave, I haven't quite found out which yet.'

'You are rather hard on everything to-day, Yevgeny Vassilyevitch.'

'And the dear good peasants are taking your father in, to a dead certainty. You know the Russian proverb, "The Russian peasant will cheat God Himself." '

'I begin to agree with my uncle,' remarked Arkady; 'you certainly have a poor opinion of Russians.'

'As though that mattered! The only good point in a Russian is his having the lowest possible opinion of himself. What does matter is that two and two make four, and the rest is all foolery.'

'And is nature foolery?' asked Arkady, looking pensively at the bright-coloured fields in the distance, in the beautiful soft light of the sun, which was not yet high up in the sky.

'Nature, too, is foolery in the sense you understand it. Nature's not a temple, but a workshop, and man's the workman in it.'

At that instant, the long drawn notes of a violoncello floated out to them from the house. Someone was playing Schubert's *Expectation* with much feeling, though with an untrained hand, and the melody flowed with honey sweetness through the air.

'What's that?' cried Bazarov in amazement.

'It's my father.'

'Your father plays the violoncello?'

'Yes.'

'And how old is your father?'

'Forty-four.'

Bazarov suddenly burst into a roar of laughter.

'What are you laughing at?'

'Upon my word, a man of forty-four, a *paterfamilias* in this out-of-the-way district, playing on the violoncello!'

Bazarov went on laughing; but much as he revered his master, this time Arkady did not even smile.

43

# 10

ABOUT a fortnight passed by. Life at Maryino went on its accustomed course, while Arkady was lazy and enjoyed himself, and Bazarov worked. Everyone in the house had grown used to him, to his careless manners, and his curt and abrupt speeches. Fenitchka, in particular, was so far at home with him that one night she sent to wake him up; Mitya had had convulsions; and he had gone, and, half-joking, half-yawning, as usual, he stayed two hours with her and relieved the child. On the other hand Pavel Petrovitch had grown to detest Bazarov with all the strength of his soul; he regarded him as stuck-up, impudent, cynical, and vulgar; he suspected that Bazarov had no respect for him, that he had all but a contempt for him—him, Pavel Kirsanov! Nikolai Petrovitch was rather afraid of the young 'nihilist', and was doubtful whether his influence over Arkady was for the good; but he was glad to listen to him, and was glad to be present at his scientific and chemical experiments. Bazarov had brought with him a microscope, and busied himself for hours together with it. The servants, too, took to him, though he made fun of them; they felt, all the same, that he was one of themselves, not a master. Dunyasha was always ready to giggle with him, and used to cast significant and stealthy glances at him when she skipped by like a rabbit; Piotr, a man vain and stupid to the last degree, for ever wearing an affected frown on his brow, a man whose whole merit consisted in the fact that he looked civil, could spell out a page of reading, and was diligent in brushing his coat—even he smirked and brightened up directly Bazarov paid him any attention; the boys on the farm simply ran after the 'doctor' like puppies. The old man Prokofitch was the only one who did not like him; he handed him the dishes at table with a surly face, called him a 'butcher' and 'an upstart', and declared that with his great whiskers he looked like a pig in a sty. Prokofitch in his own way was quite as much of an aristocrat as Pavel Petrovitch.

The best days of the year had come—the first days of June. The weather kept splendidly fine; in the distance, it is true, the cholera was threatening, but the inhabitants of that province had had time to get used to its visits. Bazarov used to get up very early and go out for two or three miles, not for a walk—he couldn't bear walking without an object—but to collect specimens of plants and insects. Sometimes he took Arkady with him. On the way home an argument usually sprang up, and Arkady was usually vanquished by it, though he said more than his companion.

One day they had lingered rather late; Nikolai Petrovitch went to meet them in the garden, and as he reached the arbour he suddenly heard the quick steps and voices of the two young men. They were walking on the other side of the arbour, and could not see him.

'You don't know my father well enough,' said Arkady.

'Your father's a nice chap,' said Bazarov, 'but he's behind the times; his day is done.'

Nikolai Petrovitch listened intently. . . . Arkady made no answer.

The man whose day was done remained two minutes motionless, and stole slowly home.

'The day before yesterday I saw him reading Pushkin,' Bazarov was continuing meanwhile. 'Explain to him, please, that that's no earthly use. He's not a boy, you know; it's time to throw up that rubbish. And what an idea to be a romantic at this time of day! Give him something sensible to read.'

'What ought I to give him?' asked Arkady.

'Oh, I think Büchner's *Stoff und Kraft* to begin with.'

'I think so too,' observed Arkardy approvingly, '*Stoff und Kraft* is written in popular language. . . .'

'So it seems,' Nikolai Petrovitch said the same day after dinner to his brother, as he sat in his study, 'you and I are behind the times, our day's over. Well, well. Perhaps

45

Barazov is right; but one thing, I confess, makes me feel sore: I did so hope, precisely now, to get on to such close intimate terms with Arkady, and it turns out I'm left behind, and he has gone forward, and we can't understand one another.

'How has he gone forward? And in what way is he superior to us already?' cried Pavel Petrovitch impatiently. 'It's that high and mighty gentleman, that nihilist, who's knocked all that into his head. I hate that doctor fellow; in my opinion, he's simply a quack; I'm convinced, for all his tadpoles, he's not got very far even in medicine.'

'No, brother, you mustn't say that; Bazarov is clever, and knows his subject.'

'And his conceit's something revolting,' Pavel Petrovitch broke in again.

'Yes,' observed Nikolai Petrovitch, 'he is conceited. But there's no doing without that, it seems; only that's what I did not take into account. I thought I was doing everything to keep up with the times; I have started a model farm; I have done well by the peasants, so that I am positively called a "Red Radical" all over the province; I read, I study, I try in every way to keep abreast with the requirements of the day—and they say my day's over. And, brother, I begin to think that it is.'

'Why so?'

'I'll tell you why. This morning I was sitting reading Pushkin. . . . I remember, it happened to be *The Gipsies* . . . all of a sudden Arkady came up to me, and, without speaking, with such a kindly compassion on his face, as gently as if I were a baby, took the book away from me, and laid another before me—a German book . . . smiled, and went away, carrying Pushkin off with him.'

'Upon my word! What book did he give you?'

'This one here.'

And Nikolai Petrovitch pulled the famous treatise of Büchner, in the ninth edition, out of his coat-tail pocket.

Pavel Petrovitch turned it over in his hands. 'H'm!' he

46

growled. 'Arkady Nikolaevitch is taking your education in hand. Well, did you try reading it?'

'Yes, I tried it.'

'Well, what did you think of it?'

'Either I'm stupid, or it's all—nonsense. I must be stupid, I suppose.'

'Haven't you forgotten your German?' queried Pavel Petrovitch.

'Oh, I understand the German.'

Pavel Petrovitch again turned the book over in his hands, and glanced from under his brows at his brother. Both were silent.

'Oh, by the way,' began Nikolai Petrovitch, obviously wishing to change the subject, 'I've got a letter from Kolyazin.'

'Matvy Ilyitch?'

'Yes. He has come to——to inspect the province. He's quite a bigwig now; and writes to me that, as a relation, he should like to see us again, and invites you and me and Arkady to the town.'

'Are you going?' asked Pavel Petrovitch.

'No; are you?'

'No, I shan't go either. Much object there would be in dragging oneself over forty miles on a wild-goose chase. *Mathieu* wants to show himself in all his glory. Damn him! he will have the whole province doing him homage; he can get on without the likes of us. A grand dignity, indeed, a privy councillor! If I had stayed in the service, if I had drudged on in official harness, I should have been a general-adjutant by now. Besides, you and I are behind the times, you know.'

'Yes, brother; it's time, it seems, to order a coffin and cross one's arms on one's breast,' remarked Nikolai Petrovitch, with a sigh.

'Well, I'm not going to give in quite so soon,' muttered his brother. 'I've got a tussle with that doctor fellow before me, I feel sure of that.'

A tussle came off that same day at evening tea. Pavel

47

Petrovitch came into the drawing-room, all ready for the fray, irritable and determined. He was only waiting for an excuse to fall upon the enemy; but for a long while an excuse did not present itself. As a rule, Bazarov said little in the presence of the 'old Kirsanovs' (that was how he spoke of the brothers), and that evening he felt out of humour, and drank off cup after cup of tea without a word. Pavel Petrovitch was all aflame with impatience; his wishes were fulfilled at last.

The conversation turned on one of the neighbouring landowners. 'Rotten aristocratic snob,' observed Bazarov indifferently. He had met him in Petersburg.

'Allow me to ask you,' began Pavel Petrovitch, and his lips were trembling, 'according to your ideas, have the words "rotten" and "aristocrat" the same meaning?'

'I said "aristocratic snob",' replied Bazarov, lazily swallowing a sip of tea.

'Precisely so; but I imagine you have the same opinion of aristocrats as of aristocratic snobs. I think it my duty to inform you that I do not share that opinion. I venture to assert that everyone knows me for a man of liberal ideas and devoted to progress; but, exactly for that reason, I respect artistocrats—real aristocrats. Kindly remember, sir' (at these words Bazarov lifted his eyes and looked at Pavel Petrovitch), 'kindly remember, sir,' he repeated, with acrimony—'the English aristocracy. They do not abate one iota of their rights, and for that reason they respect the rights of others; they demand the performance of what is due to them, and for that reason they perform their own duties. The aristocracy has given freedom to England, and maintains it for her.'

'We've heard that story a good many times,' replied Bazarov; 'but what are you trying to prove by that?'

'I am tryin' to prove by that, sir'—(when Pavel Petrovitch was angry he intentionally clipped his words in this way, though, of course, he knew very well that such forms are not strictly grammatical. In this fashionable whim could be discerned a survival of the habits of the times of Alexander. The exquisites of those days, on the rare occasions when they spoke their own language, made use of such slipshod forms; as much as to say, 'We, of course, are born Russians, at the same time we are great swells, who are at liberty to neglect the rules of scholars')—'I am tryin' to prove by that, sir, that without the sense of personal dignity, without self-respect—and these two sentiments are well developed in the aristocrat—there is no secure foundation for the social . . . *bien public* . . . the social fabric. Personal character, sir—that is the chief thing; a man's personal character must be firm as a rock, since everything is built on it. I am very well aware, for instance, that you are pleased to consider my habits, my dress, my refinements, in fact, ridiculous; but all that proceeds from a sense of self-respect, from a sense of duty—yes, indeed, of duty. I live in the country, in the wilds, but I will not lower myself. I respect the dignity of man in myself.'

'Let me ask you, Pavel Petrovitch,' commented Bazarov; 'you respect yourself, and sit with your hands folded; what sort of benefit does that do to the *bien public?* If you didn't respect yourself, you'd do just the same.'

Pavel Petrovitch turned white. 'That's a different question. It's absolutely unnecessary for me to explain to you now why I sit with folded hands, as you are pleased to express yourself. I wish only to tell you that aristocracy is a principle, and in our days none but immoral or silly people can live without principles. I said that to Arkady the day after he came home, and I repeat it now. Isn't it so, Nikolai?'

Nikolai Petrovitch nodded his head. 'Aristocracy, Liberalism, progress, principles,' Bazarov was saying meanwhile; 'if you think of it, what a lot of foreign . . . and useless words! To a Russian they're good for nothing.'

'What is good for something according to you? If we listen to you, we shall find ourselves outside humanity, outside its laws. Come—the logic of history demands . . .'

'But what's that logic to us? We can get on without that too.'

'How do you mean?'

49

'Why, this. You don't need logic, I hope, to put a bit of bread in your mouth when you're hungry. What's the object of these abstractions to us?'

Pavel Petrovitch raised his hands in horror.

'I don't understand you, after that. You insult the Russian people. I don't understand how it's possible not to acknowledge principles, rules! By virtue of what do you act then?'

'I've told you already, uncle, that we don't accept any authorities,' put in Arkady.

'We act by virtue of what we recognise as beneficial,' observed Bazarov. 'At the present time, negation is the most beneficial of all—and we deny——'

'Everything?'

'Everything!'

'What? not only art and poetry . . . but even . . . horrible to say . . .'

'Everything,' repeated Bazarov, with indescribable composure.

Pavel Petrovitch stared at him. He had not expected this; while Arkady fairly blushed with delight.

'Allow me, though,' began Nikolai Petrovitch. 'You deny everything; or, speaking more precisely, you destroy everything. . . . But one must construct too, you know.'

'That's not our business now. . . . The ground wants clearing first.'

'The present condition of the people requires it,' added Arkady, with dignity; 'we are bound to carry out these requirements, we have no right to yield to the satisfaction of our personal egoism.'

This last phrase obviously displeased Barazov; there was a flavour of philosophy, that is to say, romanticism about it, for Barazov called philosophy, too, romanticism; but he did not think it necessary to correct his young disciple.

'No, no!' cried Pavel Petrovitch, with sudden energy. 'I'm not willing to believe that you, young men, know the Russian people really, that you are the representatives of their requirements, their efforts! No; the Russian people is not what you imagine it. Tradition it holds sacred; it is a patriarchal people; it cannot live without faith . . .'

'I'm not going to dispute that,' Bazarov interrupted. 'I'm even ready to agree that in that you're right.'

'But if I am right . . .'

'And, all the same, that proves nothing.'

'It just proves nothing,' repeated Arkady, with the confidence of a practised chess-player who has foreseen an apparently dangerous move on the part of his adversary, and so is not at all taken aback by it.

'How does it prove nothing?' muttered Pavel Petrovitch, astounded. 'You must be going against the people then?'

'And what if we are?' shouted Bazarov. 'The people imagine that, when it thunders, the prophet Ilya's riding across the sky in his chariot. What then? Are we to agree with them? Besides, the people's Russian; but am I not Russian too?'

'No, you are not Russian, after all you have just been saying! I can't acknowledge you as Russian.'

'My grandfather ploughed the land,' answered Bazarov with haughty pride. 'Ask any one of your peasants which of us—you or me—he'd more readily acknowledge as a fellow-countryman. You don't even know how to talk to them.'

'While you talk to him and despise him at the same time.'

'Well, suppose he deserves contempt. You find fault with my attitude, but how do you know that I have got it by chance, that it's not a product of that very national spirit in the name of which you wage war on it?'

'What an idea! Much use in nihilists!'

'Whether they're of use or not, is not for us to decide. Why, even you suppose you're not a useless person.'

'Gentlemen, gentlemen, no personalities, please!' cried Nikolai Petrovitch, getting up.

Pavel Petrovitch smiled, and laying his hand on his brother's shoulder, forced him to sit down again.

'Don't be uneasy,' he said; 'I shall not forget myself, just through that sense of dignity which is made fun of so merci-

lessly by our friend—our friend, the doctor. Let me ask,'
he resumed, turning again to Bazarov; 'you suppose, possibly,
that your doctrine is a novelty? That is quite a mistake.
The materialism you advocate has been more than once in
vogue already, and has always proved insufficient . . .'

'A foreign word again!' broke in Bazarov. He was beginning to feel vicious, and his face assumed a peculiar coarse
coppery hue. 'In the first place, we advocate nothing; that's
not our way.'

'What do you do, then?'

'I'll tell you what we do. Not long ago we used to say
that our officials took bribes, that we had no roads, no com-
merce, no real justice . . .'

'Oh, I see, you are reformers—that's what that's called, I
fancy. I too should agree to many of your reforms, but . . .'

'Then we suspected that talk, perpetual talk, and nothing
but talk, about our social diseases was not worth while, that
it all led to nothing but superficiality and pedantry; we saw
that our leading men, so-called advanced people and
reformers, are no good; that we busy ourselves over
foolery, talk rubbish about art, unconscious creativeness,
parliamentarism, trial by jury, and the deuce knows what
all; while, all the while, it's a question of getting bread to
eat, while we're stifling under the grossest superstition, while
all our enterprises come to grief simply because there aren't
honest men enough to carry them on, while the very emancipation our Government's busy upon will hardly come to any
good, because peasants are glad to rob even themselves to get
drunk at the gin-shop.'

'Yes,' interposed Pavel Petrovitch, 'yes; you were convinced of all this, and decided not to undertake anything
seriously yourselves.'

'We decided not to undertake anything,' repeated Bazarov
grimly. He suddenly felt vexed with himself for having, without reason, been so expansive before this gentleman.

'But to confine yourselves to abuse?'

'To confine ourselves to abuse.'

'And that is called nihilism?'

'And that's called nihilism,' Bazarov repeated again, this time with peculiar rudeness.

Pavel Petrovitch puckered up his face a little. 'So that's it!' he observed in a strangely composed voice. 'Nihilism is to cure all our woes, and you, you are our heroes and saviours. But why do you abuse others, those reformers even? Don't you do as much talking as everyone else?'

'Whatever faults we have, we do not err in that way,' Bazarov muttered between his teeth.

'What, then? Do you act, or what? Are you preparing for action?'

Bazarov made no answer. Something like a tremor passed over Pavel Petrovitch, but he at once regained control of himself.

'Hm! . . . Action, destruction . . .' he went on. 'But how destroy without even knowing why?'

'We shall destroy, because we are a force,' observed Arkady.

Pavel Petrovitch looked at his nephew and laughed.

'Yes, a force is not to be called to account,' said Arkady, drawing himself up.

'Unhappy boy!' wailed Pavel Petrovitch; he was positively incapable of maintaining his firm demeanour any longer. 'If you could only realise what it is you are doing for your country. No; it's enough to try the patience of an angel! Force! There's force in the savage Kalmuck, in the Mongolian; but what is it to us? What is precious to us is civilisation; yes, yes, sir, its fruits are precious to us. And don't tell me those fruits are worthless; the poorest dauber, *un barbouilleur,* the man who plays dance music for five farthings an evening, is of more use than you, because they are the representatives of civilisation, and not of brute Mongolian force! You fancy yourselves advanced people, and all the while you are only fit for the Kalmuck's hovel! Force! And recollect, you forcible gentlemen, that you're only four men and a half, and the others are millions, who won't let

53

you trample their sacred traditions under foot, who will crush you and walk over you!'

'If we're crushed, serve us right,' observed Bazarov. 'But that's an open question. We are not so few as you suppose.'

'What? You seriously suppose you will come to terms with a whole people?'

'All Moscow was burnt down, you know, by a farthing dip,' answered Bazarov.

'Yes, yes. First a pride almost Satanic, then ridicule— that, that's what it is attracts the young, that's what gains an ascendancy over the inexperienced hearts of boys! Here's one of them sitting beside you, ready to worship the ground under your feet. Look at him! (Arkady turned away and frowned.) And this plague has spread far already. I have been told that in Rome our artists never set foot in the Vatican. Raphael they regard as almost a fool, because, if you please, he's an authority; while they're all the while most disgustingly sterile and unsuccessful, men whose imagination does not soar beyond "Girls at a Fountain", however they try! And the girls even out of drawing. They are fine fellows to your mind, are they not?'

'To my mind,' retorted Bazarov, 'Raphael's not worth a brass farthing; and they're no better than he.'

'Bravo! bravo! Listen, Arkady . . . that's how young men of to-day ought to express themselves! And if you come to think of it, how could they fail to follow you! In old days, young men had to study; they didn't want to be called dunces, so they had to work hard whether they liked it or not. But now, they need only say, "Everything in the world is foolery!" and the trick's done. Young men are delighted. And, to be sure, they were simply geese before, and now they have suddenly turned nihilists.'

'Your praiseworthy sense of personal dignity has given way,' remarked Bazarov phlegmatically, while Arkady was hot all over and his eyes were flashing. 'Our argument has gone too far; it's better to cut it short, I think. I shall be quite ready to agree with you,' he added, getting up, 'when

54

you bring forward a single institution in our present mode of life, in family or in social life, which does not call for complete and unqualified destruction.'

'I will bring forward millions of such institutions,' cried Pavel Petrovitch—'millions! Well—the Mir, for instance.'

A cold smile curved Bazarov's lips. 'Well, as regards the Mir,' he commented; 'you had better talk to your brother. He has seen by now, I should fancy, what sort of thing the Mir is in fact—its common guarantee, its sobriety, and other features of the kind.'

'The family, then, the family as it exists among our peasants!' cried Pavel Petrovitch.

'And that subject, too, I imagine, it will be better for yourselves not to go into in detail. Don't you realise all the advantages of the head of the family choosing his daughters-in-law? Take my advice, Pavel Petrovitch, allow yourself two days to think about it; you're not likely to find anything on the spot. Go through all our classes, and think well over each, while I and Arkady will . . .'

'Will go on turning everything into ridicule,' broke in Pavel Petrovitch.

'No, will go on dissecting frogs. Come, Arkady; good-bye for the present, gentlemen!'

The two friends walked off. The brothers were left alone, and at first they only looked at one another.

'So that,' began Pavel Petrovitch, 'so that's what our young men of this generation are! They are like that—our successors!'

'Our successors!' repeated Nikolai Petrovitch, with a dejected smile. He had been sitting on thorns, all through the argument, and had done nothing but glance stealthily, with a sore heart, at Arkady. 'Do you know what I was reminded of, brother? I once had a dispute with our poor mother; she stormed, and wouldn't listen to me. At last I said to her, "Of course, you can't understand me; we belong," I said, "to two different generations." She was dreadfully offended, while I thought, "There's no help for it. It's a bitter

55

pill, but she has to swallow it.'' You see, now, our turn has come, and our successors can say to us, ''You are not of our generation; swallow your pill.'' '

'You are beyond everything in your generosity and modesty,' replied Pavel Petrovitch. 'I'm convinced, on the contrary, that you and I are far more in the right than these young gentlemen, though we do perhaps express ourselves in old-fashioned language, *vieilli,* and have not the same insolent conceit. . . . And the swagger of the young men nowadays! You ask one, ''Do you take red wine or white?'' ''It is my custom to prefer red!'' he answers in a deep bass, with a face as solemn as if the whole universe had its eyes on him at that instant. . . .'

'Do you care for any more tea?' asked Fenitchka, putting her head in at the door; she had not been able to make up her mind to come into the drawing-room while there was the sound of voices in dispute there.

'No, you can tell them to take the samovar,' answered Nikolai Petrovitch, and he got up to meet her. Pavel Petrovitch said *'bon soir'* to him abruptly, and went away to his study.

FATHERS AND CHILDREN

# 11

HALF an hour later Nikolai Petrovitch went into the garden to his favourite arbour. He was overtaken by melancholy thoughts. For the first time he realised clearly the distance between him and his son; he foresaw that every day it would grow wider and wider. In vain, then, had he spent whole days sometimes in the winter at Petersburg over the newest books; in vain had he listened to the talk of the young men; in vain had he rejoiced when he succeeded in putting in his word too in their heated discussions. 'My brother says we are right,' he thought, 'and apart from all vanity, I do think myself that they are farther from the truth than we are, though at the same time I feel there is something behind them we have not got, some superiority over us. . . . Is it youth? No; not only youth. Doesn't their superiority consist in there being fewer traces of the slave-owner in them than in us?'

Nikolai Petrovitch's head sank despondently, and he passed his hand over his face.

'But to renounce poetry?' he thought again; 'to have no feeling for art, for nature . . .'

And he looked round, as though trying to understand how it was possible to have no feeling for nature. It was already evening; the sun was hidden behind a small copse of aspens which lay a quarter of a mile from the garden; its shadow stretched indefinitely across the still fields. A peasant on a white nag went at a trot along the dark, narrow path close beside the copse; his whole figure was clearly visible even to the patch on his shoulder, in spite of his being in the shade; the horse's hoofs flew along bravely. The sun's rays from the farther side fell full on the copse and, piercing through its thickets, threw such a warm light on the aspen trunks that they looked like pines, and their leaves were almost a dark blue, while above them rose a pale blue sky, faintly tinged by the glow of sunset. The swallows flew high; the wind had quite died away, belated bees hummed slowly and drowsily among the lilac blossom; a swarm of midges hung like a cloud over a solitary branch which stood out against the sky. 'How beautiful, my God!' thought Nikolai Petrovitch, and his favourite verses were almost on his lips; he remembered Arkady's *Stoff und Kraft*—and was silent, but still he sat there, still he gave himself up to the sorrowful consolation of solitary thought. He was fond of dreaming; his country life had developed the tendency in him. How short a time ago he had been dreaming like this, waiting for his son at the posting station, and what a change already since that day; their relations, that were then undefined, were defined now—and how defined! Again his dead wife came back to

57

his imagination, but not as he had known her for many years, not as the good domestic housewife, but as a young girl with a slim figure, innocently inquiring eyes, and a tight twist of hair on her childish neck. He remembered how he had seen her for the first time. He was still a student then. He had met her on the staircase of his lodgings, and, jostling by accident against her, he tried to apologise, and could only mutter, *'Pardon, monsieur,'* while she bowed, smiled, and suddenly seemed frightened, and ran away, though at the bend of the staircase she had glanced rapidly at him, assumed a serious air, and blushed. Afterwards, the first timid visits, the half-words, the half-smiles, and embarrassment; and melancholy, and yearnings, and at last that breathing rapture. . . . Where had it all vanished? She had been his wife, he had been happy as few on earth are happy. . . . 'But,' he mused, 'these sweet, first moments, why could one not live an eternal, undying life in them?'

He did not try to make his thought clear to himself; but he felt that he longed to keep that blissful time by something stronger than memory; he longed to feel his Marya near him again, to have the sense of her warmth and breathing, and already he could fancy that over him. . . .

'Nikolai Petrovitch,' came the sound of Fenitchka's voice close by him; 'where are you?'

He started. He felt no pang, no shame. He never even admitted the possibility of comparison between his wife and Fenitchka, but he was sorry she had thought of coming to look for him. Her voice had brought back to him at once his grey hairs, his age, his reality. . . .

The enchanted world into which he was just stepping, which was just rising out of the dim mists of the past, was shaken— and vanished.

'I'm here,' he answered; 'I'm coming, run along.' 'There it is, the traces of the slave-owner,' flashed through his mind. Fenitchka peeped into the arbour at him without speaking, and disappeared; while he noticed with astonishment that the night had come on while he had been dreaming. Everything around was dark and hushed. Fenitchka's face had glimmered so pale and slight before him. He got up, and was about to go home; but the emotion stirred in his heart could not be soothed at once, and he began slowly walking about the garden, sometimes looking at the ground at his feet, and then raising his eyes towards the sky, where swarms of stars were twinkling. He walked a great deal, till he was almost tired out, while the restlessness within him, a kind of yearning, vague, melancholy restlessness, still was not appeased. Oh, how Bazarov would have laughed at him, if he had known what was passing within him then! Arkady himself would have condemned him. He, a man of forty-four years old, an agriculturist and a farmer, was shedding tears, causeless tears; this was a hundred times worse than the violoncello.

Nikolai Petrovitch continued walking, and could not make up his mind to go into the house, into the snug peaceful nest which looked out at him so hospitably from all its lighted windows; he had not the force to tear himself away from the darkness, the garden, the sense of the fresh air in his face, from that melancholy, that restless craving.

At a turn in the path, he was met by Pavel Petrovitch. 'What's the matter with you?' he asked Nikolai Petrovitch; 'you are as white as a ghost; you are not well; why don't you go to bed?'

Nikolai Petrovitch explained to him briefly his state of feeling and moved away. Pavel Petrovitch went to the end of the garden, and he too grew thoughtful, and he too raised his eyes towards the heavens. But in his beautiful dark eyes, nothing was reflected but the light of the stars. He was not born an idealist, and his fastidiously dry and sensuous soul, with its French tinge of cynicism, was not capable of dreaming. . . .

'Do you know what?' Bazarov was saying to Arkady the same night. 'I've got a splendid idea. Your father was saying to-day that he'd had an invitation from your illustrious relative. Your father's not going; let us be off to X——; you know the worthy man invites you, too. You see what fine

59

weather it is; we'll stroll about and look at the town. We'll have five or six days outing and enjoy ourselves.'

'And you'll come back here again?'

'No; I must go to my father's. You know, he lives about twenty-five miles from X——. I've not seen him for a long while, and my mother too; I must cheer the old people up. They've been good to me, especially my father; he's awfully funny. I'm their only one too.'

'And will you be long with them?'

'I don't suppose so. It will be dull, of course.'

'And you'll come to us on your way back?'

'I don't know . . . I'll see. Well, what do you say? Shall we go?'

'If you like,' observed Arkady languidly.

In his heart he was highly delighted with his friend's suggestion, but he thought it a duty to conceal his feeling. He was not a nihilist for nothing!

The next day he set off with Bazarov to X——. The younger part of the household at Maryino were sorry at their going; Dunyasha even cried . . . but the old folks breathed more easily.

FATHERS AND CHILDREN

# 12

THE town of X—— to which our friends set off was in the jurisdiction of a governor who was a young man, and at once a progressive and a despot, as often happens with Russians. Before the end of the first year of his government, he had managed to quarrel not only with the marshal of nobility, a retired officer of the guards, who kept open house and a stud of horses, but even with his own subordinates. The feuds arising from this cause assumed at last such proportions that the ministry in Petersburg had found it necessary to send down a trusted personage with a commission to investigate it all on the spot. The choice of the authorities fell upon Matvy Ilyitch Kolyazin, the son of the Kolyazin under whose protection the brothers Kirsanov had once found themselves. He, too, was a 'young man'; that is to say, he had not long passed forty, but he was already on the high road to becoming a statesman, and wore a star on each side of his breast—one, to be sure, a foreign star, not of the first magnitude. Like the governor whom he had come down to pass judgment upon, he was reckoned a progressive; and though he was already a bigwig, he was not like the majority of bigwigs. He had the highest opinion of himself; his vanity knew no bounds, but he behaved simply, looked affable, listened condescendingly, and laughed so good-naturedly that on a first acquaintance he might even be taken for 'a jolly good fellow'. On important occasions, however, he knew, as the saying is, how to make his authority felt. 'Energy is essential,' he used to say then, *'l'énergie est la première qualité d'un homme d'état;'* and for all that, he was usually taken in, and any moderately experienced official could turn him round his finger. Matvy Ilyitch used to speak with great respect of Guizot, and tried to impress everyone with the idea that he did not belong to the class of *routiniers* and high-and-dry bureaucrats, that not a single phenomenon of social life passed unnoticed by him. . . . All such phrases were very familiar to him. He even followed, with dignified indifference, it is true, the development of contemporary literature; so a grown-up man who meets a procession of small boys in the street will sometimes walk after it. In reality, Matvy Ilyitch had not got much beyond those political men of the days of Alexander who used to prepare for an evening party at Madame Svyetchin's by reading a page of Condillac; only his methods were different, more modern. He was an adroit courtier, a great hypocrite, and nothing more; he had no special aptitude for affairs, and no intellect, but he knew how to manage his own business successfully; no one could get the better of him there, and, to be sure, that's the principal thing.

61

Matvy Ilyitch received Arkady with the good-nature, we might even call it playfulness, characteristic of the enlightened higher official. He was astonished, however, when he heard that the cousins he had invited had remained at home in the country. 'Your father was always a queer fellow,' he remarked, playing with the tassels of his magnificent velvet dressing-gown, and suddenly turning to a young official in a discreetly buttoned-up uniform, he cried, with an air of concentrated attention, 'What?' The young man, whose lips were glued together from prolonged silence, got up and looked in perplexity at his chief. But, having nonplussed his subordinate, Matvy Ilyitch paid him no further attention. Our higher officials are fond as a rule of nonplussing their subordinates; the methods to which they have recourse to attain that end are rather various. The following means, among others, is in great vogue, *'is quite a favourite,'* as the English say; a high official suddenly ceases to understand the simplest words, assuming total deafness. He will ask, for instance, 'What's to-day?'

He is respectfully informed, 'To-day's Friday, your Ex-s-s-s-lency.'

'Eh? What? What's that? What do you say?' the great man repeats with intense attention.

'To-day's Friday, your Ex—s—s—lency.'

'Eh? What? What's Friday? What Friday?'

'Friday, your Ex—s—s—s—lency, the day of the week.'

'What, do you pretend to teach me, eh?'

Matvy Ilyitch was a higher official all the same, though he was reckoned a liberal.

'I advise you, my dear boy, to go and call on the Governor,' he said to Arkady; 'you understand, I don't advise you to do so because I adhere to old-fashioned ideas of the necessity of paying respect to authorities, but simply because the Governor's a very decent fellow; besides, you probably want to make acquaintance with the society here. . . . You're not a bear, I hope? And he's giving a great ball the day after to-morrow.'

'Will you be at the ball?' inquired Arkady.

'He gives it in my honour,' answered Matvy Ilyitch, almost pityingly. 'Do you dance?'

'Yes; I dance, but not well.'

'That's a pity! There are pretty girls here, and it's a disgrace for a young man not to dance. Again, I don't say that through any old-fashioned ideas; I don't in the least imagine that a man's wit lies in his feet, but Byronism is ridiculous, *il a fait son temps.*'

'But, uncle, it's not through Byronism, I . . .'

'I will introduce you to the ladies here; I will take you under my wing,' interrupted Matvy Ilyitch, and he laughed complacently. 'You'll find it warm, eh?'

A servant entered and announced the arrival of the superintendent of the Crown domains, a mild-eyed old man, with deep creases round his mouth, who was excessively fond of nature, especially on a summer day, when, in his words, 'every little busy bee takes a little bribe from every little flower.' Arkady withdrew.

He found Bazarov at the tavern where they were staying, and was a long while persuading him to go with him to the Governor's. 'Well, there's no help for it,' said Bazarov at last. 'It's no good doing things by halves. We came to look at the gentry; let's look at them!'

The Governor received the young men affably, but he did not ask them to sit down, nor did he sit down himself. He was in an everlasting fuss and hurry; in the morning he used to put on a tight uniform and an excessively stiff cravat; he never ate or drank enough; he was for ever making arrangements. He invited Kirsanov and Bazarov to his ball, and within a few minutes invited them a second time, regarding them as brothers, and calling them Kisarov.

They were on their way home from the Governor's, when suddenly a short man, in a Slavophil national dress, leaped out of a trap that was passing them, and crying, 'Yevgeny Vassilyitch!' dashed up to Bazarov.

'Ah! it's you, Herr Sitnikov,' observed Bazarov, still

63

stepping along on the pavement; 'by what chance did you come here?'

'Fancy, absolutely by chance,' he replied, and returning to the trap, he waved his hand several times, and shouted, 'Follow, follow us! My father had business here,' he went on, hopping across the gutter, 'and so he asked me. . . . I heard to-day of your arrival, and have already been to see you. . . .' (The friends did, in fact, on returning to their room, find there a card, with the corners turned down, bearing the name of Sitnikov, on one side in French, on the other in Slavonic characters.) 'I hope you are not coming from the Governor's?'

'It's no use to hope; we come straight from him.'

'Ah! in that case I will call on him too. . . . Yevgeny Vassilyitch, introduce me to your . . . to the . . .'

'Sitnikov, Kirsanov,' mumbled Barazov, not stopping.

'I am greatly flattered,' began Sitnikov, walking sideways, smirking, and hurriedly pulling off his really over-elegant gloves. 'I have heard so much. . . . I am an old acquaintance of Yevgeny Vassilyitch, and, I may say—his disciple. I am indebted to him for my regeneration. . . .'

Arkady looked at Bazarov's disciple. There was an expression of excitement and dullness imprinted on the small but pleasant features of his well-groomed face; his small eyes, that seemed squeezed in, had a fixed and uneasy look, and his laugh, too, was uneasy—a sort of short, wooden laugh.

'Would you believe it,' he pursued, 'when Yevgeny Vassilyitch for the first time said before me that it was not right to accept any authorities, I felt such enthusiasm . . . as though my eyes were opened! Here, I thought, at last I have found a man! By the way, Yevgeny Vassilyitch, you positively must come to know a lady here who is really capable of understanding you, and for whom your visit would be a real festival; you have heard of her, I suppose?'

'Who is it?' Bazarov brought out unwillingly.

'Kukshina, *Eudoxie*, Evdoksya Kukshin. She's a remarkable nature, *émancipée* in the true sense of the word, an advanced woman. Do you know what? We'll all go together to see her now. She lives only two steps from here. We will have lunch there. I suppose you have not lunched yet?'

'No; not yet.'

'Well, that's capital. She has separated, you understand, from her husband; she is not dependent on anyone.'

'Is she pretty?' Bazarov cut in.

'N . . . no, one couldn't say that.'

'Then, what the devil are you asking us to see her for?'

'Fie; you must have your joke. . . . She will give us a bottle of champagne.'

'Oh, that's it. One can see the practical man at once. By the way, is your father still in the gin business?'

'Yes,' said Sitnikov, hurriedly, and he gave a shrill spasmodic laugh. 'Well? Will you come?'

'I don't really know.'

'You wanted to see people, go along,' said Arkady in an undertone.

'And what do you say to it, Mr. Kirsanov?' Sitnikov put in. 'You must come too; we can't go without you.'

'But how can we burst in upon her all at once?'

'That's no matter. Kukshina's a brick!'

'There will be a bottle of champagne?' asked Bazarov.

'Three!' cried Sitnikov; 'that I answer for.'

'What with?'

'My own head.'

'Your father's purse would be better. However, we are coming.'

# 13

THE small gentleman's house in the Moscow style in which Avdotya Nikitishna, otherwise Evdoksya, Kukshin lived was in one of the streets of X—— which had been lately burnt down; it is well known that our provincial towns are burnt down every five years. At the door, above a visiting-card nailed on all askew, there was a bell-handle to be seen, and in the hall the visitors were met by someone, not exactly a servant, nor exactly a companion, in a cap—unmistakable tokens of the progressive tendencies of the lady of the house. Sitnikov inquired whether Avdotya Nikitishna was at home.

'Is that you, *Victor?*' sounded a shrill voice from the adjoining room. 'Come in.'

The woman in the cap disappeared at once.

'I'm not alone,' observed Sitnikov, with a sharp look at Arkady and Bazarov as he briskly pulled off his overcoat, beneath which appeared something of the nature of a coach-man's velvet jacket.

'No matter,' answered the voice. *'Entrez.'*

The young men went in. The room into which they walked was more like a working study than a drawing-room. Papers, letters, fat numbers of Russian journals, for the most part uncut, lay at random on the dusty tables; white cigarette ends lay scattered in every direction. On a leather-covered sofa, a lady, still young, was half reclining. Her fair hair was rather dishevelled; she wore a silk gown, not perfectly tidy, heavy bracelets on her short arms, and a lace handkerchief on her head. She got up from the sofa, and carelessly drawing a velvet cape trimmed with yellowish ermine over her shoulders, she said languidly, 'Good-morning, *Victor,*' and pressed Sitnikov's hand.

'Bazarov, Kirsanov,' he announced abruptly in imitation of Bazarov.

'Delighted,' answered Madame Kukshin, and fixing on Bazarov a pair of round eyes, between which was a forlorn little turned-up red nose, 'I know you,' she added, and pressed his hand too.

Bazarov scowled. There was nothing repulsive in the little plain person of the emancipated woman; but the expression of her face produced a disagreeable effect on the spectator.

66

One felt impelled to ask her, 'What's the matter; are you hungry? Or bored? Or shy? What are you in a fidget about?' Both she and Sitnikov had always the same uneasy air. She was extremely unconstrained, and at the same time awkward; she obviously regarded herself as a good-natured, simple creature, and all the while, whatever she did, it always struck one that it was not just what she wanted to do; everything with her seemed, as children say, done on purpose, that's to say, not simply, not naturally.

'Yes, yes, I know you, Bazarov,' she repeated. (She had the habit—peculiar to many provincial and Moscow ladies—of calling men by their surnames from the first day of acquaintance with them.) 'Will you have a cigar?'

'A cigar's all very well,' put in Sitnikov, who by now was lolling in an armchair, his legs in the air; 'but give us some lunch. We're awfully hungry; and tell them to bring us up a little bottle of champagne.'

'Sybarite,' commented Evdoksya, and she laughed. (When she laughed the gum showed above her upper teeth.) 'Isn't it true, Bazarov; he's a Sybarite?'

'I like comfort in life,' Sitnikov brought out, with dignity. 'That does not prevent my being a Liberal.'

'No, it does; it does prevent it!' cried Evdoksya. She gave directions, however, to her maid, both as regards the lunch and the champagne.

'What do you think about it?' she added, turning to Bazarov. 'I'm persuaded you share my opinion.'

'Well, no,' retorted Bazarov; 'a piece of meat's better than a piece of bread even from the chemical point of view.'

'You are studying chemistry? That is my passion. I've even invented a new sort of composition myself.'

'A composition? You?'

'Yes. And do you know for what purpose? To make dolls' heads so that they shouldn't break. I'm practical, too, you see. But everything's not quite ready yet. I've still to read Liebig. By the way, have you read Kislyakov's article on Female Labour, in the *Moscow Gazette?* Read it, please.

You're interested in the woman question, I suppose? And in the schools too? What does your friend do? What is his name?'

Madame Kukshin shed her questions one after another with affected negligence, not waiting for an answer; spoilt children talk so to their nurses.

'My name's Arkady Nikolaitch Kirsanov,' said Arkady, 'and I'm doing nothing.'

Evdoksya giggled. 'How charming! What, don't you smoke? Victor, do you know, I'm very angry with you.'

'What for?'

'They tell me you've begun singing the praises of George Sand again. A retrograde woman, and nothing else! How can people compare her with Emerson! She hasn't an idea on education, nor physiology, nor anything. She'd never, I'm persuaded, heard of embryology, and in these days—what can be done without that?' (Evdoksya even threw up her hands.) 'Ah, what a wonderful article Elisyevitch has written on that subject! He's a gentleman of genius.' (Evdoksya constantly made use of the word 'gentleman' instead of the word 'man'.) 'Bazarov, sit by me on the sofa. You don't know, perhaps, I'm awfully afraid of you.'

'Why so? Allow me to ask.'

'You're a dangerous gentleman; you're such a critic. Good God! yes! why, how absurd, I'm talking like some country lady. I really am a country lady, though. I manage my property myself; and only fancy, my bailiff Erofay's a wonderful type, quite like Cooper's Pathfinder; something in him so spontaneous! I've come to settle here finally; it's an intolerable town, isn't it? But what's one to do?'

'The town's like every town,' Bazarov remarked coolly.

'All its interests are so petty, that's what's so awful! I used to spend the winters in Moscow . . . but now my lawful spouse, Monsieur Kukshin's residing there. And besides, Moscow nowadays . . . there, I don't know—it's not the same as it was. I'm thinking of going abroad; last year I was on the point of setting off.'

'To Paris, I suppose?' queried Bazarov.

'To Paris and to Heidelberg.'

'Why to Heidelberg?'

'How can you ask? Why, Bunsen's there!'

To this Bazarov could find no reply.

'*Pierre* Sapozhnikov . . . do you know him?'

'No, I don't.'

'Not know *Pierre* Sapozhnikov . . . he's always at Lidia Hestatov's.'

'I don't know her either.'

'Well, it was he undertook to escort me. Thank God, I'm independent; I've no children. . . . What was that I said: *thank God!* It's no matter though.'

Evdoksya rolled a cigarette up between her fingers, which were brown with tobacco stains, put it to her tongue, licked it up, and began smoking. The maid came in with a tray.

'Ah, here's lunch! Will you have an appetiser first? Victor, open the bottle; that's in your line.'

'Yes, it's in my line,' muttered Sitnikov, and again he gave vent to the same convulsive laugh.

'Are there any pretty women here?' inquired Bazarov, as he drank off a third glass.

'Yes, there are,' answered Evdoksya; 'but they're all such empty-headed creatures. *Mon amie,* Odintsova, for instance, is nice-looking. It's a pity her reputation's rather doubtful. . . . That wouldn't matter, though, but she's no independence in her views, no width, nothing . . . of all that. The whole system of education wants changing. I've thought a great deal about it; our women are very badly educated.'

'There's no doing anything with them,' put in Sitnikov; 'one ought to despise them, and I do despise them fully and completely!' (The possibility of feeling and expressing contempt was the most agreeable sensation to Sitnikov; he used to attack women in especial, never suspecting that it was to be his fate a few months later to be cringing before his wife merely because she had been born a Princess Durdoleosov.) 'Not a single one of them would be capable of understanding our conversation; not a single one deserves to be spoken of by serious men like us!'

'But there's not the least need for them to understand our conversation,' observed Bazarov.

'Whom do you mean?' put in Evdoksya.

'Pretty women.'

'What? Do you adopt Proudhon's ideas, then?'

Bazarov drew himself up haughtily. 'I don't adopt anyone's ideas; I have my own.'

'Damn all authorities!' shouted Sitnikov, delighted to have a chance of expressing himself boldly before the man he slavishly admired.

'But even Macaulay,' Madame Kukshin was beginning . . .

'Damn Macaulay,' thundered Sitnikov. 'Are you going to stand up for the silly hussies?'

'For silly hussies, no, but for the rights of women, which I have sworn to defend to the last drop of my blood.'

'Damn!'—but here Sitnikov stopped. 'But I don't deny them,' he said.

'No, I see you're a Slavophil.'

'No, I'm not a Slavophil, though, of course . . .'

'No, no, no. You are a Slavophil. You're an advocate of patriarchal despotism. You want to have the whip in your hand!'

'A whip's an excellent thing,' remarked Bazarov; 'but we've got to the last drop.'

'Of what?' interrupted Evdoksya.

'Of champagne, most honoured Avdotya Nikitishna, of champagne—not of your blood.'

'I can never listen calmly when women are attacked,' pursued Evdoksya. 'It's awful, awful. Instead of attacking them, you'd better read Michelet's book, *De l'amour*. That's exquisite! Gentlemen, let us talk of love,' added Evdoksya letting her arm fall languidly on the rumpled sofa cushion.

A sudden silence followed. 'No, why should we talk of love?' said Bazarov; 'but you mentioned just now a Madame

Odintsov . . . That was what you called her, I think? Who is that lady?'

'She's charming, charming!' piped Sitnikov. 'I will introduce you. Clever, rich, a widow. It's a pity she's not yet advanced enough; she ought to see more of our Evdoksya. I drink to your health, *Eudoxie!* Let us clink glasses! *Et toc, et toc, et tin-tin-tin! Et toc, et toc, et tin-tin-tin!!!*'

'Victor, you're a wretch.'

The lunch dragged on a long while. The first bottle of champagne was followed by another, a third, and even a fourth. . . . Evdoksya chattered without pause; Sitnikov seconded her. They had much discussion upon the question whether marriage was a prejudice or a crime, and whether men were born equal or not, and precisely what individuality consists in. Things came at last to Evdoksya, flushed from the wine she had drunk, tapping with her flat finger-tips on the keys of a discordant piano, and beginning to sing in a hoarse voice, first gipsy songs, and then Seymour Schiff's song, 'Granada lies slumbering'; while Sitnikov tied a scarf round his head, and represented the dying lover at the words—

> 'And thy lips to mine
> In burning kiss entwine'

Arkady could not stand it at last. 'Gentlemen, it's getting something like Bedlam,' he remarked aloud. Bazarov, who had at rare intervals put in an ironical word in the conversation—he paid more attention to the champagne—gave a loud yawn, got up, and, without taking leave of their hostess, he walked off with Arkady. Sitnikov jumped up and followed them.

'Well, what do you think of her?' he inquired, skipping obsequiously from right to left of them. 'I told you, you see, a remarkable personality! If only we had more women like that! She is, in her own way, an expression of the highest morality.'

'And is that establishment of your governor's an expression of the highest morality too?' observed Bazarov, pointing to a gin-shop which they were passing at that instant.

Sitnikov again went off into a shrill laugh. He was greatly ashamed of his origin, and did not know whether to feel flattered or offended at Bazarov's unexpected familiarity.

# 14

A FEW days later the ball at the Governor's took place. Matvy Ilyitch was the real 'hero of the occasion'. The marshal of nobility declared to all and each that he had come simply out of respect for him; while the Governor, even at the ball, even while he remained perfectly motionless, was still 'making arrangements'. The affability of Matvy Ilyitch's demeanour could only be equalled by its dignity. He was gracious to all, to some with a shade of disgust, to others with a shade of respect; he was all bows and smiles *'en vrai chevalier français'* before the ladies, and was continually giving vent to a hearty, sonorous, unshared laugh, such as befits a high official. He slapped Arkady on the back, and called him loudly 'nephew'; vouchsafed Bazarov—who was attired in a rather old evening coat—a sidelong glance in passing, absent but condescending, and an indistinct but affable grunt in which nothing could be distinguished but 'I . . .' and 'very much'; gave Sitnikov a finger and a smile, though with his head already averted; even to Madame Kukshin, who made her appearance at the ball with dirty gloves, no crinoline, and a bird of Paradise in her hair, he said *'enchanté'*. There were crowds of people, and no lack of dancing men; the civilians were for the most part standing close along the walls, but the officers danced assiduously, especially one of them who had spent six weeks in Paris, where he had mastered various daring interjections of the kind of—*'zut'*, *'Ah, fichtr-re'*, *'pst, pst, mon bibi'*, and such. He pronounced them to perfection with genuine Parisian

72

*chic,* and at the same time he said *'si j'aurais'* for *'si j'avais'*, *'absolument'* in the sense of 'absolutely', expressing himself, in fact, in that Great Russo-French jargon which the French ridicule so when they have no reason for assuring us that we speak French like angels, *'comme des anges.'*

Arkady, as we are aware, danced badly, while Bazarov did not dance at all; they both took up their position in a corner; Sitnikov joined himself on to them, with an expression of contemptuous scorn on his face, and giving vent to spiteful comments, he looked insolently about him, and seemed to be really enjoying himself. Suddenly his face changed, and turning to Arkady, he said, with some show of embarrassment it seemed, 'Odintsova is here!'

Arkady looked round, and saw a tall woman in a black dress standing at the door of the room. He was struck by the dignity of her carriage. Her bare arms lay gracefully beside her slender waist; gracefully some light sprays of fuchsia drooped from her shining hair on to her sloping shoulders; her clear eyes looked out from under a rather overhanging white brow, with a tranquil and intelligent expression— tranquil it was precisely, not pensive—and on her lips was a scarcely perceptible smile. There was a kind of gracious and gentle force about her face.

'Do you know her?' Arkady asked Sitnikov.

'Intimately. Would you like me to introduce you?'

'Please . . . after this quadrille.'

Bazarov's attention, too, was directed to Madame Odintsov.

'That's a striking figure,' he remarked. 'Not like the other females.'

After waiting till the end of the quadrille, Sitnikov led Arkady up to Madame Odintsov; but he hardly seemed to be intimately acquainted with her; he was embarrassed in his sentences, while she looked at him in some surprise. But her face assumed an expression of pleasure when she heard Arkady's surname. She asked him whether he was not the son of Nikolai Petrovitch.

'Yes.'

73

'I have seen your father twice, and have heard a great deal about him,' she went on; 'I am glad to make your acquaintance.'

At that instant some adjutant flew up to her and begged for a quadrille. She consented.

'Do you dance then?' asked Arkady respectfully.

'Yes, I dance. Why do you suppose I don't dance? Do you think I am too old?'

'Really, how could I possibly. . . . But in that case, let me ask you for a mazurka.'

Madame Odintsov smiled graciously. 'Certainly,' she said, and she looked at Arkady, not exactly with an air of superiority, but as married sisters look at very young brothers. Madame Odintsov was a little older than Arkady—she was twenty-nine—but in her presence he felt himself a schoolboy, a little student, so that the difference in age between them seemed of more consequence. Matvy Ilyitch approached her with a majestic air and ingratiating speeches. Arkady moved away, but he still watched her; he could not take his eyes off her even during the quadrille. She talked with equal ease to her partner and to the grand official, softly turned her head and eyes, and twice laughed softly. Her nose—like almost all Russian noses—was a little thick; and her complexion was not perfectly clear; Arkady made up his mind, for all that, that he had never before met such an attractive woman. He could not get the sound of her voice out of his ears; the very folds of her dress seemed to hang upon her differently from all the rest—more gracefully and amply—and her movements were distinguished by a peculiar smoothness and naturalness.

Arkady felt some timidity in his heart when at the first sounds of the mazurka he began to sit it out beside his partner; he had prepared to enter into a conversation with her, but he only passed his hand through his hair, and could not find a single word to say. But his timidity and agitation did not last long; Madame Odintsov's tranquillity gained upon him too; before a quarter of an hour had passed he was telling her freely about his father, his uncle, his life in Petersburg and

74

in the country. Madame Odintsov listened to him with courteous sympathy, slightly opening and closing her fan; his talk was broken off when partners came for her; Sitnikov, among others, twice asked her. She came back, sat down again, took up her fan, and her bosom did not even heave more rapidly, while Arkady fell to chattering again, filled through and through by the happiness of being near her, talking to her, looking at her eyes, her lovely brow, all her sweet, dignified, clever face. She said little, but her words showed a knowledge of life; from some of her observations Arkady gathered that this young woman had already felt and thought much. . . .

'Who is that you were standing with?' she asked him, 'when Mr. Sitnikov brought you to me?'

'Did you notice him?' Arkady asked in his turn. 'He has a splendid face, hasn't he? That's Bazarov, my friend.'

Arkady fell to discussing 'his friend'. He spoke of him in such detail, and with such enthusiasm, that Madame Odintsov turned towards him and looked attentively at him. Meanwhile, the mazurka was drawing to a close. Arkady felt sorry to part from his partner; he had spent nearly an hour so happily with her! He had, it is true, during the whole time continually felt as though she were condescending to him, as though he ought to be grateful to her . . . but young hearts are not weighed down by that feeling.

The music stopped. *'Merci,'* said Madame Odintsov, getting up. 'You promised to come and see me; bring your friend with you. I shall be curious to see the man who has the courage to believe in nothing.'

The Governor came up to Madame Odintsov, announced that supper was ready, and, with a careworn face, offered her his arm. As she went away, she turned to give a last smile and bow to Arkady. He bowed low, looked after her (how graceful her figure seemed to him, draped in the greyish lustre of the black silk!), and thinking, 'This minute she has forgotten my existence,' was conscious of an exquisite humility in his soul.

'Well?' Bazarov questioned him, directly he had gone back to him in the corner. 'Did you have a good time? A gentleman has just been talking to me about that lady; he said, "She's—oh, fie! fie!" but I fancy the fellow was a fool. What do you think, what is she?—oh, fie! fie!'

'I don't quite understand that definition,' answered Arkady.

'Oh, my! What innocence!'

'In that case, I don't understand the gentleman you quote. Madame Odintsov is very sweet, no doubt, but she behaves so coldly and severely, that . . .'

'Still waters . . . you know!' put in Bazarov. 'That's just what gives it piquancy. You like ices, I expect?'

'Perhaps,' muttered Arkady. 'I can't give an opinion about that. She wishes to make your acquaintance, and has asked me to bring you to see her.'

'I can imagine how you've described me! But you did very well. Take me. Whatever she may be—whether she's simply a provincial lioness, or "advanced" after Kukshina's fashion—anyway she's got a pair of shoulders such as I've not set eyes on for a long while.'

Arkady was wounded by Bazarov's cynicism, but—as often happens—he reproached his friend not precisely for what he did not like in him . . .

'Why are you unwilling to allow free-thinking in women?' he said in a low voice.

'Because, my boy, as far as my observations go, the only free-thinkers among women are frights.'

The conversation was cut short at this point. Both the young men went away immediately after supper. They were pursued by a nervously malicious but somewhat faint-hearted laugh from Madame Kukshin; her vanity had been deeply wounded by neither of them having paid any attention to her. She stayed later than anyone at the ball, and at four o'clock in the morning she was dancing a polka-mazurka with Sitnikov in the Parisian style. This edifying spectacle was the final event of the Governor's ball.

# 15

'LET'S see what species of mammalia this specimen belongs to,' Bazarov said to Arkady the following day, as they mounted the staircase of the hotel in which Madame Odintsov was staying. 'I scent out something wrong here.'

'I'm surprised at you!' cried Arkady. 'What? You, you, Barazov, clinging to the narrow morality which . . .'

'What a funny fellow you are!' Bazarov cut him short, carelessly. 'Don't you know that "something wrong" means "something right" in my dialect and for me? It's an advantage for me, of course. Didn't you tell me yourself this morning that she made a strange marriage, though, to my mind, to marry a rich old man is by no means a strange thing to do, but, on the contrary, very sensible. I don't believe the gossip of the town; but I should like to think, as our cultivated Governor says, that it's well-grounded.'

Arkady made no answer, and knocked at the door of the apartments. A young servant in livery conducted the two friends into a large room, badly furnished, like all rooms in Russian hotels, but filled with flowers. Soon Madame Odintsov herself appeared in a simple morning dress. She seemed still younger by the light of the spring sunshine. Arkady presented Bazarov, and noticed with secret amazement that he seemed embarrassed, while Madame Odintsov remained perfectly tranquil, as she had been the previous day. Bazarov himself was conscious of being embarrassed, and was irritated by it. 'Here's a go!—frightened of a petticoat!' he thought, and lolling, quite like Sitnikov, in an easy-chair, he began talking with an exaggerated appearance of ease, while Madame Odintsov kept her clear eyes fixed on him.

Anna Sergyevna Odintsov was the daughter of Sergay Nikolaevitch Loktev, notorious for his personal beauty, his speculations, and his gambling propensities, who after cutting a figure and making a sensation for fifteen years in Petersburg and Moscow, finished by ruining himself completely at cards, and was forced to retire to the country, where, however, he soon after died, leaving a very small property to his two daughters—Anna, a girl of twenty, and Katya, a child of twelve. Their mother, who came of an impoverished line of princes—the H——s—had died at Petersburg when her husband was in his heyday. Anna's position after her father's death was very difficult. The brilliant education she had received in Petersburg had not fitted her for putting up with the cares of domestic life and economy, for an obscure existence in the country. She knew positively no one in the whole neighbourhood, and there was no one she could consult. Her father had tried to avoid all contact with the neighbours; he despised them in his way, and they despised him in theirs. She did not lose her head, however, and promptly sent for a sister of her mother's, Princess Avdotya Stepanovna H——, a spiteful and arrogant old lady, who, on installing herself in her niece's house, appropriated all the best rooms for her own use, scolded and grumbled from morning till night, and would not go a walk even in the garden unattended by her one serf, a surly footman in a threadbare pea-green livery with light blue trimming and a three-cornered hat. Anna put up patiently with all her aunt's whims, gradually set to work on her sister's education, and was, it seemed, already getting reconciled to the idea of wasting her life in the wilds. . . . But destiny had decreed another fate for her. She chanced to be seen by Odintsov, a very wealthy man of forty-six, an eccentric hypochondriac, stout, heavy, and sour, but not stupid, and not ill-natured; he fell in love with her, and offered her his hand. She consented to become his wife, and he lived six years with her, and on his death settled all his property upon her. Anna Sergyevna remained in the country for nearly a year after his death; then she went abroad with her sister, but only stopped in Germany; she got tired of it, and came back to live at her favourite Nikolskoe, which was nearly thirty miles from the town of X——. There she had

78

a magnificent, splendidly furnished house and a beautiful garden, with conservatories; her late husband had spared no expense to gratify his fancies. Anna Sergyevna went very rarely to the town, generally only on business, and even then she did not stay long. She was not liked in the province; there had been a fearful outcry at her marriage with Odintsov, all sorts of fictions were told about her; it was asserted that she had helped her father in his cardsharping tricks, and even that she had gone abroad for excellent reasons, that it had been necessary to conceal the lamentable consequences . . . 'You understand?' the indignant gossips would wind up. 'She has gone through the fire,' was said of her; to which a noted provincial wit usually added: 'And through all the other elements?' All this talk reached her; but she turned a deaf ear to it; there was much independence and a good deal of determination in her character.

Madame Odintsov sat leaning back in her easy-chair, and listened with folded hands to Bazarov. He, contrary to his habit, was talking a good deal, and obviously trying to interest her—again a surprise for Arkady. He could not make up his mind whether Bazarov was attaining his object. It was difficult to conjecture from Anna Sergyevna's face what impression was being made on her; it retained the same expression, gracious and refined; her beautiful eyes were lighted up by attention, but by quiet attention. Bazarov's bad manners had impressed her unpleasantly for the first minutes of the visit like a bad smell or a discordant sound; but she saw at once that he was nervous, and that even flattered her. Nothing was repulsive to her but vulgarity, and no one could have accused Bazarov of vulgarity. Arkady was fated to meet with surprises that day. He had expected that Bazarov would talk to a clever woman like Madame Odintsov about his opinions and his views; she had herself expressed a desire to listen to the man 'who dares to have no belief in anything'; but, instead of that, Bazarov talked about medicine, about homœopathy, and about botany. It turned out that Madame Odintsov had not wasted her time in solitude; she had read a good many excellent books, and spoke herself in excellent Russian. She turned the conversation upon music; but noticing that Bazarov did not appreciate art, she quietly brought it back to botany, even though Arkady was just launching into a discourse upon the significance of national melodies. Madame Odintsov treated him as though he were a younger brother; she seemed to appreciate his good-nature and youthful simplicity—and that was all. For over three hours, a lively conversation was kept up, ranging freely over various subjects.

The friends at last got up and began to take leave. Anna Sergyevna looked cordially at them, held out her beautiful, white hand to both, and, after a moment's thought, said with a doubtful but delightful smile, 'If you are not afraid of being dull, gentlemen, come and see me at Nikolskoe.'

'Oh, Anna Sergyevna,' cried Arkady, 'I shall think it the greatest happiness . . .'

'And you, Monsieur Bazarov?'

Bazarov only bowed, and a last surprise was in store for Arkady; he noticed that his friend was blushing.

'Well?' he said to him in the street; 'are you still of the same opinion—that she's . . .'

'Who can tell? See how correct she is!' retorted Bazarov; and after a brief pause he added, 'She's a perfect grand-duchess, a royal personage. She only needs a train on behind, and a crown on her head.'

'Our grand-duchesses don't talk Russian like that,' remarked Arkady.

'She's seen ups and downs, my dear boy; she's known what it is to be hard up!'

'Anyway, she's charming,' observed Arkady.

'What a magnificent body!' pursued Bazarov. 'Shouldn't I like to see it on the dissecting-table.'

'Hush, for mercy's sake, Yevgeny! that's beyond everything.'

'Well, don't get angry, you baby. I meant it's first-rate. We must go to stay with her.'

'When?'

'Well, why not the day after to-morrow. What is there to do here? Drink champagne with Kukshina? Listen to your cousin, the Liberal dignitary? . . . Let's be off the day after to-morrow. By the way, too—my father's little place is not far from there. This Nikolskoe's on the S—— road, isn't it?'

'Yes.'

'*Optime*, why hesitate? leave that to fools and prigs! I say, what a splendid body!'

Three days later the two friends were driving along the road to Nikolskoe. The day was bright, and not too hot, and the sleek posting-horses trotted smartly along, switching their tied and plaited tails. Arkady looked at the road, and, not knowing why, he smiled.

'Congratulate me,' cried Bazarov suddenly, 'to-day's the 22nd of June, my guardian angel's day. Let's see how he will watch over me. To-day they expect me at home,' he added, dropping his voice. . . . 'Well, they can go on expecting. . . . What does it matter!'

# 16

THE country house in which Anna Sergyevna lived stood on an exposed hill at no great distance from a yellow stone church with a green roof, white columns, and a fresco over the principal entrance representing the 'Resurrection of Christ' in the 'Italian' style. Sprawling in the foreground of the picture was a swarthy warrior in a helmet specially conspicuous for his rotund contours. Behind the church a long village stretched in two rows, with chimneys peeping out here and there above the thatched roofs. The manor-house was built in the same style as the church, the style known among us as that of Alexander; the house too was painted yellow, and had a green roof, and white columns, and a pediment with

an escutcheon on it. The architect had designed both buildings with the approval of the deceased Odintsov, who could
not endure—as he expressed it—idle and arbitrary innovations. The house was enclosed on both sides by the dark trees
of an old garden; an avenue of lopped pines led up to the
entrance.

Our friends were met in the hall by two tall footmen in
livery; one of them at once ran for the steward. The steward,
a stout man in a black dress coat, promptly appeared and
led the visitors by a staircase covered with rugs to a special
room, in which two bedsteads were already prepared for them
with all necessaries for the toilet. It was clear that order
reigned supreme in the house; everything was clean, everywhere there was a peculiar delicate fragrance, just as there
is in the reception rooms of ministers.

'Anna Sergyevna asks you to come to her in half an hour,'
the steward announced; 'will there be orders to give meanwhile?'

'No orders,' answered Bazarov; 'perhaps you will be so
good as to trouble yourself to bring me a glass of vodka.'

'Yes, sir,' said the steward, looking in some perplexity,
and he withdrew, his boots creaking as he walked.

'What *grand genre!*' remarked Bazarov. 'That's what it's
called in your set, isn't it? She's a grand-duchess, and that's
all about it.'

'A nice grand-duchess,' retorted Arkady, 'at the very first
meeting she invited such great aristocrats as you and me to
stay with her.'

'Especially me, a future doctor, and a doctor's son, and a
village sexton's grandson. . . . You know, I suppose, I'm
the grandson of a sexton? Like the great Speransky,' added
Bazarov after a brief pause, contracting his lips. 'At any
rate she likes to be comfortable; oh, doesn't she, this lady!
Oughtn't we to put on evening dress?'

Arkady only shrugged his shoulders . . . but he too was
conscious of a little nervousness.

Half an hour later Bazarov and Arkady went together into

the drawing-room. It was a large lofty room, furnished rather luxuriously but without particularly good taste. Heavy, expensive furniture stood in the ordinary stiff arrangement along the walls, which were covered with cinnamon-coloured paper with gold flowers on it; Odintsov had ordered the furniture from Moscow through a friend and agent of his, a spirit merchant. Over a sofa in the centre of one wall hung a portrait of a faded light-haired man—and it seemed to look with displeasure at the visitors. 'It must be the late lamented,' Barazov whispered to Arkady, and, turning up his nose, he added, 'Hadn't we better bolt . . . ?' But at that instant the lady of the house entered. She wore a light barège dress; her hair smoothly combed back behind her ears gave a girlish expression to her pure and fresh face.

'Thank you for keeping your promise,' she began. 'You must stay a little while with me; it's really not bad here. I will introduce you to my sister; she plays the piano well. That is a matter of indifference to you, Monsieur Bazarov; but you, I think, Monsieur Kirsanov, are fond of music. Besides my sister I have an old aunt living with me, and one of our neighbours comes in sometimes to play cards; that makes up all our circle. And now let us sit down.'

Madame Odintsov delivered all this little speech with peculiar precision, as though she had learned it by heart; then she turned to Arkady. It appeared that her mother had known Arkady's mother, and had even been her confidante in her love for Nikolai Petrovitch. Arkady began talking with great warmth of his dead mother; while Bazarov fell to turning over albums. 'What a tame cat I'm getting!' he was thinking to himself.

A beautiful greyhound, with a blue collar on, ran into the drawing-room, tapping on the floor with his paws, and after him entered a girl of eighteen, black-haired and dark-skinned, with a rather round but pleasing face and small dark eyes. In her hands she held a basket filled with flowers.

'This is my Katya,' said Madame Odintsov, indicating her with a motion of her head. Katya made a slight curtsy, placed herself beside her sister, and began picking out flowers. The greyhound, whose name was Fifi, went up to both of the visitors, in turn wagging his tail and thrusting his cold nose into their hands.

'Did you pick all that yourself?' asked Madame Odintsov.

'Yes,' answered Katya.

'Is auntie coming to tea?'

'Yes.'

When Katya spoke, she had a very charming smile, sweet, timid, and candid, and looked up from under her eyebrows with a sort of humorous severity. Everything about her was still young and undeveloped; the voice, and the bloom on her whole face, and the rosy hands, with white palms, and the rather narrow shoulders. . . . She was constantly blushing and getting out of breath.

Madame Odintsov turned to Bazarov. 'You are looking at pictures from politeness, Yevgeny Vassilyitch,' she began. 'That does not interest you. You had better come nearer to us, and let us have a discussion about something.'

Bazarov went closer. 'What subject have you decided upon for discussion?' he said.

'What you like. I warn you, I am dreadfully argumentative.'

'You?'

'Yes. That seems to surprise you. Why?'

'Because, as far as I can judge, you have a calm, cool character, and one must be impulsive to be argumentative.'

'How can you have had time to understand me so soon? In the first place, I am impatient and obstinate—you should ask Katya; and secondly, I am very easily carried away.'

Bazarov looked at Anna Sergyevna. 'Perhaps; you must know best. And so you are inclined for a discussion—by all means. I was looking through the views of the Saxon mountains in your album, and you remarked that that couldn't interest me. You said so, because you suppose me to have no feeling for art, and as a fact I haven't any; but these views

84

might be interesting to me from a geological standpoint, for the formation of the mountains, for instance.'

'Excuse me; but as a geologist, you would sooner have recourse to a book, to a special work on the subject, and not to a drawing.'

'The drawing shows me at a glance what would be spread over ten pages in a book.'

Anna Sergyevna was silent for a little.

'And so you haven't the least artistic feeling?' she observed, putting her elbow on the table, and by that very action bringing her face nearer to Bazarov. 'How can you get on without it?'

'Why, what is it wanted for, may I ask?'

'Well, at least to enable one to study and understand men.'

Bazarov smiled. 'In the first place, experience of life does that; and in the second, I assure you, studying separate individuals is not worth the trouble. All people are like one another, in soul as in body; each of us has brain, spleen, heart, and lungs made alike; and the so-called moral qualities are the same in all; the slight variations are of no importance. A single human specimen is sufficient to judge of all by. People are like trees in a forest; no botanist would think of studying each individual birch tree.'

Katya, who was arranging the flowers, one at a time in a leisurely fashion, lifted her eyes to Bazarov with a puzzled look, and meeting his rapid and careless glance, she crimsoned up to her ears. Anna Sergyevna shook her head.

'The trees in a forest,' she repeated. 'Then according to you there is no difference between the stupid and the clever person, between the good-natured and ill-natured?'

'No, there is a difference, just as between the sick and the healthy. The lungs of a consumptive patient are not in the same condition as yours and mine, though they are made on the same plan. We know approximately what physical diseases come from; moral diseases come from bad education, from all the nonsense people's heads are stuffed with from childhood up, from the defective state of society; in short,

85

reform society, and there will be no diseases.'

Bazarov said all this with an air, as though he were all the while thinking to himself, 'Believe me or not, as you like, it's all one to me!' He slowly passed his fingers over his whiskers, while his eyes strayed about the room.

'And you conclude,' observed Anna Sergyevna, 'that when society is reformed, there will be no stupid nor wicked people?'

'At any rate, in a proper organisation of society, it will be absolutely the same whether a man is stupid or clever, wicked or good.'

'Yes, I understand; they will all have the same spleen.'

'Precisely so, madam.'

Madame Odintsov turned to Arkady. 'And what is your opinion, Arkady Nikolaevitch?'

'I agree with Yevgeny,' he answered.

Katya looked up at him from under her eyelids.

'You amaze me, gentlemen,' commented Madame Odintsov, 'but we will have more talk together. But now I hear my aunt coming in to tea; we must spare her.'

Anna Sergyevna's aunt, Princess H——, a thin little woman with a pinched-up face, drawn together like a fist, and staring ill-natured-looking eyes under a grey front, came in, and, scarcely bowing to the guests, she dropped into a wide velvet-covered arm-chair, upon which no one but herself was privileged to sit. Katya put a foot-stool under her feet; the old lady did not thank her, did not even look at her, only her hands shook under the yellow shawl, which almost covered her feeble body. The Princess liked yellow; her cap, too, had bright yellow ribbons.

'How have you slept, aunt?' inquired Madame Odintsov, raising her voice.

'That dog in here again,' the old lady muttered in reply, and, noticing Fifi was making two hesitating steps in her direction, she cried, 'Ss . . . ss!'

Katya called Fifi and opened the door for him.

Fifi rushed out delighted, in the expectation of being taken out for a walk; but when he was left alone outside the door,

he began scratching and whining. The princess scowled.
Katya was about to go out. . . .

'I expect tea is ready,' said Madame Odintsov.

'Come, gentlemen; aunt, will you go in to tea?'

The princess got up from her chair without speaking and
led the way out of the drawing-room. They all followed her
into the dining-room. A little page in livery drew back, with
a scraping sound, from the table an arm-chair covered with
cushions, devoted to the princess's use; she sank into it;
Katya, in pouring out the tea, handed her first a cup
emblazoned with a heraldic crest. The old lady put some
honey in her cup (she considered it both sinful and extravagant
to drink tea with sugar in it, though she never spent a farthing
herself on anything), and suddenly asked in a hoarse voice,
'And what does Prince Ivan write?'

No one made her any reply. Bazarov and Arkady soon
guessed that they paid no attention to her though they treated
her respectfully.

'Because of her grand family,' thought Bazarov. . . .

After tea, Anna Sergyevna suggested they should go out
for a walk; but it began to rain a little, and the whole party,
with the exception of the princess, returned to the drawing-
room. The neighbour, the devoted card-player, arrived; his
name was Porfiry Platonitch, a stoutish, greyish man with
short, spindly legs, very polite and ready to be amused. Anna
Sergyevna, who still talked principally with Bazarov, asked
him whether he'd like to try a contest with them in the old-
fashioned way at preference. Bazarov assented, saying that
he ought to prepare himself beforehand for the duties awaiting him as a country doctor.

'You must be careful,' observed Anna Sergyevna; 'Porfiry
Platonitch and I will beat you. And you, Katya,' she added,
'play something to Arkady Nikolaevitch; he is fond of music,
and we can listen, too.'

Katya went unwillingly to the piano; and Arkady, though
he certainly was fond of music, unwillingly followed her; it
seemed to him that Madame Odintsov was sending him away,

and already, like every young man at his age, he felt a vague and oppressive emotion surging up in his heart, like the forebodings of love. Katya raised the top of the piano, and, not looking at Arkady, she said in a low voice—

'What am I to play to you?'

'What you like,' answered Arkady indifferently.

'What sort of music do you like best?' repeated Katya, without changing her attitude.

'Classical,' Arkady answered in the same tone of voice.

'Do you like Mozart?'

'Yes, I like Mozart.'

Katya pulled out Mozart's Sonata-Fantasia in C minor. She played very well, though rather over-correctly and precisely. She sat upright and immovable, her eyes fixed on the notes and her lips tightly compressed, only at the end of the sonata her face glowed, her hair came loose, and a little lock fell on to her dark brow.

Arkady was particularly struck by the last part of the sonata, the part in which, in the midst of the bewitching gaiety of the careless melody, the pangs of such mournful, almost tragic suffering suddenly break in. . . . But the ideas stirred in him by Mozart's music had no reference to Katya. Looking at her, he simply thought, 'Well, that young lady doesn't play badly, and she's not bad-looking either.'

When she had finished the sonata, Katya, without taking her hands from the keys, asked, 'Is that enough?' Arkady declared that he could not venture to trouble her again, and began talking to her about Mozart; he asked her whether she had chosen that sonata herself, or someone had recommended it to her. But Katya answered him in monosyllables; she withdrew into herself, went back into her shell. When this happened to her, she did not very quickly come out again; her face even assumed at such times an obstinate, almost stupid expression. She was not exactly shy, but diffident, and rather over-awed by her sister, who had educated her, and who had no suspicion of the fact. Arkady was reduced at last to calling Fifi to him, and with an affable smile patting him

88

on the head to give himself an appearance of being at home.

Katya set to work again upon her flowers.

Bazarov meanwhile was losing and losing. Anna Sergyevna played cards in masterly fashion; Porfiry Platonitch, too, could hold his own in the game. Bazarov lost a sum which, though trifling in itself, was not altogether pleasant for him. At supper Anna Sergyevna again turned the conversation on botany.

'We will go for a walk to-morrow morning,' she said to him; 'I want you to teach me the Latin names of the wild flowers and their species.'

'What use are the Latin names to you?' asked Bazarov.

'Order is needed in everything,' she answered.

'What an exquisite woman Anna Sergyevna is!' cried Arkady, when he was alone with his friend in the room assigned to them.

'Yes,' answered Bazarov, 'a female with brains. Yes, and she's seen life too.'

'In what sense do you mean that, Yevgeny Vassilitch?'

'In a good sense, a good sense, my dear friend, Arkady Nikolaeitch! I'm convinced she manages her estate capitally too. But what's splendid is not her, but her sister.'

'What, that little dark thing?'

'Yes, that little dark thing. She now is fresh and untouched, and shy and silent, and anything you like. She's worth educating and developing. You might make something fine out of her; but the other's—a stale loaf.'

Arkady made no reply to Bazarov, and each of them got into bed with rather singular thoughts in his head.

Anna Sergyevna, too, thought of her guests that evening. She liked Bazarov for the absence of gallantry in him, and even for his sharply defined views. She found in him something new, which she had not chanced to meet before, and she was curious.

Anna Sergyevna was a rather strange creature. Having no prejudices of any kind, having no strong convictions even, she never gave way or went out of her way for anything.

She had seen many things very clearly; she had been interested in many things, but nothing had completely satisfied her; indeed, she hardly desired complete satisfaction. Her intellect was at the same time inquiring and indifferent; her doubts were never soothed to forgetfulness, and they never grew strong enough to distract her. Had she not been rich and independent, she would perhaps have thrown herself into the struggle, and have known passion. But life was easy for her, though she was bored at times, and she went on passing day after day with deliberation, never in a hurry, placid, and only rarely disturbed. Dreams sometimes danced in rainbow colours before her eyes even, but she breathed more freely when they died away, and did not regret them. Her imagination indeed overstepped the limits of what is reckoned permissible by conventional morality; but even then her blood flowed as quietly as ever in her fascinatingly graceful, tranquil body. Sometimes, coming out of her fragrant bath all warm and enervated, she would fall to musing on the nothingness of life, the sorrow, the labour, the malice of it. . . . Her soul would be filled with sudden daring, and would flow with generous ardour, but a draught would blow from a half-closed window, and Anna Sergyevna would shrink into herself, and feel plaintive and almost angry, and there was only one thing she cared for at that instant—to get away from that horrid draught.

Like all women who have not succeeded in loving, she wanted something, without herself knowing what. Strictly speaking, she wanted nothing; but it seemed to her that she wanted everything. She could hardly endure the late Odintsov (she had married him from prudential motives, though probably she would not have consented to become his wife if she had not considered him a good sort of man), and had conceived a secret repugnance for all men, whom she could only figure to herself as slovenly, heavy, drowsy, and feebly importunate creatures. Once, somewhere abroad, she had met a handsome young Swede, with a chivalrous expression, with honest blue eyes under an open brow; he had made a powerful impression on her, but it had not prevented her from going back to Russia.

'A strange man this doctor!' she thought as she lay in her luxurious bed on lace pillows under a light silk coverlet. . . . Anna Sergyevna had inherited from her father a little of his inclination for splendour. She had fondly loved her sinful but good-natured father, and he had idolised her, used to joke with her in a friendly way as though she were an equal, and to confide in her fully, to ask her advice. Her mother she scarcely remembered.

'This doctor is a strange man!' she repeated to herself. She stretched, smiled, clasped her hands behind her head, then ran her eyes over two pages of a stupid French novel, dropped the book—and fell asleep, all pure and cold, in her pure and fragrant linen.

The following morning Anna Sergyevna went off botanising with Bazarov directly after lunch, and returned just before dinner; Arkady did not go off anywhere, and spent about an hour with Katya. He was not bored with her; she offered of herself to repeat the sonata of the day before; but when Madame Odintsov came back at last, when he caught sight of her, he felt an instantaneous pang at his heart. She came through the garden with a rather tired step; her cheeks were glowing and her eyes shining more brightly than usual under her round straw hat. She was twirling in her fingers the thin stalk of a wild flower, a light mantle had slipped down to her elbows, and the wide grey ribbons of her hat were clinging to her bosom. Bazarov walked behind her, self-confident and careless as usual, but the expression of his face, cheerful and even friendly as it was, did not please Arkady. Muttering between his teeth, 'Good-morning!' Bazarov went away to his room, while Madame Odintsov shook Arkady's hand abstractedly, and also walked past him.

'Good-morning!' thought Arkady . . . 'As though we had not seen each other already to-day!'

# 17

TIME, it is well known, sometimes flies like a bird, sometimes crawls like a worm; but man is wont to be particularly happy when he does not even notice whether it passes quickly or slowly. It was in that way Arkady and Bazarov spent a fortnight at Madame Odintsov's. The good order she had established in her house and in her life partly contributed to this result. She adhered strictly to this order herself, and forced others to submit to it. Everything during the day was done at a fixed time. In the morning, precisely at eight o'clock, all the party assembled for tea; from morning-tea till lunch-time everyone did what he pleased, the hostess herself was engaged with her bailiff (the estate was on the rent-system), her steward, and her head housekeeper. Before dinner the party met again for conversation or reading; the evening was devoted to walking, cards, and music; at half-past ten Anna Sergyevna retired to her own room, gave her orders for the following day, and went to bed. Bazarov did not like this measured, somewhat ostentatious punctuality in daily life, 'like moving along rails,' he pronounced it to be; the footmen in livery, the decorous stewards offended his democratic sentiments. He declared that if one went so far, one might as well dine in the English style at once—in tail-coats and white ties. He once spoke plainly upon the subject to Anna Sergyevna. Her attitude was such that no one hesitated to speak his mind freely before her. She heard him out; and then her comment was, 'From your point of view, you are right—and perhaps, in that respect, I am too much of a lady; but there's no living in the country without order, one would be devoured by ennui,' and she continued to go her own way. Bazarov grumbled, but the very reason life was so easy for him and Arkady at Madame Odintsov's was that everything in the house 'moved on rails'. For all that, a change had taken place in both the young men since the first days of their stay at Nikolskoe. Bazarov, in whom Anna Sergyevna was obviously interested, though she seldom agreed with him, began to show signs of an unrest, unprecedented in him; he was easily put out of temper, and unwilling to talk, he looked irritated, and could not sit still in one place, just as though he were possessed by some secret longing; while Arkady, who had made up his mind conclusively that he was in love with Madame Odintsov, had begun to yield to a gentle melancholy. This melancholy did not, however, prevent him from becoming friendly with Katya; it even impelled him to get into friendly, affectionate terms with her. '*She* does not appreciate me? So be it! . . . But here is a good creature, who does not repulse me,' he thought, and his heart again knew the sweetness of magnanimous emotions. Katya vaguely realised that he was seeking a sort of consolation in her company, and did not deny him or herself the innocent pleasure of a half-shy, half-confidential friendship. They did not talk to each other in Anna Sergyevna's presence; Katya always shrank into herself under her sister's sharp eyes; while Arkady, as befits a man in love, could pay attention to nothing else when near the object of his passion; but he was happy with Katya alone. He was conscious that he did not possess the power to interest Madame Odintsov, he was shy and at a loss when he was left alone with her, and she did not know what to say to him; he was too young for her. With Katya, on the other hand, Arkady felt at home; he treated her condescendingly, encouraged her to express the impressions made on her by music, reading novels, verses, and other such trifles, without noticing or realising that these trifles were what interested him too. Katya, on her side, did not try to drive away melancholy. Arkady was at his ease with Katya, Madame Odintsov with Bazarov, and thus it usually came to pass that the two couples, after being a little while together, went off on their separate ways, especially during the walks. Katya adored nature, and Arkady loved it, though he did not dare to acknowledge it; Madame Odintsov was, like Bazarov, rather indifferent to the beauties of nature. The almost continual separation of the two friends was not without its consequences; the relations between them began to change. Bazarov gave up talking to Arkady about Madame Odintsov, gave up even abusing her 'aristocratic ways'; Katya, it is true, he praised as before, and only advised him to restrain her sentimental tendencies, but his praises were hurried, his advice dry, and in general he talked less to Arkady than before . . . he seemed to avoid him, seemed ill at ease with him.

Arkady observed it all, but he kept his observations to himself.

The real cause of all this 'newness' was the feeling inspired in Bazarov by Madame Odintsov, a feeling which tortured and maddened him, and which he would at once have denied, with scornful laughter and cynical abuse, if anyone had ever so remotely hinted at the possibility of what was taking place in him. Bazarov had a great love for women and for feminine beauty; but love in the ideal, or, as he expressed it, romantic, sense he called lunacy, unpardonable imbecility he regarded chivalrous sentiments as something of the nature of deformity or disease, and had more than once expressed his wonder that Toggenburg and all the minnesingers and troubadours had not been put into a lunatic asylum. 'If a woman takes your fancy,' he used to say, 'try and gain your end; but if you can't —well, turn your back on her—there are lots of good fish in the sea.' Madame Odintsov had taken his fancy; the rumours about her, the freedom and independence of her ideas, her unmistakable liking for him, all seemed to be in his favour, but he soon saw that with her he would not 'gain his ends', and to turn his back on her he found, to his own bewilderment, beyond his power. His blood was on fire directly if he merely thought of her; he could easily have mastered his blood, but something else was taking root in him, something he had never admitted, at which he had always jeered, at which all his pride revolted. In his conversations with Anna Sergyevna he expressed more strongly than ever his calm contempt for everything idealistic; but when he was alone, with indignation he recognised idealism in himself. Then he would set off to the forest and walk with long strides about it, smashing the twigs that came in his way, and cursing under his breath both her and himself; or he would get into the hay-loft in the barn, and, obstinately closing his eyes, try to force himself to sleep, in which, of course, he did not always succeed. Suddenly his fancy would bring before him those chaste hands twining one day about his neck, those proud lips responding to his kisses, those intellectual eyes dwelling with tenderness—yes, with tenderness—on his, and his head went round, and he forgot himself for an instant, till indignation boiled up in him again. He caught himself in all sorts of 'shameful' thoughts, as though he were driven on by a devil mocking him. Sometimes he fancied that there was a change taking place in Madame Odintsov too; that there were signs in the expression of her face of something special; that, perhaps . . . but at that point he would stamp, or grind his teeth, and clench his fists.

Meanwhile Bazarov was not altogether mistaken. He had struck Madame Odintsov's imagination; he interested her, she thought a great deal about him. In his absence, she was not dull, she was impatient for his coming, but she always grew more lively on his appearance; she liked to be left alone with him, and she liked talking to him, even when he irritated her or offended her taste, her refined habits. She was, as it were, eager at once to sound him and to analyse herself.

One day, walking in the garden with her, he suddenly announced, in a surly voice, that he intended going to his father's place very soon. She turned white, as though something had given her a pang, and such a pang that she wondered and pondered long after what could be the meaning of it. Bazarov had spoken of his departure with no idea of putting her to the test, of seeing what would come of it; he never 'fabricated'. On the morning of that day he had an interview with his father's bailiff, who had taken care of him when he was a child, Timofeitch. This Timofeitch, a little old man of much experience and astuteness, with faded yellow hair, a weather-beaten red face, and tiny tear-drops in his

95

shrunken eyes, unexpectedly appeared before Bazarov, in his shortish overcoat of stout greyish-blue cloth, girt with a strip of leather, and in tarred boots.

'Hullo, old man; how are you?' cried Bazarov.

'How do you do, Yevgeny Vassilyitch?' began the little old man, and he smiled with delight, so that his whole face was all at once covered with wrinkles.

'What have you come for? They sent for me, eh?'

'Upon my word, sir, how could we?' mumbled Timofeitch. (He remembered the strict injunctions he had received from his master on starting.) 'We were sent to the town on business, and we'd heard news of your honour, so here we turned off on our way, that's to say—to have a look at your honour . . . as if we could think of disturbing you!'

'Come, don't tell lies!' Bazarov cut him short. 'Is this the road to the town, do you mean to tell me?' Timofeitch hesitated, and made no answer. 'Is my father well?'

'Thank God, yes.'

'And my mother?'

'Anna Vlasyevna too, glory be to God.'

'They are expecting me, I suppose?'

The little old man held his tiny head on one side.

'Ah, Yevgeny Vassilyitch, it makes one's heart ache to see them; it does really.'

'Come, all right, all right! shut up! Tell them I'm coming soon.'

'Yes, sir,' answered Timofeitch, with a sigh.

As he went out of the house, he pulled his cap down on his head with both hands, clambered into a wretched-looking racing droshky, and went off at a trot, but not in the direction of the town.

On the evening of the same day, Madame Odintsov was sitting in her own room with Bazarov, while Arcady walked up and down the hall listening to Katya's playing. The princess had gone upstairs to her own room; she could not bear guests as a rule, and 'especially this new riff-raff lot,' as she called them. In the common rooms she only sulked; but she made up for it in her own room by breaking out into such abuse before her maid that the cap danced on her head, wig and all. Madame Odintsov was well aware of all this.

'How is it you are proposing to leave us?' she began; 'how about your promise?'

Bazarov started. 'What promise?'

'Have you forgotten? You meant to give me some lessons in chemistry.'

'It can't be helped! My father expects me; I can't loiter any longer. However, you can read Pelouse et Frémy, *Notions générales de Chimie;* it's a good book, and clearly written. You will find everything you need in it.'

'But do you remember; you assured me a book cannot take the place of . . . I've forgotten how you put it, but you know what I mean . . . do you remember?'

'It can't be helped!' repeated Bazarov.

'Why go away?' said Madame Odintsov, dropping her voice.

He glanced at her. Her head had fallen on to the back of her easy-chair, and her arms, bare to the elbow, were folded on her bosom. She seemed paler in the light of the single lamp covered with a perforated paper shade. An ample white gown hid her completely in its soft folds; even the tips of her feet, also crossed, were hardly seen.

'And why stay?' answered Bazarov.

Madame Odintsov turned her head slightly. 'You ask why. Have you not enjoyed yourself with me? Or do you suppose you will not be missed here?'

'I am sure of it.'

Madame Odintsov was silent a minute. 'You are wrong in thinking that. But I don't believe you. You could not say that seriously.' Bazarov still sat immovable. 'Yevgeny Vassilyitch, why don't you speak?'

'Why, what am I to say to you? People are not generally worth being missed, and I less than most.'

'Why so?'

'I'm a practical, uninteresting person. I don't know how to talk.'

97

'You are fishing, Yevgeny Vassilyitch.'

'That's not a habit of mine. Don't you know yourself that I've nothing in common with the elegant side of life, the side you prize so much?'

Madame Odintsov bit the corner of her handkerchief.

'You may think what you like, but I shall be dull when you go away.'

'Arkady will remain,' remarked Bazarov. Madame Odintsov shrugged her shoulders slightly. 'I shall be dull,' she repeated.

'Really? In any case you will not feel dull for long.'

'What makes you suppose that?'

'Because you told me yourself that you are only dull when your regular routine is broken in upon. You have ordered your existence with such unimpeachable regularity that there can be no place in it for dullness or sadness . . . for any unpleasant emotions.'

'And do you consider I am so unimpeachable . . . that's to say, that I have ordered my life with such regularity?'

'I should think so. Here's an example; in a few minutes it will strike ten, and I know beforehand that you will drive me away.'

'No; I'm not going to drive you away, Yevgeny Vassilyitch. You may stay. Open that window. . . . I feel half-stifled.'

Bazarov got up and gave a push to the window. It flew up with a loud crash. . . . He had not expected it to open so easily; besides, his hands were shaking. The soft, dark night looked into the room with its almost black sky, its faintly rustling trees, and the fresh fragrance of the pure open air.

'Draw the blind and sit down,' said Madame Odintsov; 'I want to have a talk with you before you go away. Tell me something about yourself; you never talk about yourself.'

'I try to talk to you upon improving subjects, Anna Sergyevna.'

'You are very modest. . . . But I should like to know something about you, about your family, about your father, for whom you are forsaking us.'

'Why is she talking like that?' thought Bazarov.

'All that's not in the least interesting,' he uttered aloud, 'especially for you; we are obscure people. . . .'

'And you regard me as an aristocrat?'

Bazarov lifted his eyes to Madame Odintsov.

'Yes,' he said with exaggerated sharpness.

She smiled. 'I see you know me very little, though you do maintain that all people are alike, and it's not worth while to study them. I will tell you my life some time or other . . . but first you tell me yours.'

'I know you very little,' repeated Bazarov. 'Perhaps you are right; perhaps, really, everyone is a riddle. You, for instance; you avoid society, you are oppressed by it, and you have invited two students to stay with you. What makes you, with your intellect, with your beauty, live in the country?'

'What? What was it you said?' Madame Odintsov interposed eagerly. 'With my . . . beauty?'

Bazarov scowled. 'Never mind that,' he muttered; 'I meant to say that I don't exactly understand why you have settled in the country?'

'You don't understand it. . . . But you explain it to yourself in some way?'

'Yes . . . I assume that you remain continually in the same place because you indulge yourself, because you are very fond of comfort and ease, and very indifferent to everything else.'

Madame Odintsov smiled again. 'You would absolutely refuse to believe that I am capable of being carried away by anything?'

Bazarov glanced at her from under his brows.

'By curiosity, perhaps; but not otherwise.'

'Really? Well, now I understand why we are such friends; you are just like me, you see.'

'We are such friends . . .' Bazarov articulated in a choked voice.

'Yes! . . . Why, I'd forgotten you wanted to go away.'

Bazarov got up. The lamp burnt dimly in the middle of

the dark, luxurious, isolated room; from time to time the blind was shaken, and there flowed in the freshness of the insidious night; there was heard its mysterious whisperings. Madame Odintsov did not move in a single limb; but she was gradually possessed by concealed emotion.

It communicated itself to Bazarov. He was suddenly conscious that he was alone with a young and lovely woman. . . .

'Where are you going?' she said slowly.

He answered nothing, and sank into a chair.

'And so you consider me a placid, pampered, spoiled creature,' she went on in the same voice, never taking her eyes off the window. 'While I know so much about myself, that I am unhappy.'

'You unhappy? What for? Surely you can't attach any importance to idle gossip?'

Madame Odintsov frowned. It annoyed her that he had given such a meaning to her words.

'Such gossip does not even affect me, Yevgeny Vassil-yevitch, and I am too proud to allow it to disturb me. I am unhappy because . . . I have no desires, no passion for life. You look at me incredulously; you think that's said by an "aristocrat", who is all in lace, and sitting in a velvet arm-chair. I don't conceal the fact: I love what you call comfort, and at the same time I have little desire to live. Explain that contradiction as best you can. But all that's romanticism in your eyes.'

Bazarov shook his head. 'You are in good health, independent, rich; what more would you have? What do you want?'

'What do I want?' echoed Madame Odintsov, and she sighed. 'I am very tired, I am old, I feel as if I have had a very long life. Yes, I am old,' she added, softly drawing the ends of her lace over her bare arms. Her eyes met Bazarov's eyes, and she faintly blushed. 'Behind me I have already so many memories: my life in Petersburg, wealth, then poverty, then my father's death, marriage, then the inevitable tour in due order. . . . So many memories, and nothing to remember, and before me, before me—a long, long road, and no goal. . . . I have no wish to go on.'

'Are you so disillusioned?' queried Bazarov.

'No, but I am dissatisfied,' Madame Odintsov replied, dwelling on each syllable. 'I think if I could interest myself strongly in something. . . .'

'You want to fall in love,' Bazarov interrupted her, 'and you can't love; that's where your unhappiness lies.'

Madame Odintsov began to examine the sleeve of her lace.

'Is it true I can't love?' she said.

'I should say not! Only I was wrong in calling that an unhappiness. On the contrary, anyone's more to be pitied when such a mischance befalls him.'

'Mischance, what?'

'Falling in love.'

'And how do you come to know that?'

'By hearsay,' answered Bazarov angrily.

'You're flirting,' he thought; 'you're bored, and teasing me for want of something to do, while I . . .' His heart really seemed as though it were being torn to pieces.

'Besides, you are perhaps too exacting,' he said, bending his whole frame forward and playing with the fringe of the chair.

'Perhaps. My idea is everything or nothing. A life for a life. Take mine, give up thine, and that without regret or turning back. Or else better have nothing.'

'Well?' observed Bazarov; 'that's fair terms, and I'm surprised that so far you . . . have not found what you wanted.'

'And do you think it would be easy to give oneself up wholly to anything whatever?'

'Not easy, if you begin reflecting, waiting and attaching value to yourself; prizing yourself, I mean; but to give oneself up without reflection is very easy.'

'How can one help prizing oneself? If I am of no value, who could need my devotion?'

'That's not my affair; that's the other's business to discover what is my value. The chief thing is to be able to devote oneself.'

Madame Odintsov bent forward from the back of her chair. 'You speak,' she began, 'as though you had experienced all that.'

'It happened to come up, Anna Sergyevna; all that, as you know, is not in my line.'

'But you could devote yourself?'

'I don't know. I shouldn't like to boast.'

Madame Odintsov said nothing, and Bazarov was mute. The sounds of the piano floated up to them from the drawing-room.

'How is it Katya is playing so late?' observed Madame Odintsov.

Bazarov got up. 'Yes, it is really late now; it's time for you to go to bed.'

'Wait a little; why are you in a hurry? . . . I want to say one word to you.'

'What is it?'

'Wait a little,' whispered Madame Odintsov. Her eyes rested on Bazarov; it seemed as though she were examining him attentively.

He walked across the room, then suddenly went up to her, hurriedly said 'Good-bye,' squeezed her hand so that she almost screamed, and was gone. She raised her crushed fingers to her lips, breathed on them, and suddenly, impulsively getting up from her low chair, she moved with rapid steps towards the door, as though she wished to bring Bazarov back. . . . A maid came into the room with a decanter on a silver tray. Madame Odintsov stood still, told her she could go, and sat down again, and again sank into thought. Her hair slipped loose and fell in a dark coil down her shoulders. Long after, the lamp was still burning in Anna Sergyevna's room, and for long she stayed without moving, only from time to time chafing her hands, which ached a little from the cold of the night.

Bazarov went back two hours later to his bedroom with his boots wet with dew, dishevelled and ill-humoured. He found Arkady at the writing-table with a book in his hands, his coat buttoned up to the throat.

'You're not in bed yet?' he said, in a tone, it seemed, of annoyance.

'You stopped a long while with Anna Sergyevna this evening,' remarked Arkady, not answering him.

'Yes, I stopped with her all the while you were playing the piano with Katya Sergyevna.'

'I did not play . . .' Arkady began, and he stopped. He felt the tears were coming into his eyes, and he did not like to cry before his sarcastic friend.

FATHERS AND CHILDREN

# 18

THE following morning when Madame Odintsov came down to morning tea, Bazarov sat a long while bending over his cup, then suddenly he glanced up at her. . . . She turned to him as though he had struck her a blow, and he fancied that her face was a little paler since the night before. She quickly went off to her own room, and did not appear till lunch. It rained from early morning; there was no possibility of going for a walk. The whole company assembled in the drawing-room. Arkady took up the new number of a journal and began reading it aloud. The princess, as was her habit, tried to express her amazement in her face, as though he were doing something improper, then glared angrily at him; but he paid no attention to her.

'Yevgeny Vassilyevitch,' said Anna Sergyevna, 'come to my room. . . . I want to ask you. . . . You mentioned a text-book yesterday . . .'

She got up and went to the door. The princess looked round

with an expression that seemed to say, 'Look at me; see how shocked I am!' and again glared at Arkady; but he raised his voice and, exchanging glances with Katya, near whom he was sitting, he went on reading.

Madame Odintsov went with rapid steps to her study. Bazarov followed her quickly, not raising his eyes, and only with his ears catching the delicate swish and rustle of her silk gown gliding before him. Madame Odintsov sank into the same easy-chair in which she had sat the previous evening, and Bazarov took up the same position as before.

'What was the name of that book?' she began, after a brief silence.

'Pelouse et Frémy, *Notions générales,*' answered Bazarov. 'I might, though, recommend you also Ganot, *Traité élémentaire de physique expérimentale.* In that book the illustrations are clearer, and in general it's a text-book.'

Madame Odintsov stretched out her hand. 'Yevgeny Vassilyitch, I beg your pardon, but I didn't invite you in here to discuss text-books. I wanted to continue our conversation of last night. You went away so suddenly. . . . It will not bore you . . .'

'I am at your service, Anna Sergyevna. But what were we talking about last night?'

Madame Odintsov flung a sidelong glance at Bazarov.

'We were talking of happiness, I believe. I told you about myself. By the way, I mentioned the word "happiness". Tell me why it is that even when we are enjoying music, for instance, or a fine evening, or a conversation with sympathetic people, it all seems an imitation of some measureless happiness existing apart somewhere rather than actual happiness—such, I mean, as we ourselves are in possession of. Why is it? Or perhaps you have no feeling like that?'

'You know the saying, "Happiness is where we are not",' replied Bazarov; 'besides, you told me yesterday you are discontented. I certainly never have such ideas come into my head.'

'Perhaps they seem ridiculous to you?'

'No; but they don't come into my head.'

'Really? Do you know, I should very much like to know what you do think about?'

'What? I don't understand.'

'Listen; I have long wanted to speak openly to you. There's no need to tell you—you are conscious of it yourself—that you are not an ordinary man; you are still young—all life is before you. What are you preparing yourself for? What future is awaiting you? I mean to say—what object do you want to attain? What are you going forward to? What is in your heart? in short, who are you? What are you?'

'You surprise me, Anna Sergyevna. You are aware that I am studying natural science, and who I . . .'

'Well, who are you?'

'I have explained to you already that I am going to be a district doctor.'

Anna Sergyevna made a movement of impatience.

'What do you say that for? You don't believe it yourself. Arkady might answer me in that way, but not you.'

'Why, in what is Arkady . . .'

'Stop! Is it possible you could content yourself with such a humble career, and aren't you always maintaining yourself that you don't believe in medicine? You—with your ambition —a district doctor! You answer me like that to put me off, because you have no confidence in me. But, do you know, Yevgeny Vassilyitch, that I could understand you; I have been poor myself, and ambitious, like you; I have been perhaps through the same trials as you.'

'That is all very well, Anna Sergyevna, but you must pardon me for . . . I am not in the habit of talking freely about myself at any time as a rule, and between you and me there is such a gulf . . .'

'What sort of gulf? You mean to tell me again that I am an aristocrat? No more of that, Yevgeny Vassilyitch; I thought I had proved to you . . .'

'And even apart from that,' broke in Bazarov, 'what could induce one to talk and think about the future, which for the most part does not depend on us? If a chance turns up of doing something—so much the better; and if it doesn't turn up—at least one will be glad one didn't gossip idly about it beforehand.'

'You call a friendly conversation idle gossip? . . . Or perhaps you consider me as a woman unworthy of your confidence? I know you despise us all.'

'I don't despise you, Anna Sergyevna, and you know that.'

'No, I don't know anything . . . but let us suppose so. I understand your disinclination to talk of your future career; but as to what is taking place within you now . . .'

'Taking place!' repeated Bazarov, 'as though I were some sort of government or society! In any case, it is utterly uninteresting; and besides, can a man always speak of everything that "takes place" in him?'

'Why, I don't see why you can't speak freely of everything you have in your heart.'

'Can *you?*' asked Bazarov.

'Yes,' answered Anna Sergyevna, after a brief hesitation.

Bazarov bowed his head. 'You are more fortunate than I am.'

Anna Sergyevna looked at him questioningly. 'As you please,' she went on, 'but still something tells me that we have not come together for nothing; that we shall be great friends. I am sure this—what should I say, constraint, reticence in you will vanish at last.'

'So you have noticed reticence . . . as you expressed it . . . constraint?'

'Yes.'

Bazarov got up and went to the window. 'And would you like to know the reason of this reticence? Would you like to know what is passing within me?'

'Yes,' repeated Madame Odintsov, with a sort of dread she did not at the time understand.

'And you will not be angry?'

'No.'

'No?' Bazarov was standing with his back to her. 'Let

me tell you then that I love you like a fool, like a madman.
. . . There, you've forced it out of me.'

Madame Odintsov held both her hands out before her; but
Bazarov was leaning with his forehead pressed against the
window-pane. He breathed hard; his whole body was visibly
trembling. But it was not the tremor of youthful timidity,
not the sweet alarm of the first declaration that possessed him;
it was passion struggling in him, strong and painful—passion
not unlike hatred, and perhaps akin to it. . . . Madame
Odintsov felt both afraid and sorry for him.

'Yevgeny Vassilyitch!' she said, and there was the ring of
unconscious tenderness in her voice.

He turned quickly, flung a searching look at her, and,
snatching both her hands, he drew her suddenly to his breast.

She did not at once free herself from his embrace, but an
instant later she was standing far away in a corner, and looking from there at Bazarov. He rushed at her . . .

'You have misunderstood me,' she whispered hurriedly, in
alarm. It seemed if he had made another step she would have
screamed. . . . Bazarov bit his lips, and went out.

Half an hour later, a maid gave Anna Sergyevna a note
from Bazarov; it consisted simply of one line: 'Am I to go
to-day, or can I stop till to-morrow?'

'Why should you go? I did not understand you—you did
not understand me,' Anna Sergyevna answered him, but to
herself she thought: 'I did not understand myself either.'

She did not show herself till dinner-time, and kept walking to and fro in her room, stopping sometimes at the window,
sometimes at the looking-glass, and slowly rubbing her handkerchief over her neck, on which she still seemed to feel a
burning spot. She asked herself what had induced her to
'force' on Bazarov's words, his confidence, and whether she
had suspected nothing . . . 'I am to blame,' she decided
aloud, 'but I could not have foreseen this.' She fell to musing,
and blushed crimson, remembering Bazarov's almost animal
face when he had rushed at her. . . .

'Or?' she uttered suddenly aloud, and she stopped short

and shook back her curls. . . . She caught sight of herself in the glass; her head thrown back, with a mysterious smile on the half-closed eyes and lips, told her, it seemed, in a flash something at which she herself was confused. . . .

'No,' she made up her mind at last. 'God knows what it would lead to; he couldn't be played with; peace is anyway the best thing in the world.'

Her peace of mind was not shaken; but she felt gloomy, and even shed a few tears once, though she could not have said why—certainly not for the insult done her. She did not feel insulted; she was more inclined to feel guilty. Under the influence of various vague emotions, the sense of life passing by, the desire of novelty, she had forced herself to go up to a certain point, forced herself to look behind herself, and had seen behind her not even an abyss, but what was empty . . . or revolting.

### FATHERS AND CHILDREN

# 19

GREAT as was Madame Odintsov's self-control, and superior as she was to every kind of prejudice, she felt awkward when she went into the dining-room to dinner. The meal went off fairly successfully, however. Porfiry Platonovitch made his appearance and told various anecdotes; he had just come back from the town. Among other things, he informed them that the Governor had ordered his secretaries on special commissions to wear spurs, in case he might send them off anywhere for greater speed on horseback. Arkady talked in an undertone to Katya, and diplomatically attended to the princess's wants. Bazarov maintained a grim and obstinate silence. Madame Odintsov looked at him twice, not stealthily, but straight in the face, which was bilious and forbidding, with downcast eyes, and contemptuous determination stamped on every feature, and thought: 'No . . . no . . . no.' . . . After dinner, she went with the whole company into the garden, and seeing that Bazarov wanted to speak to her, she took a few steps to one side and stopped. He went up to her, but even then he did not raise his eyes, and said hoarsely:

'I have to apologise to you, Anna Sergyevna. You must be in a fury with me.'

'No, I'm not angry with you, Yevgeny Vassilyitch,' answered Madame Odintsov; 'but I am sorry.'

'So much the worse. Anyway, I'm sufficiently punished. My position, you will certainly agree, is most foolish. You wrote to me, "Why go away?" But I cannot stay, and don't wish to. To-morrow I shall be gone.'

'Yevgeny Vassilyitch, why are you . . .'

'Why am I going away?'

'No; I didn't mean to say that.'

'There's no recalling the past, Anna Sergyevna . . . and this was bound to come about sooner or later. Consequently I must go. I can only conceive of one condition upon which I could remain; but that condition will never be. Excuse my impertinence, but you don't love me, and you never will love me, I suppose?'

Bazarov's eyes glittered for an instant under their dark brows.

Anna Sergyevna did not answer him. 'I'm afraid of this man,' flashed through her brain.

'Good-bye, then,' said Bazarov, as though he guessed her thought, and he went back into the house.

Anna Sergyevna walked slowly after him, and calling Katya to her, she took her arm. She did not leave her side till quite evening. She did not play cards, and was constantly laughing, which did not at all accord with her pale and perplexed face. Arkady was bewildered, and looked on at her as all young people look on—that's to say, he was constantly asking himself, 'What is the meaning of that?' Bazarov shut himself up in his room; he came back to tea, however. Anna Sergyevna longed to say some friendly word to him, but she did not know how to address him. . . .

An unexpected incident relieved her from her embarrassment: a steward announced the arrival of Sitnikov.

It is difficult to do justice in words to the strange figure cut by the young apostle of progress as he fluttered into the room. Though, with his characteristic impudence, he had made up his mind to go into the country to visit a woman whom he hardly knew, who had never invited him, but with whom, according to information he had gathered, such talented and intimate friends were staying, he was nevertheless trembling to the marrow of his bones; and instead of bringing out the apologies and compliments he had learned by heart beforehand, he muttered some absurdity about Evdoksya Kukshin having sent him to inquire after Anna Sergyevna's health, and Arkady Nikolaevitch's too, having always spoken to him in the highest terms. . . . At this point he faltered and lost his presence of mind so completely that he sat down on his own hat. However, since no one turned him out, and Anna Sergyevna even presented him to her aunt and her sister, he soon recovered himself and began to chatter volubly. The introduction of the commonplace is often an advantage in life; it relieves over-strained tension, and sobers too self-confident or self-sacrificing emotions by recalling its close kinship with them. With Sitnikov's appearance everything became somehow duller and simpler; they all even ate a more solid supper, and retired to bed half an hour earlier than usual.

'I might now repeat to you,' said Arkady, as he lay down in bed, to Bazarov, who was also undressing, 'what you once said to me, "Why are you so melancholy?" One would think you had fulfilled some sacred duty.' For some time past a sort of pretence of free-and-easy banter had sprung up between the two young men, which is always an unmistakable sign of secret displeasure or unexpressed suspicions.

'I'm going to my father's to-morrow,' said Bazarov.

Arkady raised himself and leaned on his elbow. He felt both surprised and for some reason or other pleased. 'Ah!' he commented, 'and is that why you're sad?'

Bazarov yawned. 'You'll get old if you know too much.'

'And Anna Sergyevna?' persisted Arkady.

'What about Anna Sergyevna?'

'I mean, will she let you go?'

'I'm not her paid man.'

Arkady grew thoughtful, while Bazarov lay down and turned his face to the wall.

Some minutes went by in silence. 'Yevgeny?' cried Arkady suddenly.

'Well?'

'I will leave with you to-morrow too.'

Bazarov made no answer.

'Only I will go home,' continued Arkady. 'We will go together as far as Hohlovsky, and there you can get horses at Fedot's. I should be delighted to make the acquaintance of your people, but I'm afraid of being in their way and yours. You are coming to us again later, of course?'

'I've left all my things with you,' Bazarov said, without turning round.

'Why doesn't he ask me why I am going, and just as suddenly as he?' thought Arkady. 'In reality, why am I going, and why is he going?' he pursued his reflections. He could find no satisfactory answer to his own question, though his heart was filled with some bitter feeling. He felt it would be hard to part from this life to which he had grown so accustomed; but for him to remain alone would be rather odd. 'Something has passed between them,' he reasoned to himself; 'what good would it be for me to hang on after he's gone? She's utterly sick of me; I'm losing the last that remained to me.' He began to imagine Anna Sergyevna to himself, then other features gradually eclipsed the lovely image of the young widow.

'I'm sorry to lose Katya too!' Arkady whispered to his pillow, on which a tear had already fallen. . . . All at once he shook back his hair and said aloud—

"What the devil made that fool of a Sitnikov turn up here?'

Bazarov at first stirred a little in his bed, then he uttered the following rejoinder: 'You're still a fool, my boy, I see. Sitnikovs are indispensable to us. I—do you understand? I need dolts like him. It's not for the gods to bake bricks, in fact!' . . .

'Oho!' Arkady thought to himself, and then in a flash all the fathomless depths of Bazarov's conceit dawned upon him. 'Are you and I gods then? at least, you're a god; am not I a dolt then?'

'Yes,' repeated Bazarov; 'you're still a fool.'

Madame Odintsov expressed no special surprise when Arkady told her the next day that he was going with Bazarov; she seemed tired and absorbed. Katya looked at him silently and seriously; the princess went so far as to cross herself under her shawl so that he could not help noticing it. Sitnikov, on the other hand, was completely disconcerted. He had only just come in to lunch in a new and fashionable get-up, not on this occasion of a Slavophil cut; the evening before he had astonished the man told off to wait on him by the amount of linen he had brought with him, and now all of a sudden his comrades were deserting him! He took a few tiny steps, doubled back like a hunted hare at the edge of a copse, and abruptly, almost with dismay, almost with a wail, announced that he proposed going too. Madame Odintsov did not attempt to detain him.

'I have a very comfortable carriage,' added the luckless young man, turning to Arkady; 'I can take you, while Yevgeny Vassilyitch can take your coach, so it will be even more convenient.'

'But, really, it's not at all in your way, and it's a long way to my place.'

'That's nothing, nothing; I've plenty of time; besides, I have business in that direction.'

'Gin-selling?' asked Arkady, rather too contemptuously.

But Sitnikov was reduced to such desperation that he did not even laugh as usual. 'I assure you, my carriage is exceedingly comfortable,' he muttered; 'and there will be room for all.'

'Don't wound Monsieur Sitnikov by a refusal,' commented Anna Sergyevna.

Arkady glanced at her, and bowed his head significantly.

The visitors started off after lunch. As she said good-bye to Bazarov, Madame Odintsov held out her hand to him, and said, 'We shall meet again, shan't we?'

'As you command,' answered Bazarov.

'In that case, we shall.'

Arkady was the first to descend the steps; he got into Sitnikov's carriage. A steward tucked him in respectfully, but he could with pleasure have killed him, or have burst into tears. Bazarov took his seat in the coach. When they reached Hohlovsky, Arkady waited till Fedot, the keeper of the posting-station, had put in the horses, and going up to the coach, he said, with his old smile, to Bazarov, 'Yevgeny, take me with you; I want to come to you.'

'Get in,' Bazarov brought out through his teeth.

Sitnikov, who had been walking to and fro round the wheels of his carriage, whistling briskly, could only gape when he heard these words; while Arkady coolly pulled his luggage out of the carriage, took his seat beside Bazarov, and bowing politely to his former fellow-traveller, he called, 'Whip up!' The coach rolled away, and was soon out of sight. . . . Sitnikov, utterly confused, looked at his coachman, but the latter was flicking his whip about the tail of the off horse. Then Sitnikov jumped into the carriage, and growling at two passing peasants, 'Put on your caps, idiots!' he drove to the town, where he arrived very late, and where, next day, at Madame Kukshin's, he dealt very severely with two 'disgusting stuck-up churls'.

When he was seated in the coach by Bazarov, Arkady pressed his hand warmly, and for a long while he said nothing. It seemed as though Bazarov understood and appreciated both the pressure and the silence. He had not slept all the previous night, and had not smoked, and had eaten scarcely anything for several days, His profile, already thinner, stood out darkly and sharply under his cap, which was pulled down to his eyebrows.

'Well, brother,' he said at last, 'give us a cigarette. But look, I say, is my tongue yellow?'

'Yes, it is,' answered Arkady.

'Hm . . . and the cigarette's tasteless. The machine's out of gear.'

'You look changed lately, certainly,' observed Arkady.

'It's nothing! we shall soon be all right. One thing's a bother—my mother's so tender-hearted; if you don't grow as round as a tub, and eat ten times a day, she's quite upset. My father's all right, he's known all sorts of ups and downs himself. No, I can't smoke,' he added, and he flung the cigarette into the dust of the road.

'Do you think it's twenty miles?' asked Arkady.

'Yes. But ask this sage here.' He indicated the peasant sitting on the box, a labourer of Fedot's.

But the sage only answered, 'Who's to know—miles hereabout aren't measured,' and went on swearing in an undertone at the shaft horse for 'kicking with her head-piece,' that is, shaking with her head down.

'Yes, yes,' began Bazarov; 'it's a lesson to you, my young friend, an instructive example. God knows, what rot it is! Every man hangs on a thread, the abyss may open under his feet any minute, and yet he must go and invent all sorts of discomforts for himself, and spoil his life.'

'What are you alluding to?' asked Arkady.

'I'm not alluding to anything; I'm saying straight out that we've both behaved like fools. What's the use of talking about it! Still, I've noticed in hospital practice, the man who's furious at his illness—he's sure to get over it.'

'I don't quite understand you,' observed Arkady; 'I should have thought you had nothing to complain of.'

'And since you don't quite understand me, I'll tell you this—to my mind, it's better to break stones on the highroad than to let a woman have the mastery of even the end of one's little finger. That's all . . .' Bazarov was on the point of uttering his favourite word, 'romanticism', but he checked himself, and said, 'rubbish. You don't believe me now, but

114

I tell you: you and I have been in feminine society, and very nice we found it; but to throw up society like that is for all the world like a dip in cold water on a hot day. A man hasn't time to attend to such trifles; a man ought not to be tame, says an excellent Spanish proverb. Now, you, I suppose, my sage friend,' he added, turning to the peasant sitting on the box—'you've a wife?'

The peasant showed both the friends his dull blear-eyed face.

'A wife? Yes. Every man has a wife.'

'Do you beat her?'

'My wife? Everything happens sometimes. We don't beat her without good reason!'

'That's excellent. Well, and does she beat you?'

The peasant gave a tug at the reins. 'That's a strange thing to say, sir. You like your joke.' . . . He was obviously offended.

'You hear, Arkady Nikolaevitch! But we have taken a beating . . . that's what comes of being educated people.'

Arkady gave a forced laugh, while Bazarov turned away, and did not open his mouth again the whole journey.

The twenty miles seemed to Arkady quite forty. But at last, on the slope of some rising ground, appeared the small hamlet where Bazarov's parents lived. Beside it, in a young birch copse, could be seen a small house with a thatched roof. Two peasants stood with their hats on at the first hut, abusing each other. 'You're a great sow,' said one; 'and worse than a little sucking pig.'

'And your wife's a witch,' retorted the other.

'From their unconstrained behaviour,' Bazarov remarked to Arkady, 'and the playfulness of their retorts, you can guess that my father's peasants are not too much oppressed. Why, there he is himself coming out on the steps of his house. They must have heard the bells. It's he; it's he—I know his figure. Ay, ay! how grey he's grown though, poor chap!'

# 20

BAZAROV leaned out of the coach, while Arkady thrust his head out behind his companion's back, and caught sight on the steps of the little manor-house of a tall, thinnish man with dishevelled hair, and a thin hawk nose, dressed in an old military coat not buttoned up. He was standing, his legs wide apart, smoking a long pipe and screwing up his eyes to keep the sun out of them.

The horses stopped.

'Arrived at last,' said Bazarov's father, still going on smoking though the pipe was fairly dancing up and down between his fingers. 'Come, get out; get out; let me hug you.'

He began embracing his son . . . 'Enyusha, Enyusha,' was heard a trembling woman's voice. The door was flung open, and in the doorway was seen a plump, short, little old woman in a white cap and a short striped jacket. She moaned, staggered, and would certainly have fallen, had not Bazarov supported her. Her plump little hands were instantly twined round his neck, her head was pressed to his breast, and there was a complete hush. The only sound heard was her broken sobs.

Old Bazarov breathed hard and screwed his eyes up more than ever.

'There, that's enough, that's enough, Arisha! give over,' he said, exchanging a glance with Arkady, who remained motionless in the coach, while the peasant on the box even turned his head away; 'that's not at all necessary, please give over.'

'Ah, Vassily Ivanitch,' faltered the old woman, 'for what ages, my dear one, my darling, Enyusha,' . . . and, not unclasping her hands, she drew her wrinkled face, wet with tears and working with tenderness, a little away from Bazarov, and gazed at him with blissful and comic-looking eyes, and again fell on his neck.

'Well, well, to be sure, that's all in the nature of things,' commented Vassily Ivanitch, 'only we'd better come indoors. Here's a visitor come with Yevgeny. You must excuse it,' he added, turning to Arkady, and scraping with his foot; 'you understand, a woman's weakness; and, well, a mother's heart . . .'

His lips and eyebrows too were twitching, and his beard was quivering . . . but he was obviously trying to control himself and appear almost indifferent.

'Let's come in, mother, really,' said Bazarov, and he led the enfeebled old woman into the house. Putting her into a comfortable arm-chair, he once more hurriedly embraced his father and introduced Arkady to him.

'Heartily glad to make your acquaintance,' said Vassily Ivanovitch, 'but you mustn't expect great things; everything here in my house is done in a plain way, on a military footing. Arina Vlasyevna, calm yourself, pray; what weakness! The gentleman our guest will think ill of you.'

'My dear sir,' said the old lady through her tears, 'your name and your father's I haven't the honour of knowing . . .'

'Arkady Nikolaitch,' put in Vassily Ivanitch solemnly, in a low voice.

'You must excuse a silly old woman like me.' The old woman blew her nose, and bending her head to right and to left, carefully wiped one eye after the other. 'You must excuse me. You see, I thought I should die, that I should not live to see my da . . arling.'

'Well, here we have lived to see him, madam,' put in Vassily Ivanovitch. 'Tanyushka,' he turned to a bare-legged little girl of thirteen in a bright red cotton dress, who was timidly peeping in at the door, 'bring your mistress a glass of water—on a tray, do you hear?—and you, gentlemen,' he added, with a kind of old-fashioned playfulness, 'let me ask you into the study of a retired old veteran.'

'Just once more let me embrace you, Enyusha,' moaned

Arina Vlasyevna. Bazarov bent down to her. 'Why, what a handsome fellow you have grown!'

'Well, I don't know about being handsome,' remarked Vassily Ivanovitch, 'but he's a man, as the saying is, *ommfay*. And now I hope, Arina Vlasyevna, that having satisfied your maternal heart, you will turn your thoughts to satisfying the appetites of our dear guests, because, as you're aware, even nightingales can't be fed on fairy tales.'

The old lady got up from her chair. 'This minute, Vassily Ivanovitch, the table shall be laid. I will run myself to the kitchen and order the samovar to be brought in; everything shall be ready, everything. Why, I have not seen him, not given him food or drink, these three years; is that nothing?'

'There, mind, good mother, bustle about; don't put us to shame; while you, gentlemen, I beg you to follow me. Here's Timofeitch come to pay his respects to you, Yevgeny. He, too, I dare say, is delighted, the old dog. Eh, aren't you delighted, old dog? Be so good as to follow me.'

And Vassily Ivanovitch went bustling forward, scraping and flapping with his slippers trodden down at heel.

His whole house consisted of six tiny rooms. One of them— the one to which he led our friends—was called the study. A thick-legged table, littered over with papers black with the accumulation of ancient dust as though they had been smoked, occupied all the space between the two windows; on the walls hung Turkish firearms, whips, a sabre, two maps, some anatomical diagrams, a portrait of Hoffland, a monogram woven in hair in a blackened frame, and a diploma under glass; a leather sofa, torn and worn into hollows in parts, was placed between two huge cupboards of birchwood; on the shelves books, boxes, stuffed birds, jars, and phials were huddled together in confusion; in one corner stood a broken galvanic battery.

'I warned you, my dear Arkady Nikolaitch,' began Vassily Ivanitch, 'that we live, so to say, bivouacking. . . .'

'There, stop that, what are you apologising for?' Bazarov interrupted. 'Kirsanov knows very well we're not Crœsuses, and that you have no butler. Where are we going to put him, that's the question?'

'To be sure, Yevgeny; I have a capital room there in the little lodge; he will be very comfortable there.'

'Have you had a lodge put up then?'

'Why, where the bath-house is,' put in Timofeitch.

'That is next to the bathroom,' Vassily Ivanitch added hurriedly. 'It's summer now . . . I will run over there at once, and make arrangements; and you, Timofeitch, meanwhile bring in their things. You, Yevgeny, I shall of course offer my study. *Suum cuique.*'

'There you have him! A comical old chap, and very good-natured,' remarked Bazarov, directly Vassily Ivanitch had gone. 'Just such a queer fish as yours, only in another way. He chatters too much.'

'And your mother seems an awfully nice woman,' observed Arkady.

'Yes, there's no humbug about her. You'll see what a dinner she'll give us.'

'They didn't expect you to-day, sir; they've not brought any beef,' observed Timofeitch, who was just dragging in Bazarov's box.

'We shall get on very well without beef. It's no use crying for the moon. Poverty, they say, is no vice.'

'How many serfs has your father?' Arkady asked suddenly.

'The estate's not his, but mother's; there are fifteen serfs, if I remember.'

'Twenty-two in all,' Timofeitch added, with an air of displeasure.

The flapping of slippers was heard, and Vassily Ivanovitch reappeared. 'In a few minutes your room will be ready to receive you,' he cried triumphantly 'Arkady . . . Nikolaitch? I think that is right? And here is your attendant,' he added, indicating a short-cropped boy, who had come in with him in a blue full-skirted coat with ragged elbows and a pair of boots which did not belong to him. 'His name is Fedka. Again, I repeat, even though my son tells me not to, you mustn't expect great things. He knows how to fill a pipe, though. You smoke, of course?'

'I generally smoke cigars,' answered Arkady.

'And you do very sensibly. I myself give the preference to cigars, but in these solitudes it is exceedingly difficult to obtain them.'

'There, that's enough humble pie,' Bazarov interrupted again. 'You'd much better sit here on the sofa and let us have a look at you.'

Vassily Ivanovitch laughed and sat down. He was very like his son in face, only his brow was lower and narrower, and his mouth rather wider, and he was for ever restless, shrugging up his shoulder as though his coat cut him under the armpits, blinking, clearing his throat, and gesticulating with his fingers, while his son was distinguished by a kind of nonchalant immobility.

'Humble pie!' repeated Vassily Ivanovitch. 'You must not imagine, Yevgeny, I want to appeal, so to speak, to our guest's sympathies by making out we live in such a wilderness. Quite the contrary, I maintain that for a thinking man nothing is a wilderness. At least, I try as far as possible not to get rusty, so to speak, not to fall behind the age.'

Vassily Ivanovitch drew out of his pocket a new yellow silk handkerchief, which he had had time to snatch up on the way to Arkady's room, and flourishing it in the air, he proceeded: 'I am not now alluding to the fact that, for example, at the cost of sacrifices not inconsiderable for me, I have put my peasants on the rent-system and given up my land to them on half profits. I regarded that as my duty; common sense itself enjoins such a proceeding, though other proprietors do not even dream of it; I am alluding to the sciences, to culture.'

'Yes; I see you have here *The Friend of Health* for 1855,' remarked Bazarov.

'It's sent me by an old comrade out of friendship,' Vassily Ivanovitch made haste to answer; 'but we have, for instance, some idea even of phrenology,' he added, addressing himself principally, however, to Arkady, and pointing to a small plaster head on the cupboard, divided into numbered squares; 'we are not unacquainted even with Schenlein and Rademacher.'

'Why do people still believe in Rademacher in this province?' asked Bazarov.

Vassily Ivanovitch cleared his throat. 'In this province. . . . Of course, gentlemen, you know best; how could we keep pace with you? You are here to take our places. In my day, too, there was some sort of a Humouralist school, Hoffmann, and Brown too with his vitalism—they seemed very ridiculous to us, but, of course, they too had been great men at one time or other. Someone new has taken the place of Rademacher with you; you bow down to him, but in another twenty years it will be his turn to be laughed at.'

'For your consolation I will tell you,' observed Bazarov, 'that nowadays we laugh at medicine altogether, and don't bow down to anyone.'

'How's that? Why, you're going to be a doctor, aren't you?'

'Yes, but the one fact doesn't prevent the other.'

Vassily Ivanovitch poked his third finger into his pipe, where a little smouldering ash was still left. 'Well, perhaps, perhaps—I am not going to dispute. What am I? A retired army doctor, *volla-too;* now fate has made me take to farming. I served in your grandfather's brigade,' he addressed himself again to Arkady; 'yes, yes, I have seen many sights in my day. And I was thrown into all kinds of society, brought into contact with all sorts of people! I myself, the man you see before you now, have felt the pulse of Prince Wittgenstein and of Zhukovsky! They were in the southern army, in the fourteenth, you understand' (and here Vassily Ivanovitch pursed his mouth up significantly). 'Well, well, but my business was on one side; stick to your lancet, and let everything else go hang! Your grandfather was a very honourable man, a real soldier.'

'Confess, now, he was rather a blockhead,' remarked Bazarov lazily.

'Ah, Yevgeny, how can you use such an expression! Do consider. . . . Of course, General Kirsanov was not one of the . . .'

'Come, drop him,' broke in Bazarov; 'I was pleased as I was driving along here to see your birch copse; it has shot up capitally.'

Vassily Ivanovitch brightened up. 'And you must see what a little garden I've got now! I planted every tree myself. I've fruit, and raspberries, and all kinds of medicinal herbs. However clever you young gentlemen may be, old Paracelsus spoke the holy truth: *in herbis, verbis et lapidibus.* . . . I've retired from practice, you know, of course, but two or three times a week it will happen that I'm brought back to my old work. They come for advice—I can't drive them away. Sometimes the poor have recourse to me for help. And indeed there are no doctors here at all. There's one of the neighbours here, a retired major, only fancy, he doctors the people too. I asked the question, "Has he studied medicine?" And they told me, "No, he's not studied; he does it more from philanthropy." . . . Ha! ha! ha! from philanthropy! What do you think of that? Ha! ha! ha!'

'Fedka, fill me a pipe!' said Bazarov rudely.

'And there's another doctor here who just got to a patient.' Vassily Ivanovitch persisted in a kind of desperation, 'when the patient had gone *ad patres;* the servant didn't let the doctor speak; you're no longer wanted, he told him. He hadn't expected this, got confused, and asked, "Why, did your master hiccup before his death?" "Yes." "Did he hiccup much?" "Yes." "Ah, well, that's all right," and off he set back again. Ha! ha! ha!'

The old man was alone in his laughter; Arkady forced a smile on his face. Bazarov simply stretched. The conversation went on in this way for about an hour; Arkady had time to go to his room, which turned out to be the ante-room attached to the bathroom, but was very snug and clean. At last Tanyusha came in and announced that dinner was ready.

Vassily Ivanovitch was the first to get up. 'Come, gentlemen. You must be magnanimous and pardon me if I've bored you. I daresay my good wife will give you more satisfaction.'

The dinner, though prepared in haste, turned out to be very good, even abundant; only the wine was not quite up to the mark; it was almost black sherry, bought by Timofeitch in the town at a well-known merchant's, and had a faint coppery, resinous taste, and the flies were a great nuisance. On ordinary days a serf-boy used to keep driving them away with a large green branch; but on this occasion Vassily Ivanovitch had sent him away through dread of the criticism of the younger generation. Arina Vlasyevna had had time to dress; she had put on a high cap with silk ribbons and a pale blue flowered shawl. She broke down again directly she caught sight of her Enyusha, but her husband had no need to admonish her; she made haste to wipe away her tears herself, for fear of spotting her shawl. Only the young men ate anything; the master and mistress of the house had dined long ago. Fedka waited at table, obviously encumbered by having boots on for the first time; he was assisted by a woman of a masculine cast of face and one eye, by name Anfisushka, who performed the duties of housekeeper, poultry-woman, and laundress. Vassily Ivanovitch walked up and down during the whole of dinner, and with a perfectly happy, positively beatific countenance talked about the serious anxiety he felt at Napoleon's policy, and the intricacy of the Italian question. Arina Vlasyevna took no notice of Arkady. She did not press him to eat; leaning her round face, to which the full cherry-coloured lips and the little moles on the cheeks and over the eyebrows gave a very simple good-natured expression, on her little closed fist, she did not take her eyes off her son, and kept constantly sighing; she was dying to know for how long he had come, but she was afraid to ask him.

'What if he says for two days,' she thought, and her heart sank. After the roast Vassily Ivanovitch disappeared for an instant, and returned with an opened half-bottle of champagne. 'Here,' he cried, 'though we do live in the wilds, we have something to make merry with on festive occasions!' He filled three champagne glasses and a little wineglass, proposed the health of 'our inestimable guests,' and at once tossed off his glass in military fashion; while he made Arina Vlasyevna drink her wineglass to the last drop. When the time came in due course for preserves, Arkady, who could not bear anything sweet, thought it his duty, however, to taste four different kinds which had been freshly made, all the more as Bazarov flatly refused them and began at once smoking a cigarette. Then tea came on the scene with cream, butter, and cracknels; then Vassily Ivanovitch took them all into the garden to admire the beauty of the evening. As they passed a garden seat he whispered to Arkady—

'At this spot I love to meditate, as I watch the sunset; it suits a recluse like me. And there, a little farther off, I have planted some of the trees beloved of Horace.'

'What trees?' asked Bazarov, overhearing.

'Oh . . . acacias.'

Bazarov began to yawn.

'I imagine it's time our travellers were in the arms of Morpheus,' observed Vassily Ivanovitch.

'That is, it's time for bed,' Bazarov put in. 'That's a correct idea. It is time, certainly.'

As he said good-night to his mother, he kissed her on the forehead, while she embraced him, and stealthily behind his back she gave him her blessing three times. Vassily Ivanovitch conducted Arkady to his room, and wished him 'as refreshing repose as I enjoyed at your happy years'. And Arkady did as a fact sleep excellently in his bath-house; there was a smell of mint in it, and two crickets behind the stove rivalled each other in their drowsy chirping. Vassily Ivanovitch went from Arkady's room to his study, and perching on the sofa at his son's feet, he was looking forward to having a chat with him; but Bazarov at once sent him away, saying he was sleepy, and did not fall asleep till morning. With wide-open eyes he stared vindictively into the darkness; the memories of childhood had no power over him; and besides, he had not yet had time to get rid of the impression of his recent bitter emotions. Arina Vlasyevna first prayed to her heart's content, then she had a long, long conversation with Anfisushka, who stood stock-still before her mistress, and fixing her solitary eye upon her, communicated in a mysterious whisper all her observations and conjectures in regard to Yevgeny Vassilyevitch. The old lady's head was giddy with happiness and wine and tobacco smoke: her husband tried to talk to her, but with a wave of his hand gave it up in despair.

Arina Vlasyevna was a genuine Russian gentlewoman of the olden times; she ought to have lived two centuries before, in the old Moscow days. She was very devout and emotional; she believed in fortune-telling, charms, dreams, and omens of every possible kind; she believed in the prophecies of crazy people, in house-spirits, in wood-spirits, in unlucky meetings, in the evil eye, in popular remedies, she ate specially prepared salt on Holy Thursday, and believed that the end of the world was at hand; she believed that if on Easter Sunday the lights did not go out at vespers, then there would be a good crop of buckwheat, and that a mushroom will not grow after it has been looked on by the eye of man; she believed that the devil likes to be where there is water, and that every Jew has a blood-stained patch on his breast; she was afraid of mice, of snakes, of frogs, of sparrows, of leeches, of thunder, of cold water, of draughts, of horses, of goats, of red-haired people, and black cats, and she regarded crickets and dogs as unclean beasts; she never ate veal, doves, cray-fishes, cheese, asparagus, artichokes, hares, nor water-melons, because a cut water-melon suggested the head of John the Baptist, and of oysters she could not speak without a shudder; she was fond of eating—and fasted rigidly; she slept ten hours out of the twenty-four—and never went to bed at all if Vassily Ivanovitch had so much as a headache; she had never read a single book except *Alexis or the Cottage in the Forest;* she wrote one, or at the most two, letters in a year, but was great in housewifery, preserving, and jam-making, though with her own hands she never touched a thing, and was generally disinclined to move from her place. Arina Vlasyevna was very kind-hearted, and in her way not at all stupid. She knew that the world is divided into masters whose duty it is to command, and simple folk whose duty it is to serve them—and so she felt no repugnance to servility and prostrations to the ground; but she treated those in subjection to her kindly and gently, never let a single beggar go away empty-handed, and never spoke ill of anyone, though she was fond of gossip. In her youth she had been pretty, had played the clavichord, and spoken French a little; but in the course of many years' wanderings with her husband, whom she had married against her will, she had grown stout, and forgotten music and French. Her son she loved and feared unutterably; she had given up the management of the property to Vassily Ivanovitch—and now did not interfere in anything; she used to groan, wave her handkerchief, and raise her eyebrows higher and higher with horror directly her old husband began to discuss the impending government reforms and his own plans. She was apprehensive, and constantly expecting some great misfortune, and began to weep directly she remembered anything sorrowful. . . . Such women are not common nowadays. God knows whether we ought to rejoice!

# 21

On getting up Arkady opened the window, and the first object that met his view was Vassily Ivanovitch. In an Oriental dressing-gown girt round the waist with a pocket-handkerchief he was industriously digging in his garden. He perceived his young visitor, and leaning on his spade, he called, 'The best of health to you! How have you slept?'

'Capitally,' answered Arkady.

'Here am I, as you see, like some Cincinnatus, marking out a bed for late turnips. The time has come now—and thank God for it!—when everyone ought to obtain his sustenance with his own hands; it's useless to reckon on others; one must labour oneself. And it turns out that Jean Jacques Rousseau is right. Half an hour ago, my dear young gentleman, you might have seen me in a totally different position. One peasant woman, who complained of looseness—that's how they express it, but in our language, dysentery—I . . . how can I express it best? I administered opium; and for another I extracted a tooth. I proposed an anæsthetic to her . . . but she would not consent. All that I do *gratis—anamatyer (en amateur)*. I'm used to it, though; you see, I'm a plebeian, *homo novus*— not one of the old stock, not like my spouse. . . . Wouldn't you like to come this way into the shade, to breathe the morning freshness a little before tea?'

Arkady went out to him.

'Welcome once again,' said Vassily Ivanovitch, raising his hand in a military salute to the greasy skull-cap which covered his head. 'You, I know, are accustomed to luxury, to amusements, but even the great ones of this world do not disdain to spend a brief space under a cottage roof.'

'Good heavens,' protested Arkady, 'as though I were one of the great ones of this world! And I'm not accustomed to luxury.'

'Pardon me, pardon me,' rejoined Vassily Ivanovitch with a polite simper. 'Though I am laid on the shelf now, I have knocked about the world too—I can tell a bird by its flight. I am something of a psychologist too in my own way, and a physiognomist. If I had not, I will venture to say, been endowed with that gift, I should have come to grief long ago; I should have stood no chance, a poor man like me. I tell you without flattery, I am sincerely delighted at the friendship I observe between you and my son. I have just seen him; he got up as he usually does—no doubt you are aware of it—very early, and went a ramble about the neighbourhood.

Permit me to inquire—have you known my son long?'

'Since last winter.'

'Indeed. And permit me to question you further—but hadn't we better sit down? Permit me, as a father, to ask without reserve: What is your opinion of my Yevgeny?'

'Your son is one of the most remarkable men I have ever met,' Arkady answered emphatically.

Vassily Ivanovitch's eyes suddenly grew round, and his cheeks were suffused with a faint flush. The spade fell out of his hand.

'And so you expect,' he began . . .

'I'm convinced,' Arkady put in, 'that your son has a great future before him; that he will do honour to your name. I've been certain of that ever since I first met him.'

'How . . . how was that?' Vassily Ivanovitch articulated with an effort. His wide mouth was relaxed in a triumphant smile, which would not leave it.

'Would you like me to tell you how we met?'

'Yes . . . and altogether. . . .'

Arkady began to tell his tale, and to talk of Bazarov with even greater warmth, even greater enthusiasm than he had done on the evening when he danced a mazurka with Madame Odintsov.

Vassily Ivanovitch listened and listened, blinked, and rolled his handkerchief up into a ball in both his hands, cleared his throat, ruffled up his hair, and at last could stand it no longer; he bent down to Arkady and kissed him on his shoulder. 'You have made me perfectly happy,' he said, never ceasing to smile. 'I ought to tell you, I . . . idolise my son; my old wife I won't speak of—we all know what mothers are!—but I dare not show my feelings before him, because he doesn't like it. He is averse to every kind of demonstration of feeling; many people even find fault with him for such firmness of character, and regard it as a proof of pride or lack of feeling, but men like him ought not to be judged by the common standard, ought they? And here, for example, many another fellow in his place would have been a constant drag on his

128

parents; but he, would you believe it? has never from the day he was born taken a farthing more than he could help, that's God's truth!'

'He is a disinterested, honest man,' observed Arkady.

'Exactly so; he is disinterested. And I don't only idolise him, Arkady Nikolaitch, I am proud of him, and the height of my ambition is that some day there will be the following lines in his biography: "The son of a simple army doctor, who was, however, capable of divining his greatness betimes, and spared nothing for his education. . . ." ' The old man's voice broke.

Arkady pressed his hand.

'What do you think,' inquired Vassily Ivanovitch, after a short silence, 'will it be in the field of medicine that he will attain the celebrity you anticipate for him?'

'Of course, not in medicine, though even in that department he will be one of the leading scientific men.'

'In what then, Arkady Nikolaitch?'

'It would be hard to say now, but he will be famous.'

'He will be famous!' repeated the old man, and he sank into a reverie.

'Arina Vlasyevna sent me to call you in to tea,' announced Anfisushka, coming by with an immense dish of ripe raspberries.

Vassily Ivanovitch started. 'And will there be cooled cream for the raspberries?'

'Yes.'

'Cold now, mind! Don't stand on ceremony, Arkady Nikolaitch; take some more. How is it Yevgeny doesn't come?'

'I'm here,' was heard Bazarov's voice from Arkady's room.

Vassily Ivanovitch turned round quickly. 'Aha! you wanted to pay a visit to your friend; but you were too late, *amice,* and we have already had a long conversation with him. Now we must go in to tea, mother summons us. By the way, I want to have a little talk with you.'

'What about?'

'There's a peasant here; he's suffering from icterus. . . .'

'You mean jaundice?'

'Yes, a chronic and very obstinate case of icterus. I have prescribed him centaury and St. John's wort, ordered him to eat carrots, given him soda; but all that's merely palliative measures; we want some more decided treatment. Though you do laugh at medicine, I am certain you can give me practical advice. But we will talk of that later. Now come in to tea.'

Vassily Ivanovitch jumped up briskly from the garden seat, and hummed from *Robert le Diable*—

> 'The rule, the rule we set ourselves,
> To live, to live for pleasure!'

'Singular vitality!' observed Bazarov, going away from the window.

It was midday. The sun was burning hot behind a thin veil of unbroken whitish clouds. Everything was hushed; there was no sound but the cocks crowing irritably at one another in the village, producing in everyone who heard them a strange sense of drowsiness and ennui; and somewhere, high up in a tree-top, the incessant plaintive cheep of a young hawk. Arkady and Bazarov lay in the shade of a small haystack, putting under themselves two armfuls of dry and rustling but still greenish and fragrant grass.

'That aspen-tree,' began Bazarov, 'reminds me of my childhood; it grows at the edge of the clay-pits where the bricks were dug, and in those days I believed firmly that that clay-pit and aspen tree possessed a peculiar talismanic power; I never felt dull near them. I did not understand then that I was not dull because I was a child. Well, now I'm grown up, the talisman's lost its power.'

'How long did you live here altogether?' asked Arkady.

'Two years on end; then we travelled about. We led a roving life, wandering from town to town for the most part.'

'And has this house been standing long?'

'Yes. My grandfather built it—my mother's father.'

'Who was he—your grandfather?'

'Devil knows. Some second-major. He served with Suvorov, and was always telling stories about the crossing of the Alps—inventions probably.'

'You have a portrait of Suvorov hanging in the drawing-room. I like these dear little houses like yours; they're so warm and old-fashioned; and there's always a special sort of scent about them.'

'A smell of lamp-oil and clover,' Bazarov remarked, yawning. 'And the flies in those dear little houses. . . . Faugh!'

'Tell me,' began Arkady, after a brief pause, 'were they strict with you when you were a child?'

'You can see what my parents are like. They're not a severe sort.'

'Are you fond of them, Yevgeny?'

'I am, Arkady.'

'How fond they are of you!'

Bazarov was silent for a little. 'Do you know what I'm thinking about?' he brought out at last, clasping his hands behind his head.

'No. What is it?'

'I'm thinking life is a happy thing for my parents. My father at sixty is fussing around, talking about "palliative" measures, doctoring people, playing the bountiful master with the peasants—having a festive time, in fact; and my mother's happy too; her day's so chockful of duties of all sorts, and sighs and groans, that she's no time even to think of herself; while I . . .'

'While you?'

'I think; here I lie under a haystack. . . . The tiny space I occupy is so infinitely small in comparison with the rest of space, in which I am not, and which has nothing to do with me; and the period of time in which it is my lot to live is so petty beside the eternity in which I have not been, and shall not be. . . . And in this atom, this mathematical point, the blood is circulating, the brain is working and wanting something. . . . Isn't it loathsome? Isn't it petty?'

'Allow me to remark that what you're saying applies to men in general.'

'You are right,' Bazarov cut in. 'I was going to say that they now—my parents, I mean—are absorbed and don't trouble themselves about their nothingness; it doesn't sicken them . . . while I . . . I feel nothing but weariness and anger.'

'Anger? why anger?'

'Why? How can you ask why? Have you forgotten?'

'I remember everything, but still I don't admit that you have any right to be angry. You're unlucky, I'll allow, but . . .'

'Pooh! then you, Arkady Nikolaevitch, I can see, regard love like all modern young men; cluck, cluck, cluck, you call to the hen, but if the hen comes near you, you run away. I'm not like that. But that's enough of that. What can't be helped, it's shameful to talk about.' He turned over on his side. 'Aha! there goes a valiant ant dragging off a half-dead fly. Take her, brother, take her! Don't pay attention to her resistance; it's your privilege as an animal to be free from the sentiment of pity—make the most of it—not like us conscientious self-destructive animals!'

'You shouldn't say that, Yevgeny! When have you destroyed yourself?'

Bazarov raised his head. 'That's the only thing I pride myself on. I haven't crushed myself, so a woman can't crush me. Amen! It's all over! You shall not hear another word from me about it.'

Both the friends lay for some time in silence.

'Yes,' began Bazarov, 'man's a strange animal. When one gets a side view from a distance of the dead-alive life our "fathers" lead here, one thinks: What could be better? You eat and drink, and know you are acting in the most reasonable, most judicious manner. But if not, you're devoured by ennui. One wants to have to do with people if only to abuse them.'

'One ought so to order one's life that every moment in it

should be of significance,' Arkady affirmed reflectively.

'I dare say! What's of significance is sweet, however mistaken; one could make up one's mind to what's insignificant even. But pettiness, pettiness, that's what's insufferable.'

'Pettiness doesn't exist for a man so long as he refuses to recognise it.'

'H'm . . . what you've just said is a commonplace reversed.'

'What? What do you mean by that term?'

'I'll tell you: saying, for instance, that education is beneficial, that's a commonplace; but to say that education is injurious, that's a commonplace turned upside down. There's more style about it, so to say, but in reality it's one and the same.''

'And the truth is—where, which side?'

'Where? Like an echo I answer, 'Where?''

'You're in a melancholy mood to-day, Yevgeny.'

'Really? The sun must have softened my brain, I suppose, and I can't stand so many raspberries either.'

'In that case, a nap's not a bad thing,' observed Arkady.

'Certainly; only don't look at me; every man's face is stupid when he's asleep.'

'But isn't it all the same to you what people think of you?'

'I don't know what to say to you. A real man ought not to care; a real man is one whom it's no use thinking about, whom one must either obey or hate.'

'It's funny! I don't hate anybody,' observed Arkady, after a moment's thought.

'And I hate so many. You are a soft-hearted, mawkish creature; how could you hate anyone? . . . You're timid; you don't rely on yourself much.'

'And you,' interrupted Arkady, 'do you expect much of yourself? Have you a high opinion of yourself?'

Bazarov paused. 'When I meet a man who can hold his own beside me,' he said, dwelling on every syllable, 'then I'll change my opinion of myself. Yes, hatred! You said, for instance, to-day as we passed our bailiff Philip's cottage—it's the one that's so nice and clean—well, you said, Russia will come to perfection when the poorest peasant has a house like that, and every one of us ought to work to bring it about. . . . And I felt such a hatred for this poorest peasant, this Philip or Sidor, for whom I'm to be ready to jump out of my skin, and who won't even thank me for it . . . and why should he thank me? Why, suppose he does live in a clean house, while the nettles are growing out of me—well what do I gain by it?'

'Hush, Yevgeny . . . if one listened to you to-day one would be driven to agreeing with those who reproach us for want of principles.'

'You talk like your uncle. There are no general principles—you've not made out that even yet! There are feelings. Everything depends on them.'

'How so?'

'Why, I, for instance, take up a negative attitude, by virtue of my sensations; I like to deny—my brain's made on that plan, and that's all about it! Why do I like chemistry? Why do you like apples?—by virtue of our sensations. It's all the same thing. Deeper than that men will never penetrate. Not everyone will tell you that, and, in fact, I shan't tell you so another time.'

'What? and is honesty a matter of the senses?'

'I should rather think so.'

'Yevgeny!' Arkady was beginning in a dejected voice . . .

'Well? What? Isn't it to your taste?' broke in Bazarov. 'No, brother. If you've made up your mind to mow down everything, don't spare your own legs. But we've talked enough metaphysics. "Nature breathes the silence of sleep," said Pushkin.'

'He never said anything of the sort,' protested Arkady.

'Well, if he didn't, as a poet he might have—and ought to have said it. By the way, he must have been a military man.'

'Pushkin never was a military man!'

'Why on every page of him there's, "To arms! to arms! for Russia's honour!"'

'Why, what stories you invent! I declare, it's positive calumny.'

'Calumny? That's a mighty matter! What a word he's found to frighten me with! Whatever charge you make against a man, you may be certain he deserves twenty times worse than that in reality.'

'We had better go to sleep,' said Arkady, in a tone of vexation.

'With the greatest pleasure,' answered Bazarov. But neither of them slept. A feeling almost of hostility had come over both the young men. Five minutes later, they opened their eyes and glanced at one another in silence.

'Look,' said Arkady suddenly, 'a dry maple leaf has come off and is falling to the earth; its movement is exactly like a butterfly's flight. Isn't it strange? Gloom and decay—like brightness and life.'

'Oh, my friend, Arkady Nikolaitch!' cried Bazarov, 'one thing I entreat of you; no fine talk.'

'I talk as best I can. . . . And, I declare, it's perfect despotism. An idea came into my head; why shouldn't I utter it?'

'Yes; and why shouldn't I utter my ideas? I think that fine talk's positively indecent.'

'And what is decent? Abuse?'

'Ha! ha! you really do intend, I see, to walk in your uncle's footsteps. How pleased that worthy imbecile would have been if he had heard you!'

'What did you call Pavel Petrovitch?'

'I called him, very justly, an imbecile.'

'But this is unbearable!' cried Arkady.

'Aha! family feeling spoke there,' Bazarov commented coolly. 'I've noticed how obstinately it sticks to people. A man's ready to give up everything and break every prejudice; but to admit that his brother, for instance, who steals handkerchiefs, is a thief—that's too much for him. And when one comes to think of it: my brother, mine—and no genius . . . that's an idea no one can swallow.'

'It was a simple sense of justice spoke in me and not in the least family feeling,' retorted Arkady passionately. 'But since that's a sense you don't understand, since you haven't that sensation, you can't judge of it.'

'In other words, Arkady Kirsanov is too exalted for my comprehension. I bow down before him and say no more.'

'Don't, please, Yevgeny; we shall really quarrel at last.'

'Ah, Arkady! do me a kindness. I entreat you, let us quarrel for once in earnest. . . .'

'But then perhaps we should end by . . .'

'Fighting?' put in Bazarov. 'Well? Here, on the hay, in these idyllic surroundings, far from the world and the eyes of men, it wouldn't matter. But you'd be no match for me. I'd have you by the throat in a minute.'

Bazarov spread out his long, cruel fingers. . . . Arkady turned round and prepared, as though in jest, to resist. . . . But his friend's face struck him as so vindictive—there was such menace in grim earnest in the smile that distorted his lips, and in his glittering eyes, that he felt instinctively afraid.

'Ah! so this is where you have got to!' the voice of Vassily Ivanovitch was heard saying at that instant, and the old army doctor appeared before the young men, garbed in a home-made linen pea-jacket, with a straw hat, also home-made, on his head. 'I've been looking everywhere for you. . . . Well, you've picked out a capital place, and you're excellently employed. Lying on the "earth, gazing up to heaven". Do you know, there's a special significance in that?'

'I never gaze up to heaven except when I want to sneeze,' growled Bazarov, and turning to Arkady he added in an undertone, 'Pity he interrupted us.'

'Come, hush!' whispered Arkady, and he secretly squeezed his friend's hand. But no friendship can long stand such shocks.

'I look at you, my youthful friends,' Vassily Ivanovitch was saying meantime, shaking his head, and leaning his folded arms on a rather cunningly bent stick of his own carving, with a

Turk's figure for a top—'I look, and I cannot refrain from admiration. You have so much strength, such youth and bloom, such abilities, such talents! Positively, a Castor and Pollux!'

'Get along with you—going off into mythology!' commented Bazarov. 'You can see at once that he was a great Latinist in his day! Why, I seem to remember, you gained the silver medal for Latin prose—didn't you?'

'The Dioscuri, the Dioscuri!' repeated Vassily Ivanovitch.

'Come, shut up, father; don't show off.'

'Once in a way it's surely permissible,' murmured the old man. 'However, I have not been seeking for you, gentlemen, to pay you compliments; but with the object, in the first place, of announcing to you that we shall soon be dining; and secondly, I wanted to prepare you, Yevgeny. . . . You are a sensible man, you know the world, and you know what women are, and consequently you will excuse. . . . Your mother wished to have a Te Deum sung on the occasion of your arrival. You must not imagine that I am inviting you to attend this thanksgiving—it is over indeed now; but Father Alexey . . .'

'The village parson?'

'Well, yes, the priest; he . . . is to dine . . . with us. . . . I did not anticipate this, and did not even approve of it . . . but it somehow came about . . . he did not understand me. . . . And, well . . . Arina Vlasyevna . . . Besides, he's a worthy, reasonable man.'

'He won't eat my share at dinner, I suppose?' queried Bazarov.

Vassilly Ivanovitch laughed. 'How you talk!'

'Well, that's all I ask. I'm ready to sit down to table with any man.'

Vassily Ivanovitch set his hat straight. 'I was certain before I spoke,' he said, 'that you were above any kind of prejudice. Here am I, an old man at sixty-two, and I have none.' (Vassily Ivanovitch did not dare to confess that he had himself desired the thanksgiving service. He was no less religious than his wife.) 'And Father Alexey very much wanted to make your acquaintance. You will like him, you'll see. He's no objection even to cards, and he sometimes—but this is between ourselves . . . positively smokes a pipe.'

'All right. We'll have a round of whist after dinner, and I'll clean him out.'

'He! he! he! We shall see! That remains to be seen.'

'I know you're an old hand,' said Bazarov, with a peculiar emphasis.

Vassily Ivanovitch's bronzed cheeks were suffused with an uneasy flush.

'For shame, Yevgeny. . . . Let bygones be bygones. Well, I'm ready to acknowledge before this gentleman I had that passion in my youth; and I have paid for it too! How hot it is, though! Let me sit down with you. I shan't be in your way, I hope?'

'Oh, not at all,' answered Arkady.

Vassily Ivanovitch lowered himself, sighing, into the hay. 'Your present quarters remind me, my dear sirs,' he began, 'of my military bivouacking existence, the ambulance halts, somewhere like this under a haystack, and even for that we were thankful.' He sighed. 'I have had many, many experiences in my life. For example, if you will allow me, I will tell you a curious episode of the plague in Bessarabia.'

'For which you got the Vladimir cross?' put in Bazarov. 'We know, we know. . . . By the way, why is it you're not wearing it?'

'Why, I told you that I have no prejudices,' muttered Vassily Ivanovitch (he had only the evening before had the red ribbon picked off his coat), and he proceeded to relate the episode of the plague. 'Why, he's fallen asleep,' he whispered all at once to Arkady, pointing to Yevgeny, and winking good-naturedly. 'Yevgeny! get up,' he went on aloud. 'Let's go to dinner.'

Father Alexey, a good-looking stout man with thick, carefully-combed hair, with an embroidered girdle round his lilac silk cassock, appeared to be a man of much tact and adaptability. He made haste to be the first to offer his hand to Arkady and Bazarov, as though understanding beforehand that they did not want his blessing, and he behaved himself in general without constraint. He neither derogated from his own dignity, nor gave offence to others; he vouchsafed a passing smile at the seminary Latin, and stood up for his bishop; drank two small glasses of wine, but refused a third; accepted a cigar from Arkady, but did not proceed to smoke it, saying he would take it home with him. The only thing not quite agreeable about him was a way he had of constantly raising his hand with care and deliberation to catch the flies on his face, sometimes succeeding in smashing them. He took his seat at the green table, expressing his satisfaction at so doing in measured terms, and ended by winning from Bazarov two roubles and a half in paper money; they had no idea of even reckoning in silver in the house of Arina Vlasyevna. . . . She was sitting, as before, near her son (she did not play cards), her cheek, as before, propped on her little fist; she only got up to order some new dainty to be served. She was afraid to caress Bazarov, and he gave her no encouragment, he did not invite her caresses; and besides, Vassily Ivanovitch had advised her not to 'worry' him too much. 'Young men are not fond of that sort of thing,' he declared to her. (It's needless to say what the dinner was like that day; Timofeitch in person had galloped off at early dawn for beef; the bailiff had gone off in another direction for turbot, gremille, and crayfish; for mushrooms alone forty-two farthings had been paid the peasant women in copper); but Arina Vlasyevna's eyes, bent steadfastly on Bazarov, did not express only devotion and tenderness; in them was to be seen sorrow also, mingled with awe and curiosity; there was to be seen too a sort of humble reproachfulness.

Bazarov, however, was not in a humour to analyse the exact expression of his mother's eyes; he seldom turned to her, and then only with some short question. Once he asked her for her hand 'for luck'; she gently laid her soft, little hand on his rough, broad palm.

'Well,' she asked, after waiting a little, 'has it been any use?'

139

'Worse luck than ever,' he answered, with a careless laugh.

'He plays too rashly,' pronounced Father Alexey, as it were compassionately, and he stroked his beard.

'Napoleon's rule, good Father, Napoleon's rule,' put in Vassily Ivanovitch, leading an ace.

'It brought him to St. Helena, though,' observed Father Alexey, as he trumped the ace.

'Wouldn't you like some currant tea, Enyusha?' inquired Arina Vlasyevna.

Bazarov merely shrugged his shoulders.

'No!' he said to Arkady the next day, 'I'm off from here to-morrow. I'm bored; I want to work, but I can't work here. I will come to your place again; I've left all my apparatus there too. In your house one can at any rate shut oneself up. While here my father repeats to me, "My study is at your disposal—nobody shall interfere with you", and all the time he himself is never a yard away. And I'm ashamed somehow to shut myself away from him. It's the same thing too with mother. I hear her sighing the other side of the wall, and if one goes in to her, one's nothing to say to her.'

'She will be very much grieved,' observed Arkady, 'and so will he.'

'I shall come back again to them.'

'When?'

'Why, when on my way to Petersburg.'

'I feel sorry for your mother particularly.'

'Why's that? Has she won your heart with strawberries, or what?'

Arkady dropped his eyes. 'You don't understand your mother, Yevgeny. She's not only a very good woman, she's very clever really. This morning she talked to me for half an hour, and so sensibly, interestingly.'

'I suppose she was expatiating upon me all the while?'

'We didn't talk only about you.'

'Perhaps; lookers-on see most. If a woman can keep up half-an-hour's conversation, it's always a hopeful sign. But I'm going all the same.'

'It won't be very easy for you to break it to them. They are always making plans for what we are to do in a fortnight's time.'

'No; it won't be easy. Some demon drove me to tease my father to-day; he had one of his rent-paying peasants flogged the other day, and quite right too—yes, yes, you needn't look at me in such horror—he did quite right, because he's an awful thief and drunkard; only my father had no idea that I, as they say, was cognisant of the facts. He was greatly perturbed, and now I shall have to upset him more than ever. . . . Never mind! Never say die! He'll get over it!'

Bazarov said, 'Never mind'; but the whole day passed before he could make up his mind to inform Vassily Ivanovitch of his intentions. At last, when he was just saying good-night to him in the study, he observed, with a feigned yawn——

'Oh . . . I was almost forgetting to tell you. . . . Send to Fedot's for our horses to-morrow.'

Vassily Ivanovitch was dumbfounded. 'Is Mr. Kirsanov leaving us then?'

'Yes; and I'm going with him.'

Vassily Ivanovitch positively reeled. 'You are going?'

'Yes . . . I must. Make the arrangements about the horses, please.'

'Very good . . .' faltered the old man; 'to Fedot's . . . very good . . . only . . . only. . . . How is it?'

'I must go to stay with him for a little time. I will come back here again later.'

'Ah! For a little time . . . very good.' Vassily Ivanovitch drew out his handkerchief, and, blowing his nose, doubled up almost to the ground. 'Well . . . everything shall be done. I had thought you were to be with us . . . a little longer. Three days. . . . After three years, it's rather little; rather little, Yevgeny!'

'But, I tell you, I'm coming back directly. It's necessary for me to go.'

'Necessary. . . . Well! Duty before everything. So the

horses shall be in readiness. Very good. Arina and I, of course, did not anticipate this. She has just begged some flowers from a neighbour; she meant to decorate the room for you.' (Vassily Ivanovitch did not even mention that every morning almost at dawn he took counsel with Timofeitch, standing with his bare feet in his slippers, and, pulling out with trembling fingers one dog's-eared rouble note after another, charged him with various purchases, with special reference to good things to eat, and to red wine, which, as far as he could observe, the young men liked extremely.) 'Liberty . . . is the great thing; that's my rule. . . . I don't want to hamper you . . . not . . .'

He suddenly ceased, and made for the door.

'We shall soon see each other again, father, really.'

But Vassily Ivanovitch, without turning round, merely waved his hand and was gone. When he got back to his bedroom he found his wife in bed, and began to say his prayers in a whisper, so as not to wake her up. She woke, however. 'Is that you, Vassily Ivanovitch?' she asked.

'Yes, mother.'

'Have you come from Enyusha? Do you know, I'm afraid of his not being comfortable on that sofa. I told Anfisushka to put him your travelling mattress and the new pillows; I should have given him our feather-bed, but I seem to remember he doesn't like too soft a bed. . . .'

'Never mind, mother; don't worry yourself. He's all right. Lord, have mercy on me, a sinner,' he went on with his prayer in a low voice. Vassily Ivanovitch was sorry for his old wife; he did not mean to tell her over-night what a sorrow there was in store for her.

Bazarov and Arkady set off the next day. From early morning all was dejection in the house; Anfisushka let the tray slip out of her hands; even Fedka was bewildered, and was reduced to taking off his boots. Vassily Ivanitch was more fussy than ever; he was obviously trying to put a good face on it, talked loudly, and stamped with his feet, but his face looked haggard, and his eyes were continually avoiding his son. Arina

Vlasyevna was crying quietly; she was utterly crushed, and could not have controlled herself at all if her husband had not spent two whole hours early in the morning exhorting her. When Bazarov, after repeated promises to come back certainly not later than in a month's time, tore himself at last from the embraces detaining him, and took his seat in the coach; when the horses had started, the bell was ringing, and the wheels were turning round, and when it was no longer any good to look after them, and the dust had settled, and Timofeitch, all bent and tottering as he walked, had crept back to his little room; when the old people were left alone in their little house, which seemed suddenly to have grown shrunken and decrepit too, Vassily Ivanovitch, after a few more moments of hearty waving of his handkerchief on the steps, sank into a chair, and his head dropped on to his breast. 'He has cast us off; he has forsaken us,' he faltered; 'forsaken us; he was dull with us. Alone, alone!' he repeated several times. Then Arina Vlasyevna went up to him, and, leaning her grey head against his grey head, said, 'There's no help for it, Vasya! A son is a separate piece cut off. He's like the falcon that flies home and flies away at his pleasure; while you and I are like funguses in the hollow of a tree, we sit side by side, and don't move from our place. Only I am left you unchanged for ever, as you for me.'

Vassily Ivanovitch took his hands from his face and clasped his wife, his friend, as warmly as he had never clasped in youth; she comforted him in his grief.

FATHERS AND CHILDREN

# 22

IN silence, only rarely exchanging a few insignificant words, our friends travelled as far as Fedot's. Bazarov was not altogether pleased with himself. Arkady was displeased with him. He was feeling, too, that causeless melancholy which is only known to the very young people. The coachman changed the horses, and getting up on to the box, inquired, 'To the right or to the left?'

Arkady started. The road to the right led to the town, and from there home; the road to the left led to Madame Odintsov's.

He looked at Bazarov.

'Yevgeny,' he queried; 'to the left?'

Bazarov turned away. 'What folly is this?' he muttered.

'I know it's folly,' answered Arkady. . . . 'But what does that matter? It's not the first time.'

Bazarov pulled his cap down over his brows. 'As you choose,' he said at last. 'Turn to the left,' shouted Arkady.

The coach rolled away in the direction of Nikolskoe. But having resolved on the folly, the friends were even more obstinately silent than before, and seemed positively ill-humoured.

Directly the steward met them on the steps of Madame Odintsov's house, the friends could perceive that they had acted injudiciously in giving way so suddenly to a passing impulse. They were obviously not expected. They sat rather a long while, looking rather foolish, in the drawing-room. Madame Odintsov came in to them at last. She greeted them with her customary politeness, but was surprised at their hasty return; and, so far as could be judged from the deliberation of her gestures and words, she was not over-pleased at it. They made haste to announce that they had only called on their road, and must go on farther, to the town, within four hours. She confined herself to a slight exclamation, begged Arkady to remember her to his father, and sent for her aunt. The princess appeared very sleepy, which gave her wrinkled old face an even more ill-natured expression. Katya was not well; she did not leave her room. Arkady suddenly realised that he was at least as anxious to see Katya as Anna Sergyevna herself. The four hours were spent in insignificant discussion of one thing and another; Anna Sergyevna both listened and spoke without a smile. It was only quite at parting that her former friendliness seemed, as it were, to revive.

'I have an attack of spleen just now,' she said; 'but you must not pay attention to that, and come again—I say this to both of you—before long.'

Both Bazarov and Arkady responded with a silent bow, took their seats in the coach, and without stopping again anywhere went straight home to Maryino, where they arrived safely on the evening of the following day. During the whole course of the journey neither one nor the other even mentioned the name of Madame Odintsov; Bazarov, in particular, scarcely opened his mouth, and kept staring in a side direction away from the road, with a kind of exasperated intensity.

At Maryino everyone was exceedingly delighted to see them. The prolonged absence of his son had begun to make Nikolai Petrovitch uneasy; he uttered a cry of joy, and bounced about on the sofa, dangling his legs, when Fenitchka ran to him with sparkling eyes, and informed him of the arrival of the 'young gentlemen'; even Pavel Petrovitch was conscious of some degree of agreeable excitement, and smiled condescendingly as he shook hands with the returned wanderers. Talk, questions followed; Arkady talked most, especially at supper, which was prolonged long after midnight. Nikolai Petrovitch ordered up some bottles of porter which had only just been sent from Moscow, and partook of the festive beverage till his cheeks were crimson, and he kept laughing a half-childish, half-nervous little chuckle. Even the servants were infected by the general gaiety. Dunyasha ran up and down like one possessed, and was continually slamming doors; while Piotr was, at three o'clock in the morning, still attempting to strum a Cossack waltz on the guitar. The strings gave forth a sweet and plaintive sound in the still air; but, with the exception of a small preliminary flourish, nothing came of the cultured valet's efforts; nature had given him no more musical talent than all the rest of the world.

But meanwhile things were not going over-harmoniously at Maryino, and poor Nikolai Petrovitch was having a bad time of it. Difficulties on the farm sprang up every day—senseless, distressing difficulties. The troubles with the hired labourers had become insupportable. Some asked for their wages to be settled, or for an increase of wages, while others made off with the wages they had received in advance; the horses fell sick; the harness fell to pieces as though it were burnt; the work was carelessly done; a threshing machine that had been ordered from Moscow turned out to be useless from its great weight, another was ruined the first time it was used; half the cattle sheds were burnt down through an old blind woman on the farm going in windy weather with a burning brand to fumigate her cow . . . the old woman, it is true, maintained that the whole mischief could be traced to the master's plan of introducing new-fangled cheeses and milk-products. The overseer suddenly turned lazy, and began to grow fat, as every Russian grows fat when he gets a snug berth. When he caught sight of Nikolai Petrovitch in the distance, he would fling a stick at a passing pig, or threaten a half-naked urchin, to show his zeal, but the rest of the time he was generally asleep. The peasants who had been put on the rent system did not bring their money at the time due, and stole the forest-timber; almost every night the keepers caught peasants' horses in the meadows of the 'farm', and sometimes forcibly bore them off. Nikolai Petrovitch would fix a money fine for damages, but the matter usually ended, after the horses had been kept a day or two on the master's forage, by their returning to their owners. To crown all, the peasants began quarrelling among themselves; brothers asked for a division of property, their wives could not get on together in one house; all of a sudden the squabble, as though at a given signal, came to a head, and at once the whole village came running to the counting-house steps, crawling to the master, often drunken and with battered face, demanding justice and judgment; then arose an uproar and clamour, the shrill wailing of the women mixed with the curses of the men. Then one had to examine the contending parties, and shout oneself hoarse, knowing all the while that one could never anyway arrive at a just decision. . . . There were not hands enough for the harvest; a neighbouring small owner, with the most benevolent countenance, contracted to supply him with reapers for a commission of two roubles an acre, and cheated him in the most shameless fashion; his peasant women demanded unheard-of sums, and the corn meanwhile went to waste; and here they were not getting on with the mowing, and there the Council of Guardians threatened and demanded prompt payment, in full, of interest due. . . .

'I can do nothing!' Nikolai Petrovitch cried more than once in despair. 'I can't flog them myself; and as for calling on the police captain, my principles don't allow of it, while you can do nothing with them without the fear of punishment!'

'*Du calme, du calme,*' Pavel Petrovitch would remark upon this, but even he hummed to himself, knitted his brows, and tugged at his moustache.

Bazarov held aloof from these matters, and indeed as a guest it was not for him to meddle in other people's business. The day after his arrival at Maryino, he set to work on his frogs, his infusoria, and his chemical experiments, and was for ever busy with them. Arkady, on the contrary, thought it his duty, if not to help his father, at least to make a show of being ready to help him. He gave him a patient hearing, and once offered him some advice, not with any idea of its being acted upon, but to show his interest. Farming details did not arouse any aversion in him; he used even to dream with pleasure of work on the land, but at this time his brain was swarming with other ideas. Arkady, to his own astonishment, thought incessantly of Nikolskoe; in former days he would simply have shrugged his shoulders if anyone had told him that he could ever feel dull under the same roof as Bazarov—and that roof his father's! but he actually was dull and longed to get away. He tried going long walks till he was tired, but that was no use. In conversation with his father one day, he found that Nikolai Petrovitch had in his possession rather interesting letters, written by Madame Odintsov's mother to his wife, and he gave him no rest till he got hold of the letters, for which Nikolai Petrovitch had to rummage in twenty drawers and boxes.

Having gained possession of these half-crumbling papers, Arkady felt, as it were, soothed, just as though he had caught a glimpse of the goal towards which he ought now to go. 'I mean that for both of you,' he was constantly whispering— she had added that herself! 'I'll go, I'll go, hang it all!' But he recalled the last visit, the cold reception and his former embarrassment, and timidity got the better of him. The 'go-ahead' feeling of youth, the secret desire to try his luck, to prove his powers in solitude, without the protection of anyone whatever, gained the day at last. Before ten days had passed after his return to Maryino, on the pretext of studying the working of the Sunday schools, he galloped off to the town again, and from there to Nikolskoe. Urging the driver on without intermission, he flew along, like a young officer riding to battle; and he felt both frightened and light-hearted, and was breathless with impatience. 'The great thing is—one mustn't think,' he kept repeating to himself. His driver happened to be a lad of spirit; he halted before every public-house, saying, 'A drink or not a drink?' but, to make up for it, when he had drunk he did not spare his horses. At last the lofty roof of the familiar house came in sight. . . . 'What am I to do?' flashed through Arkady's head. 'Well, there's no turning back now!' The three horses galloped in unison; the driver whooped and whistled at them. And now the bridge was groaning under the hoofs and wheels, and now the avenue of lopped pines seemed running to meet them. . . . There was a glimpse of a woman's pink dress against the dark green, a young face peeped out from under the light fringe of a parasol. . . . He recognised Katya, and she recognised him. Arkady told the driver to stop the galloping horses, leaped out of the carriage, and went up to her. 'It's you!' she cried, gradually flushing all over; 'let us go to my sister, she's here in the garden; she will be pleased to see you.'

Katya led Arkady into the garden. His meeting with her struck him as a particularly happy omen; he was delighted to see her, as though she were of his own kindred. Everything had happened so splendidly; no steward, no formal announce-

148

ment. At a turn in the path he caught sight of Anna Sergyevna. She was standing with her back to him. Hearing footsteps, she turned slowly round.

Arkady felt confused again, but the first words she uttered soothed him at once. 'Welcome back, runaway!' she said in her even, caressing voice, and came to meet him, smiling and frowning to keep the sun and wind out of her eyes. 'Where did you pick him up, Katya?'

'I have brought you something, Anna Sergyevna,' he began, 'which you certainly don't expect.'

'You have brought yourself; that's better than anything.'

FATHERS AND CHILDREN

# 23

HAVING seen Arkady off with ironical compassion, and given him to understand that he was not in the least deceived as to the real object of his journey, Bazarov shut himself up in complete solitude; he was overtaken by a fever for work. He did not dispute now with Pavel Petrovitch, especially as the latter assumed an excessively aristocratic demeanour in his presence, and expressed his opinions more in inarticulate sounds than in words. Only on one occasion Pavel Petrovitch fell into a controversy with the *nihilist* on the subject of the question then much discussed of the rights of the nobles of the Baltic province; but suddenly he stopped of his own accord, remarking with chilly politeness, 'However, we cannot understand one another; I, at least, have not the honour of understanding you.'

'I should think not!' cried Bazarov. 'A man's capable of understanding anything—how the æther vibrates, and what's going on in the sun—but how any other man can blow his nose differently from him, that he's incapable of understanding.'

'What, is that an epigram?' observed Pavel Petrovitch inquiringly, and he walked away.

However, he sometimes asked permission to be present at Bazarov's experiments, and once even placed his perfumed face, washed with the very best soap, near the microscope to see how a transparent infusoria swallowed a green speck, and busily munched it with two very rapid sort of clappers which were in its throat. Nikolai Petrovitch visited Bazarov much oftener than his brother; he would have come every day, as he expressed it, to 'study', if his worries on the farm had not taken off his attention. He did not hinder the young man in his scientific researches; he used to sit down somewhere in a corner of the room and look on attentively, occasionally permitting himself a discreet question. During dinner and supper-time he used to try to turn the conversation upon physics, geology, or chemistry, seeing that all other topics, even agriculture, to say nothing of politics, might lead, if not to collisions, at least to mutual unpleasantness. Nikolai Petrovitch surmised that his brother's dislike for Bazarov was no less. An unimportant incident, among many others, confirmed his surmises. The cholera began to make its appearance in some places in the neighbourhood, and even 'carried off' two persons from Maryino itself. In the night Pavel Petrovitch happened to have rather severe symptoms. He was in pain till the morning, but did not have recourse to Bazarov's skill. And when he met him the following day, in reply to his question, 'Why he had not sent for him?' answered, still quite pale, but scrupulously brushed and shaved, 'Why, I seem to recollect you said yourself you didn't believe in medicine.' So the days went by. Bazarov went on obstinately and grimly working . . . and meanwhile there was in Nikolai Petrovitch's house one creature to whom, if he did not open his heart, he at least was glad to talk. . . . That creature was Fenitchka.

He used to meet her for the most part early in the morning, in the garden, or the farmyard; he never used to go to her room to see her, and she had only once been to his door to inquire—ought she to let Mitya have his bath or not? It was not only that she confided in him, that she was not afraid of him—she was positively freer and more at her ease in her behaviour with him than with Nikolai Petrovitch himself. It is hard to say how it came about; perhaps it was because she unconsciously felt the absence in Bazarov of all gentility, of all that superiority which at once attracts and overawes. In her eyes he was both an excellent doctor and a simple man. She looked after her baby without constraint in his presence; and once when she was suddenly attacked with giddiness and headache, she took a spoonful of medicine from his hand. Before Nikolai Petrovitch she kept, as it were, at a distance from Bazarov; she acted in this way not from hypocrisy, but from a kind of feeling of propriety. Pavel Petrovitch she was more afraid of than ever; for some time he had begun to watch her, and would suddenly make his appearance, as though he sprang out of the earth behind her back, in his English suit, with his immovable vigilant face, and his hands in his pockets. 'It's like a bucket of cold water on one,' Fenitchka complained to Dunyasha, and the latter sighed in response, and thought of another 'heartless' man. Bazarov, without the least suspicion of the fact, had become the *cruel tyrant* of her heart.

Fenitchka liked Bazarov; but he liked her too. His face was positively transformed when he talked to her; it took a bright, almost kind expression, and his habitual nonchalance was replaced by a sort of jesting attentiveness. Fenitchka was growing prettier every day. There is a time in the life of young women when they suddenly begin to expand and blossom like summer roses; this time had come for Fenitchka. Dressed in a delicate white dress, she seemed herself slighter and whiter; she was not tanned by the sun; but the heat, from which she could not shield herself, spread a slight flush over her cheeks and ears, and, shedding a soft indolence over her whole body, was reflected in a dreamy languor in her pretty eyes. She was almost unable to work; her hands seemed to fall naturally into her lap. She scarcely walked at all, and was constantly sighing and complaining with comic helplessness.

'You should go oftener to bathe,' Nikolai Petrovitch told her. He had made a large bath covered in with an awning in the one of his ponds which had not yet quite disappeared.

'Oh, Nikolai Petrovitch! But by the time one gets to the pond, one's utterly dead, and, coming back, one's dead again. You see, there's no shade in the garden.'

'That's true, there's no shade,' replied Nikolai Petrovitch, rubbing his forehead.

One day at seven o'clock in the morning Bazarov, returning from a walk, came upon Fenitchka in the lilac arbour, which was long past flowering, but was still thick and green. She was sitting on the garden seat, and had as usual thrown a white kerchief over her head; near her lay a whole heap of red and white roses still wet with dew. He said good-morning to her.

'Ah! Yevgeny Vassilyitch!' she said, and lifted the edge of her kerchief a little to look at him, in doing which her arm was left bare to the elbow.

'What are you doing here?' said Bazarov, sitting down beside her. 'Are you making a nosegay?'

'Yes, for the table at lunch. Nikolai Petrovitch likes it.'

'But it's a long while yet to lunch-time. What a heap of flowers!'

'I gathered them now, for it will be hot then, and one can't go out. One can only just breathe now. I feel quite weak with the heat. I'm really afraid whether I'm not going to be ill.'

'What an idea! Let me feel your pulse.' Bazarov took her hand, felt for the evenly-beating pulse, but did not even begin to count its throbs. 'You'll live a hundred years!' he said, dropping her hand.

'Ah, God forbid!' she cried.

'Why? Don't you want a long life?'

'Well, but a hundred years! There was an old woman near us eighty-five years old—and what a martyr she was! Dirty and deaf and bent and coughing all the time; nothing but a burden to herself. That's a dreadful life!'

'So it's better to be young?'

'Well, isn't it?'

'But why is it better? Tell me!'

'How can you ask why? Why, here I now, while I'm young, I can do everything—go and come and carry, and needn't ask anyone for anything. . . . What can be better?'

'And to me it's all the same whether I'm young or old.'

'How do you mean—it's all the same? It's not possible what you say.'

'Well, judge for yourself, Fedosya Nikolaevna, what good is my youth to me. I live alone, a poor lonely creature . . .'

'That always depends on you.'

'It doesn't at all depend on me! At least, someone ought to take pity on me.'

Fenitchka gave a sidelong look at Bazarov, but said nothing. 'What's this book you have?' she asked after a short pause.

'That? That's a scientific book, very difficult.'

'And are you still studying? And don't you find it dull? You know everything already, I should say.'

'It seems not everything. You try to read a little.'

'But I don't understand anything here. Is it Russian?' asked Fenitchka, taking the heavily bound book in both hands. 'How thick it is!'

'Yes, it's Russian.'

'All the same, I shan't understand anything.'

'Well, I didn't give it you for you to understand it. I wanted to look at you while you were reading. When you read, the end of your little nose moves so nicely.'

Fenitchka, who had set to work to spell out in a low voice the article on 'Creosote' she had chanced upon, laughed and threw down the book . . . it slipped from the seat on to the ground.

'I like it too when you laugh,' observed Bazarov.

'Nonsense!'

'I like it when you talk. It's just like a little brook babbling.'

Fenitchka turned her head away. 'What a person you are to talk!' she commented, picking the flowers over with her

153

finger. 'And how can you care to listen to me? You have talked with such clever ladies.'

'Ah, Fedosya Nikolaevna! believe me; all the clever ladies in the world are not worth your little elbow.'

'Come, there's another invention!' murmured Fenitchka, clasping her hands.

Bazarov picked the book up from the ground.

'That's a medical book; why do you throw it away?'

'Medical?' repeated Fenitchka, and she turned to him again. 'Do you know, ever since you gave me those drops—do you remember?—Mitya has slept so well! I really can't think how to thank you; you are so good, really.'

'But you have to pay doctors,' observed Bazarov with a smile. 'Doctors, you know yourself, are grasping people.'

Fenitchka raised her eyes, which seemed still darker from the whitish reflection cast on the upper part of her face, and looked at Bazarov. She did not know whether he was joking or not.

'If you please, we shall be delighted. . . . I must ask Nikolai Petrovitch . . .'

'Why, do you think I want money?' Bazarov interposed. 'No; I don't want money from you.'

'What then?' asked Fenitchka.

'What?' repeated Bazarov. 'Guess!'

'A likely person I am to guess!'

'Well, I will tell you; I want . . . one of those roses.'

Fenitchka laughed again, and even clapped her hands, so amusing Bazarov's request seemed to her. She laughed, and at the same time felt flattered. Bazarov was looking intently at her.

'By all means,' she said at last; and, bending down to the seat, she began picking over the roses. 'Which will you have— a red or a white one?'

'Red, and not too large.'

She sat up again. 'Here, take it,' she said, but at once drew back her outstretched hand, and, biting her lip, looked towards the entrance of the arbour, then listened.

'What is it?' asked Bazarov. 'Nikolai Petrovitch?'

'No . . . Mr. Kirsanov has gone to the fields . . . besides, I'm not afraid of him . . . but Pavel Petrovitch . . . I fancied . . .'

'What?'

'I fancied he was coming here. No . . . it was no one. Take it.' Fenitchka gave Bazarov the rose.

'On what grounds are you afraid of Pavel Petrovitch?'

'He always scares me. And I know you don't like him. Do you remember, you always used to quarrel with him? I don't know what your quarrel was about, but I can see you turn him about like this and like that.'

Fenitchka showed with her hands how in her opinion Bazarov turned Pavel Petrovitch about.

Bazarov smiled. 'But if he gave me a beating,' he asked, 'would you stand up for me?'

'How could I stand up for you? but no, no one will get the better of you.'

'Do you think so? But I know a hand which could overcome me if it liked.'

'What hand?'

'Why, don't you know, really? Smell, how delicious this rose smells you gave me.'

Fenitchka stretched her little neck forward, and put her face close to the flower. . . . The kerchief slipped from her head on to her shoulders; her soft mass of dark, shining, slightly ruffled hair was visible.

'Wait a minute; I want to smell it with you,' said Bazarov. He bent down and kissed her vigorously on her parted lips.

She started, pushed him back with both her hands on his breast, but pushed feebly, and he was able to renew and prolong his kiss.

A dry cough was heard behind the lilac bushes. Fenitchka instantly moved away to the other end of the seat. Pavel Petrovitch showed himself, made a slight bow, and saying with a sort of malicious mournfulness, 'You are here,' he retreated. Fenitchka at once gathered up all her roses and went out of the arbour. 'It was wrong of you, Yevgeny Vassilyevitch,' she whispered as she went. There was a note of genuine reproach in her whisper.

Bazarov remembered another recent scene, and he felt both shame and contemptuous annoyance. But he shook his head directly, ironically congratulated himself 'on his final assumption of the part of the gay Lothario,' and went off to his own room.

Pavel Petrovitch went out of the garden and made his way with deliberate steps to the copse. He stayed there rather a long while; and when he returned to lunch, Nikolai Petrovitch inquired anxiously whether he were quite well—his face looked so gloomy.

'You know, I sometimes suffer with my liver,' Pavel Petrovitch answered tranquilly.

# 24

Two hours later he knocked at Bazarov's door.

'I must apologise for hindering you in your scientific pursuits,' he began, seating himself on a chair in the window, and leaning with both hands on a handsome walking-stick with an ivory knob (he usually walked without a stick), 'but I am constrained to beg you to spare me five minutes of your time . . . no more.'

'All my time is at your disposal,' answered Bazarov, over whose face there passed a quick change of expression directly Pavel Petrovitch crossed the threshold.

'Five minutes will be enough for me. I have come to put a single question to you.'

'A question? What is it about?'

'I will tell you, if you will kindly hear me out. At the

commencement of your stay in my brother's house, before I had renounced the pleasure of conversing with you, it was my fortune to hear your opinions on many subjects; but so far as my memory serves, neither between us, nor in my presence, was the subject of single combats and duelling in general broached. Allow me to hear what are your views on that subject?'

Bazarov, who had risen to meet Pavel Petrovitch, sat down on the edge of the table and folded his arms.

'My view is,' he said, 'that from the theoretical standpoint duelling is absurd; from the practical standpoint, now—it's quite a different matter.'

'That is, you mean to say, if I understand you right, that whatever your theoretical views on duelling, you would not in practice allow yourself to be insulted without demanding satisfaction?'

'You have guessed my meaning absolutely.'

'Very good. I am very glad to hear you say so. Your words relieve me from a state of incertitude.'

'Of uncertainty, you mean to say.'

'That is all the same; I express myself so as to be understood; I . . . am not a seminary rat. Your words save me from a rather deplorable necessity. I have made up my mind to fight you.'

Bazarov opened his eyes wide. 'Me?'

'Undoubtedly.'

'But what for, pray?'

'I could explain the reason to you,' began Pavel Petrovitch, 'but I prefer to be silent about it. To my idea your presence here is superfluous; I cannot endure you; I despise you; and if that is not enough for you . . .'

Pavel Petrovitch's eyes glittered . . . Bazarov's too were flashing.

'Very good,' he assented. 'No need of further explanations. You've a whim to try your chivalrous spirit upon me. I might refuse you this pleasure, but—so be it!'

'I am sensible of my obligation to you,' replied Pavel Petrovitch; 'and may reckon then on your accepting my challenge without compelling me to resort to violent measures.'

'That means, speaking without metaphor, to that stick?' Bazarov remarked coolly. 'That is precisely correct. It's quite unnecessary for you to insult me. Indeed, it would not be a perfectly safe proceeding. You can remain a gentleman. . . . I accept your challenge, too, like a gentleman.'

'That is excellent,' observed Pavel Petrovitch, putting his stick in the corner. 'We will say a few words directly about the conditions of our duel; but I should like first to know whether you think it necessary to resort to the formality of a trifling dispute, which might serve as a pretext for my challenge?'

'No; it's better without formalities.'

'I think so myself. I presume it is also out of place to go into the real grounds of our difference. We cannot endure one another. What more is necessary?'

'What more, indeed?' repeated Bazarov ironically.

'As regards the conditions of the meeting itself, seeing that we shall have no seconds—for where could we get them?'

'Exactly so; where could we get them?'

'Then I have the honour to lay the following proposition before you: The combat to take place early to-morrow, at six, let us say, behind the copse, with pistols, at a distance of ten paces. . . .'

'At ten paces? that will do; we hate one another at that distance.'

'We might have it eight,' remarked Pavel Petrovitch.

'We might.'

'To fire twice; and to be ready for any result, let each put a letter in his pocket, in which he accuses himself of his end.'

'Now, that I don't approve of at all,' observed Bazarov. 'There's a slight flavour of the French novel about it, something not very plausible.'

'Perhaps. You will agree, however, that it would be unpleasant to incur a suspicion of murder?'

'I agree as to that. But there is a means of avoiding that

painful reproach.  We shall have no seconds, but we can have a witness.'

'And whom, allow me to inquire?'

'Why, Piotr.'

'What Piotr?'

'Your brother's valet.  He's a man who has attained to the acme of contemporary culture, and he will perform his part with all the *comilfo* (*comme il faut*) necessary in such cases.'

'I think you are joking, sir.'

'Not at all.  If you think over my suggestion, you will be convinced that it's full of common-sense and simplicity.  You can't hide a candle under a bushel; but I'll undertake to prepare Piotr in a fitting manner, and bring him on to the field of battle.'

'You persist in jesting still,' Pavel Petrovitch declared, getting up from his chair.  'But after the courteous readiness you have shown me, I have no right to pretend to lay down. . . . And so, everything is arranged. . . . By the way, perhaps you have no pistols?'

'How should I have pistols, Pavel Petrovitch?  I'm not in the army.'

'In that case, I offer you mine.  You may rest assured that it's five years now since I shot with them.'

'That's a very consoling piece of news.'

Pavel Petrovitch took up his stick. . . . 'And now, my dear sir, it only remains for me to thank you and to leave you to your studies.  I have the honour to take leave of you.'

'Till we have the pleasure of meeting again, my dear sir,' said Bazarov, conducting his visitor to the door.

Pavel Petrovitch went out, while Bazarov remained standing a minute before the door, and suddenly exclaimed, 'Pish, well, I'm dashed! how fine, and how foolish!  A pretty farce we've been through!  Like trained dogs dancing on their hindpaws.  But to decline was out of the question; why, I do believe he'd have struck me, and then . . .' (Bazarov turned white at the very thought; all his pride was up in arms at once)—

'then it might have come to my strangling him like a cat.'
He went back to his microscope, but his heart was beating,
and the composure necessary for taking observations had disappeared. 'He caught sight of us to-day,' he thought; 'but
would he really act like this on his brother's account? And
what a mighty matter is it—a kiss? There must be something
else in it. Bah! isn't he perhaps in love with her himself?
To be sure, he's in love; it's as clear as day. What a com-
plication! It's a nuisance!' he decided at last; 'it's a bad job,
look at it which way you will. In the first place, to risk a
bullet through one's brains, and in any case to go away; and
then Arkady . . . and that dear innocent pussy, Nikolai
Petrovitch. It's a bad job, an awfully bad job.'

The day passed in a kind of peculiar stillness and languor.
Fenitchka gave no sign of her existence; she sat in her little
room like a mouse in its hole. Nikolai Petrovitch had a careworn air. He had just heard that blight had begun to appear
in his wheat, upon which he had in particular rested his hopes.
Pavel Petrovitch overwhelmed everyone, even Prokofitch, with
his icy courtesy. Bazarov began a letter to his father, but tore
it up and threw it under the table.

'If I die,' he thought, 'they will find it out; but I'm not
going to die. No, I shall struggle along in this world a good
while yet.' He gave Piotr orders to come to him on important
business the next morning directly it was light. Piotr imagined
that he wanted to take him to Petersburg with him. Bazarov
went late to bed, and all night long he was harassed by dis-
ordered dreams. . . . Madame Odintsov kept appearing in
them: now she was his mother, and she was followed by a
kitten with black whiskers, and this kitten seemed to be
Fenitchka; then Pavel Petrovitch took the shape of a great
wolf, with which he had yet to fight. Piotr waked him up
at four o'clock; he dressed at once, and went out with him.

It was a lovely, fresh morning; tiny flecked clouds hovered
overhead in little curls of foam on the pale clear blue; a fine
dew lay in drops on the leaves and grass, and sparkled like
silver on the spiders' webs; the damp, dark earth seemed

still to keep traces of the rosy dawn; from the whole sky the songs of larks came pouring in showers. Bazarov walked as far as the copse, sat down in the shade at its edge, and only then disclosed to Piotr the nature of the service he expected of him. The refined valet was mortally alarmed; but Bazarov soothed him by the assurance that he would have nothing to do but stand at a distance and look on, and that he would not incur any sort of responsibility. 'And meantime,' he added, 'only think what an important part you have to play!' Piotr threw up his hands, looked down, and leaned against a birch tree, looking green with terror.

The road from Maryino skirted the copse; a light dust lay on it, untouched by wheel or foot since the previous day. Bazarov unconsciously stared along this road, picked and gnawed a blade of grass, while he kept repeating to himself, 'What a piece of foolery!' The chill of the early morning made him shiver twice. . . . Piotr looked at him dejectedly, but Bazarov only smiled; he was not afraid.

The tramp of horses' hoofs was heard along the road. . . . A peasant came into sight from behind the trees. He was driving before him two horses hobbled together, and as he passed Bazarov he looked at him rather strangely, without touching his cap, which it was easy to see disturbed Piotr, as an unlucky omen. 'There's someone else up early too,' thought Bazarov; 'but he at least has got up for work, while we . . .'

'Fancy the gentleman's coming,' Piotr faltered suddenly.

Bazarov raised his head and saw Pavel Petrovitch. Dressed in a light check jacket and snow-white trousers, he was walking rapidly along the road; under his arm he carried a box wrapped up in green cloth.

'I beg your pardon, I believe I have kept you waiting,' he observed, bowing first to Bazarov, then to Piotr, whom he treated respectfully at that instant, as representing something in the nature of a second. 'I was unwilling to wake my man.'

'It doesn't matter,' answered Bazarov, 'we've only just arrived ourselves.'

'Ah! so much the better!' Pavel Petrovitch took a look

161

M

round. 'There's no one in sight; no one hinders us. We can proceed?'

'Let us proceed.'

'You do not, I presume, desire any fresh explanations?'

'No, I don't.'

'Would you like to load?' inquired Pavel Petrovitch, taking the pistols out of the box.

'No; you load, and I will measure out the paces. My legs are longer,' added Bazarov with a smile. 'One, two, three . . .'

'Yevgeny Vassilyevitch,' Piotr faltered with an effort (he was shaking as though he were in a fever), 'say what you like, I am going farther off.'

'Four . . . five. . . . Good. Move away, my good fellow, move away; you may get behind a tree even, and stop up your ears, only don't shut your eyes; and if anyone falls, run and pick him up. Six . . . seven . . . eight . . .' Bazarov stopped. 'Is that enough?' he said, turning to Pavel Petrovitch; 'or shall I add two paces more?'

'As you like,' replied the latter, pressing down the second bullet.

'Well, we'll make it two paces more.' Bazarov drew a line on the ground with the toe of his boot. 'There's the barrier then. By the way, how many paces may each of us go back from the barrier? That's an important question too. That point was not discussed yesterday.'

'I imagine, ten,' replied Pavel Petrovitch, handing Bazarov both pistols. 'Will you be so good as to choose?'

'I will be so good. But, Pavel Petrovitch, you must admit our combat is singular to the point of absurdity. Only look at the countenance of our second.'

'You are disposed to laugh at everything,' answered Pavel Petrovitch. 'I acknowledge the strangeness of our duel, but I think it my duty to warn you that I intend to fight seriously. *A bon entendeur, salut!*'

'Oh! I don't doubt that we've made up our minds to make away with each other; but why not laugh too and unite *utile dulci?* You talk to me in French, while I talk to you in Latin.'

'I am going to fight in earnest,' repeated Pavel Petrovitch, and he walked off to his place. Bazarov on his side counted off ten paces from the barrier, and stood still.

'Are you ready?' asked Pavel Petrovitch.

'Perfectly.'

'We can approach one another.'

Bazarov moved slowly forward, and Pavel Petrovitch, his left hand thrust in his pocket, walked towards him, gradually raising the muzzle of his pistol. . . . 'He's aiming straight at my nose,' thought Bazarov, 'and doesn't he blink down it carefully, the ruffian! Not an agreeable sensation though. I'm going to look at his watch chain.'

Something whizzed sharply by his very ear, and at the same instant there was the sound of a shot. 'I heard it, so it must be all right,' had time to flash through Bazarov's brain. He took one more step and, without taking aim, pressed the spring.

Pavel Petrovitch gave a slight start, and clutched at his thigh. A stream of blood began to trickle down his white trousers.

Bazarov flung aside the pistol, and went up to his antagonist. 'Are you wounded?' he said.

'You had the right to call me up to the barrier,' said Pavel Petrovitch, 'but that's of no consequence. According to our agreement, each of us has the right to one more shot.'

'All right, but, excuse me, that'll do another time,' answered Bazarov, catching hold of Pavel Petrovitch, who was beginning to turn pale. 'Now I'm not a duellist, but a doctor, and I must have a look at your wound before anything else. Piotr! come here, Piotr! where have you got to?'

'That's all nonsense. . . . I need no one's aid,' Pavel Petrovitch declared jerkily, 'and . . . we must . . . again . . .' He tried to pull at his moustaches, but his hand failed him, his eyes grew dim, and he lost consciousness.

'Here's a pretty pass! A fainting fit! What next!' Bazarov cried unconsciously, as he laid Pavel Petrovitch on the grass. 'Let's have a look what's wrong.' He pulled out a handkerchief, wiped away the blood, and began feeling round the wound. . . . 'The bone's not touched,' he muttered through his teeth; 'the ball didn't go deep; one muscle, *vastus externus*, grazed. He'll be dancing about in three weeks! . . . And to faint! Oh, these nervous people, how I hate them! My word, what a delicate skin!'

'Is he killed?' the quaking voice of Piotr came rustling behind his back.

Bazarov looked round. 'Go for some water as quick as you can, my good fellow, and he'll outlive us yet.'

But the modern servant seemed not to understand his words, and he did not stir. Pavel Petrovitch slowly opened his eyes. 'He will die!' whispered Piotr, and he began crossing himself.

'You are right. . . . What an imbecile countenance!' remarked the wounded gentleman with a forced smile.

'Well, go for the water, damn you!' shouted Bazarov.

'No need. . . . It was a momentary *vertigo*. . . . Help me to sit up . . . there, that's right. . . . I only need something to bind up this scratch, and I can reach home on foot, or else you can send a droshky for me. The duel, if you are willing, shall not be renewed. You have behaved honourably . . . to-day, to-day—observe.'

'There's no need to recall the past,' rejoined Bazarov; 'and as regards the future, it's not worth while for you to trouble your head about that either, for I intend being off without delay. Let me bind up your leg now; your wound's not serious, but it's always best to stop bleeding. But first I must bring this corpse to his senses.'

Bazarov shook Piotr by the collar, and sent him for a droshky.

'Mind you don't frighten my brother,' Pavel Petrovitch said to him; 'don't dream of informing him.'

Piotr flew off; while he was running for a droshky, the two antagonists sat on the ground and said nothing. Pavel Petrovitch tried not to look at Bazarov; he did not want to be reconciled to him in any case; he was ashamed of his own haughtiness, of his failure; he was ashamed of the whole position he had brought about, even while he felt it could not have ended in a more favourable manner. 'At any rate, there will be no scandal,' he consoled himself by reflecting, 'and for that I am thankful.' The silence was prolonged, a silence distressing and awkward. Both of them were ill at ease. Each was conscious that the other understood him. That is pleasant to friends, and always very unpleasant to those who are not friends, especially when it is impossible either to have things out or to separate.

'Haven't I bound up your leg too tight?' inquired Bazarov at last.

'No, not at all; it's capital,' answered Pavel Petrovitch; and, after a brief pause, he added, 'There's no deceiving my brother; we shall have to tell him we quarrelled over politics.'

'Very good,' assented Bazarov. 'You can say I insulted all anglomaniacs.'

'That will do capitally. What do you imagine that man thinks of us now?' continued Pavel Petrovitch, pointing to the same peasant, who had driven the hobbled horses past Barazov a few minutes before the duel, and going back again along the road, took off his cap at the sight of the 'gentlefolk'.

'Who can tell!' answered Bazarov; 'it's quite likely he thinks nothing. The Russian peasant is that mysterious unknown about whom Mrs. Radcliffe used to talk so much. Who is to understand him! He doesn't understand himself!'

'Ah! so that's your idea!' Pavel Petrovitch began; and suddenly he cried, 'Look what your fool of a Piotr has done! Here's my brother galloping up to us!'

Bazarov turned round and saw the pale face of Nikolai Petrovitch, who was sitting in the droshky. He jumped out of it before it had stopped, and rushed up to his brother.

'What does this mean?' he said in an agitated voice. 'Yevgeny Vassilyitch, pray, what is this?'

'Nothing,' answered Pavel Petrovitch; 'they have alarmed you for nothing. I had a little dispute with Mr. Bazarov, and I have had to pay for it a little.'

'But what was it all about, mercy on us!'

'How can I tell you? Mr. Bazarov alluded disrespectfully to Sir Robert Peel. I must hasten to add that I am the only person to blame in all this, while Mr. Bazarov has behaved most honourably. I called him out.'

'But you're covered with blood, good Heavens!'

'Well, did you suppose I had water in my veins? But this blood-letting is positively beneficial to me. Isn't that so, doctor? Help me to get into the droshky, and don't give way to melancholy. I shall be quite well to-morrow. That's it; capital. Drive on, coachman.'

Nikolai Petrovitch walked after the droshky; Bazarov was remaining where he was. . . .

'I must ask you to look after my brother,' Nikolai Petrovitch said to him, 'till we get another doctor from the town.'

Bazarov nodded his head without speaking. In an hour's time Pavel Petrovitch was already lying in bed with a skilfully bandaged leg. The whole house was alarmed; Fenitchka fainted. Nikolai Petrovitch kept stealthily wringing his hands, while Pavel Petrovitch laughed and joked, especially with Bazarov; he had put on a fine cambric night-shirt, an elegant morning wrapper, and a fez, did not allow the blinds to be drawn down, and humorously complained of the necessity of being kept from food.

Toward night, however, he began to be feverish; his head ached. The doctor arrived from the town. (Nikolai Petrovitch would not listen to his brother, and indeed Bazarov himself did not wish him to; he sat the whole day in his room, looking yellow and vindictive, and only went in to the invalid for as brief a time as possible; twice he happened to meet Fenitchka, but she shrank away from him with horror.) The new doctor advised a cooling diet; he confirmed, however, Bazarov's assertion that there was no danger. Nikolai Petrovitch told him his brother had wounded himself by accident, to which the doctor responded, 'Hm!', but having twenty-five silver roubles slipped into his hand on the spot, he observed, 'You don't say so! Well, it's a thing that often happens, to be sure.'

No one in the house went to bed or undressed. Nikolai

Petrovitch kept going in to his brother on tiptoe, retreating on tiptoe again; the latter dozed, moaned a little, told him in French, *Couchez-vous,* and asked for drink. Nikolai Petrovitch sent Fenitchka twice to take him a glass of lemonade; Pavel Petrovitch gazed at her intently, and drank off the glass to the last drop. Towards morning the fever had increased a little; there was slight delirium. At first Pavel Petrovitch uttered incoherent words; then suddenly he opened his eyes, and seeing his brother near his bed bending anxiously over him, he said, 'Don't you think, Nikolai, Fenitchka has something in common with Nellie?'

'What Nellie, Pavel dear?'

'How can you ask? Princess R——. Especially in the upper part of the face. *C'est de la même famille.'*

Nikolai Petrovitch made no answer, while inwardly he marvelled at the persistence of old passions in man. 'It's like this when it comes to the surface,' he thought.

'Ah, how I love that light-headed creature!' moaned Pavel Petrovitch, clasping his hands mournfully behind his head. 'I can't bear any insolent upstart to dare to touch . . .' he whispered a few minutes later.

Nikolai Petrovitch only sighed; he did not even suspect to whom these words referred.

Bazarov presented himself before him at eight o'clock the next day. He had already had time to pack, and to set free all his frogs, insects, and birds.

'You have come to say good-bye to me?' said Nikolai Petrovitch, getting up to meet him.

'Yes.'

'I understand you, and approve of you fully. My poor brother, of course, is to blame; and he is punished for it. He told me himself that he made it impossible for you to act otherwise. I believe that you could not avoid this duel, which . . . which to some extent is explained by the almost constant antagonism of your respective views.' (Nikolai Petrovitch began to get a little mixed up in his words.) 'My brother is a man of the old school, hot-tempered and obstinate. . . .

Thank God that it has ended as it has. I have taken every precaution to avoid publicity.'

'I'm leaving you my address, in case there's any fuss,' Bazarov remarked casually.

'I hope there will be no fuss, Yevgeny Vassilyitch. . . . I am very sorry your stay in my house should have such a . . . such an end. It is the more distressing to me through Arkady's . . .'

'I shall be seeing him, I expect,' replied Bazarov, in whom 'explanations' and 'protestations' of every sort always aroused a feeling of impatience; 'in case I don't, I beg you to say good-bye to him for me, and accept the expression of my regret.'

'And I beg . . .' answered Nikolai Petrovitch. But Bazarov went off without waiting for the end of his sentence.

When he heard of Bazarov's going, Pavel Petrovitch expressed a desire to see him, and shook his hand. But even then he remained as cold as ice; he realised that Pavel Petrovitch wanted to play the magnanimous. He did not succeed in saying good-bye to Fenitchka; he only exchanged glances with her at the window. Her face struck him as looking dejected. 'She'll come to grief, perhaps,' he said to himself. . . . 'But who knows? she'll pull through somehow, I dare say!' Piotr, however, was so overcome that he wept on his shoulder, till Bazarov damped him by asking if he'd a constant supply laid on in his eyes; while Dunyasha was obliged to run away into the wood to hide her emotion. The originator of all this woe got into a light cart, smoked a cigar, and when at the third mile, at the bend in the road, the Kirsanovs' farm, with its new house, could be seen in a long line, he merely spat, and muttering, 'Cursed snobs!' wrapped himself closer in his cloak.

Pavel Petrovitch was soon better; but he had to keep his bed for about a week. He bore his captivity, as he called it, pretty patiently, though he took great pains over his toilet, and had everything scented with eau-de-Cologne. Nikolai Petrovitch used to read him the journals; Fenitchka waited on him as before, brought him lemonade, soup, boiled eggs, and tea; but she was overcome with secret dread whenever she went into his room. Pavel Petrovitch's unexpected action had alarmed everyone in the house, and her more than anyone; Prokofitch was the only person not agitated by it; he discoursed upon how gentlemen in his day used to fight, but only with real gentlemen; low curs like that they used to order a horsewhipping in the stable for their insolence.

Fenitchka's conscience scarcely reproached her; but she was tormented at times by the thought of the real cause of the quarrel; and Pavel Petrovitch too looked at her so strangely . . . that even when her back was turned she felt his eyes upon her. She grew thinner from constant inward agitation, and, as is always the way, became still more charming.

One day—the incident took place in the morning—Pavel Petrovitch felt better, and moved from his bed to the sofa, while Nikolai Petrovitch, having satisfied himself he was better, went off to the threshing-floor. Fenitchka brought him a cup of tea, and setting it down on a little table, was about to withdraw. Pavel Petrovitch detained her.

'Where are you going in such a hurry, Fedosya Nikolaevna?' he began; 'are you busy?'

'No . . . I have to pour out tea.'

'Dunyasha will do that without you; sit a little while with a poor invalid. By the way, I must have a little talk with you.'

Fenitchka sat down on the edge of an easy-chair, without speaking.

'Listen,' said Pavel Petrovitch, tugging at his moustaches; 'I have long wanted to ask you something; you seem afraid of me?'

'I?'

'Yes, you. You never look at me, as though your conscience were not at rest.'

Fenitchka crimsoned, but looked at Pavel Petrovitch. He impressed her as looking strange, and her heart began throbbing slowly.

'Is your conscience at rest?' he questioned her.

'Why should it not be at rest?' she faltered.

'Goodness knows why! Besides, whom can you have wronged? Me? That is not likely. Any other people in the house here? That, too, is something incredible. Can it be my brother? But you love him, don't you?'

'I love him.'

'With your whole soul, with your whole heart?'

'I love Nikolai Petrovitch with my whole heart.'

'Truly? Look at me, Fenitchka.' (It was the first time he had called her that name! 'You know, it's a great sin telling lies!'

'I am not telling lies, Pavel Petrovitch. Not love Nikolai Petrovitch—I shouldn't care to live after that.'

'And will you never give him up for anyone?'

'For whom could I give him up?'

'For whom indeed! Well, how about that gentleman who has just gone away from here?'

Fenitchka got up. 'My God, Pavel Petrovitch, what are you torturing me for? What have I done to you? How can such things be said?' . . .

'Fenitchka,' said Pavel Petrovitch, in a sorrowful voice, 'you know I saw . . .'

'What did you see?'

'Well, there . . . in the arbour.'

Fenitchka crimsoned to her hair and to her ears. 'How was I to blame for that?' she articulated with an effort.

Pavel Petrovitch raised himself up. 'You were not to blame? No? Not at all?'

'I love Nikolai Petrovitch, and no one else in the world, and I shall always love him!' cried Fenitchka with sudden force, while her throat seemed fairly breaking with sobs. 'As for what you saw, at the dreadful day of judgment I will say I'm not to blame, and wasn't to blame for it, and I would rather die at once if people can suspect me of such a thing against my benefactor, Nikolai Petrovitch.'

But here her voice broke, and at the same time she felt that

Pavel Petrovitch was snatching and pressing her hand. . . .
She looked at him, and was fairly petrified. He had turned
even paler than before; his eyes were shining, and what was
most marvellous of all, one large solitary tear was rolling down
his cheek.

'Fenitchka!' he was saying in a strange whisper; 'love him,
love my brother! Don't give him up for anyone in the world;
don't listen to anyone else! Think what can be more terrible
than to love and not be loved! Never leave my poor Nikolai!'

Fenitchka's eyes were dry, and her terror had passed away,
so great was her amazement. But what were her feelings when
Pavel Petrovitch, Pavel Petrovitch himself, put her hand to
his lips and seemed to pierce into it without kissing it, only
heaving convulsive sighs from time to time. . . .

'Goodness,' she thought, 'isn't it some attack coming on
him?' . . .

At that instant his whole ruined life was stirred up within
him.

The staircase creaked under rapidly approaching footsteps.
. . . He pushed her away from him, and let his head drop
back on the pillow. The door opened, and Nikolai Petrovitch
entered, cheerful, fresh, and ruddy. Mitya, as fresh and ruddy
as his father, in nothing but his little shirt, was frisking on
his shoulder, catching the big buttons of his rough country
coat with his little bare toes.

Fenitchka simply flung herself upon him, and clasping him
and her son together in her arms, dropped her head on his
shoulder. Nikolai Petrovitch was surprised; Fenitchka, the
reserved and staid Fenitchka, had never given him a caress in
the presence of a third person.

'What's the matter?' he said, and, glancing at his brother,
he gave her Mitya. 'You don't feel worse?' he inquired, going
up to Pavel Petrovitch.

He buried his face in a cambric handkerchief. 'No . . . not
at all . . . on the contrary, I am much better.'

'You were in too great a hurry to move on to the sofa.
Where are you going?' added Nikolai Petrovitch, turning

round to Fenitchka; but she had already closed the door behind her. 'I was bringing in my young hero to show you; he's been crying for his uncle. Why has she carried him off? What's wrong with you, though? Has anything passed between you, eh?'

'Brother!' said Pavel Petrovitch solemnly.

Nikolai Petrovitch started. He felt dismayed, he could not have said why himself.

'Brother,' repeated Pavel Petrovitch, 'give me your word that you will carry out my one request.'

'What request? Tell me.'

'It is very important; the whole happiness of your life, to my idea, depends on it. I have been thinking a great deal all this time over what I want to say to you now. . . . Brother, do your duty, the duty of an honest and generous man; put an end to the scandal and bad example you are setting—you, the best of men!'

'What do you mean, Pavel?'

'Marry Fenitchka. . . . She loves you; she is the mother of your son.'

Nikolai Petrovitch stepped back a pace and flung up his hands. 'Do you say that, Pavel? you whom I have always regarded as the most determined opponent of such marriages! You say that? Don't you know that it has simply been out of respect for you that I have not done what you so rightly call my duty?'

'You were wrong to respect me in that case,' Pavel Petrovitch responded, with a weary smile. 'I begin to think Bazarov was right in accusing me of snobbishness. No, dear brother, don't let us worry ourselves about appearances and the world's opinion any more; we are old folks and humble now; it's time we laid aside vanity of all kinds. Let us, just as you say, do our duty; and mind, we shall get happiness that way into the bargain.'

Nikolai Petrovitch rushed to embrace his brother.

'You have opened my eyes completely!' he cried. 'I was right in always declaring you the wisest and kindest-hearted fellow in the world, and now I see you are just as reasonable as you are noble-hearted.'

'Quietly, quietly,' Pavel Petrovitch interrupted him; 'don't hurt the leg of your reasonable brother, who at close upon fifty has been fighting a duel like an ensign. So, then, it's a settled matter; Fenitchka is to be my . . . *belle sœur*.'

'My dearest Pavel! But what will Arkady say?'

'Arkady? he'll be in ecstasies, you may depend upon it! Marriage is against his principles, but then the sentiment of equality in him will be gratified. And, after all, what sense have class distinctions *au dix-neuvième siècle?*'

'Ah, Pavel, Pavel! let me kiss you once more! Don't be afraid, I'll be careful.'

The brothers embraced each other.

'What do you think, should you not inform her of your intention now?' queried Pavel Petrovitch.

'Why be in a hurry?' responded Nikolai Petrovitch. 'Has there been any conversation between you?'

'Conversation between us? *Quelle idée!*'

'Well, that is all right then. First of all, you must get well, and meanwhile there's plenty of time. We must think it over well, and consider . . .'

'But your mind is made up, I suppose?'

'Of course my mind is made up, and I thank you from the bottom of my heart. I will leave you now; you must rest; any excitement is bad for you. . . . But we will talk it over again. Sleep well, dear heart, and God bless you!'

'What is he thanking me like that for?' thought Pavel Petrovitch, when he was left alone. 'As though it did not depend on him! I will go away directly he is married, somewhere a long way off—to Dresden or Florence, and will live there till I——'

Pavel Petrovitch moistened his forehead with eau-de-Cologne and closed his eyes. His beautiful, emaciated head, the glaring daylight shining full upon it, lay on the white pillow like the head of a dead man. . . . And indeed he was a dead man.

# 25

At Nikolskoe Katya and Arkady were sitting in the garden on a turf seat in the shade of a tall ash tree; Fifi had placed himself on the ground near them, giving his slender body that graceful curve, which is known among dog-fanciers as 'the hare bend'. Both Arkady and Katya were silent; he was holding a half-open book in his hands, while she was picking out of a basket the few crumbs of bread left in it, and throwing them to a small family of sparrows, who with the frightened impudence peculiar to them were hopping and chirping at her very feet. A faint breeze stirring in the ash leaves kept slowly moving pale-gold flecks of sunlight up and down over the path and Fifi's tawny back; a patch of unbroken shade fell upon Arkady and Katya; only from time to time a bright streak gleamed on her hair. Both were silent, but the very way in which they were silent, in which they were sitting together, was expressive of confidential intimacy; each of them seemed not even to be thinking of his companion, while secretly rejoicing in his presence. Their faces, too, had changed since we saw them last; Arkady looked more tranquil, Katya brighter and more daring.

'Don't you think,' began Arkady, 'that the ash has been very well named in Russian *yasen;* no other tree is so lightly and brightly transparent (*yasno*) against the air as it is.'

Katya raised her eyes to look upward, and assented, 'Yes;' while Arkady thought, 'Well, she does not reproach me for *talking finely*.'

'I don't like Heine,' said Katya, glancing towards the book which Arkady was holding in his hands, 'either when he laughs or when he weeps; I like him when he's thoughtful and melancholy.'

'And I like him when he laughs,' remarked Arkady.

'That's the relics left in you of your old satirical tendencies.'

174

('Relics!' thought Arkady—'if Bazarov had heard that?')
'Wait a little; we shall transform you.'

'Who will transform me? You?'

'Who?—my sister; Porfiry Platonovitch, whom you've
given up quarrelling with; auntie, whom you escorted to
church the day before yesterday.'

'Well, I couldn't refuse! And as for Anna Sergyevna, she
agreed with Yevgeny in a great many things, you remember?'

'My sister was under his influence then, just as you were.'

'As I was? Do you discover, may I ask, that I've shaken
off his influence now?'

Katya did not speak.

'I know,' pursued Arkady, 'you never liked him.'

'I can have no opinion about him.'

'Do you know, Katerina Sergyevna, every time I hear that
answer I disbelieve it. . . . There is no man that everyone
of us could not have an opinion about! That's simply a way
of getting out of it.'

'Well, I'll say, then, I don't. . . . It's not exactly that I
don't like him, but I feel that he's of a different order from
me, and I am different from him . . . and you too are
different from him.'

'How's that?'

'How can I tell you. . . . He's a wild animal, and you and
I are tame.'

'Am I tame too?'

Katya nodded.

Arkady scratched his ear. 'Let me tell you, Katerina
Sergyevna, do you know, that's really an insult?'

'Why, would you like to be a wild——'

'Not wild, but strong, full of force.'

'It's no good wishing for that. . . . Your friend, you see,
doesn't wish for it, but he has it.'

'Hm! So you imagine he had a great influence on Anna
Sergyevna?'

'Yes. But no one can keep the upper hand of her for long,'
added Katya in a low voice.

'Why do you think that?'

'She's very proud. . . . I didn't mean that . . . she values her independence a great deal.'

'Who doesn't value it?' asked Arkady, and the thought flashed through his mind, 'What good is it?' 'What good is it?' it occurred to Katya to wonder too. When young people are often together on friendly terms, they are constantly stumbling on the same ideas.

Arkady smiled, and, coming slightly closer to Katya, he said in a whisper, 'Confess that you are a little afraid of her.'

'Of whom?'

'Her,' repeated Arkady significantly.

'And how about you?' Katya asked in her turn.

'I am too, observe I said, I am *too*.'

Katya threatened him with her finger. 'I wonder at that,' she began; 'my sister has never felt so friendly to you as just now; much more so than when you first came.'

'Really!'

'Why, haven't you noticed it? Aren't you glad of it?'

Arkady grew thoughtful.

'How have I succeeded in gaining Anna Sergyevna's good opinion? Wasn't it because I brought her your mother's letters?'

'Both that and other causes, which I shan't tell you.'

'Why?'

'I shan't say.'

'Oh! I know; you're very obstinate.'

'Yes, I am.'

'And observant.'

Katya gave Arkady a sidelong look. 'Perhaps so; does that irritate you? What are you thinking of?'

'I am wondering how you have come to be as observant as in fact you are. You are so shy, so reserved; you keep everyone at a distance.'

'I have lived a great deal alone; that drives one to reflection. But do I really keep everyone at a distance?'

Arkady flung a grateful glance at Katya.

'That's all very well,' he pursued; 'but people in your position—I mean in your circumstances—don't often have that faculty; it is hard for them, as it is for sovereigns, to get at the truth.'

'But, you see, I am not rich.'

Arkady was taken aback, and did not at once understand Katya. 'Why, of course, the property's all her sister's!' struck him suddenly; the thought was not unpleasing to him. 'How nicely you said that!' he commented.

'What?'

'You said it nicely, simply, without being ashamed or making a boast of it. By the way, I imagine there must always be something special, a kind of pride of a sort in the feeling of any man, who knows and says he is poor.'

'I have never experienced anything of that sort, thanks to my sister. I only referred to my position just now because it happened to come up.'

'Well; you must own you have a share of that pride I spoke of just now.'

'For instance?'

'For instance, you—forgive the question—you wouldn't marry a rich man, I fancy, would you?'

'If I loved him very much. . . . No, I think even then I wouldn't marry him.'

'There! you see!' cried Arkady, and after a short pause he added, 'And why wouldn't you marry him?'

'Because even in the ballads unequal matches are always unlucky.'

'You want to rule, perhaps, or . . .'

'Oh, no! why should I? On the contrary, I am ready to obey; only inequality is intolerable. To respect oneself and obey, that I can understand, that's happiness; but a subordinate existence. . . No, I've had enough of that as it is.'

'Enough of that as it is,' Arkady repeated after Katya. 'Yes, yes,' he went on, 'you're not Anna Sergyevna's sister for nothing; you're just as independent as she is; but you're more reserved. I'm certain you wouldn't be the first to give expression to your feeling, however strong and holy it might be . . .'

'Well, what would you expect?' asked Katya.

'You're equally clever; and you've as much, if not more, character than she.'

'Don't compare me with my sister, please,' interposed Katya hurriedly; 'that's too much to my disadvantage. You seem to forget my sister's beautiful and clever, and . . . you in particular, Arkady Nikolaevitch, ought not to say such things, and with such a serious face too.'

'What do you mean by "you in particular"—and what makes you suppose I am joking?'

'Of course you are joking.'

'You think so? But what if I'm persuaded of what I say? if I believe I have not put it strongly enough even?'

'I don't understand you.'

'Really? Well, now I see; I certainly took you to be more observant than you are.'

'How?'

Arkady made no answer, and turned away, while Katya looked for a few more crumbs in the basket, and began throwing them to the sparrows; but she moved her arm too vigorously, and they flew away, without stopping to pick them up.

'Katerina Sergyevna!' began Arkady, suddenly; 'it's of no consequence to you, probably; but, let me tell you, I put you not only above your sister, but above everyone in the world.'

He got up and went quickly away, as though he were frightened at the words that had fallen from his lips.

Katya let her two hands drop together with the basket on to her lap, and with bent head she stared a long while after Arkady. Gradually a crimson flush came faintly out upon her cheeks; but her lips did not smile, and her dark eyes had a look of perplexity and some other, as yet undefined, feeling.

'Are you alone?' she heard the voice of Anna Sergyevna near her; 'I thought you came into the garden with Arkady.'

Katya slowly raised her eyes to her sister (elegantly, even elaborately, dressed, she was standing in the path and tickling Fifi's ears with the tip of her open parasol), and slowly replied. 'Yes, I'm alone.'

'So I see,' she answered with a smile; 'I suppose he has gone to his room.'

'Yes.'

'Have you been reading together?'

'Yes.'

Anna Sergyevna took Katya by the chin and lifted her face up.

'You have not been quarrelling, I hope?'

'No,' said Katya, and she quietly removed her sister's hand.

'How solemnly you answer! I expected to find him here, and meant to suggest his coming a walk with me. That's what he is always asking for. They have sent you some shoes from the town; go and try them on; I noticed only yesterday your old ones are quite shabby. You never think enough about it, and you have such charming little feet! Your hands are nice too . . . though they're large; so you must make the most of your little feet. But you're not vain.'

Anna Sergyevna went farther along the path with a light rustle of her beautiful gown; Katya got up from the grass, and, taking Heine with her, went away too—but not to try on her shoes.

'Charming little feet!' she thought, as she slowly and lightly mounted the stone steps of the terrace, which were burning with the heat of the sun; 'charming little feet you call them. . . . Well, he shall be at them.'

But all at once a feeling of shame came upon her, and she ran swiftly upstairs.

Arkady had gone along the corridor to his room; a steward had overtaken him, and announced that Mr. Bazarov was in his room.

'Yevgeny!' murmured Arkady, almost with dismay; 'has he been here long?'

'Mr. Bazarov arrived this minute, sir, and gave orders not

to announce him to Anna Sergyevna, but to show him straight up to you.'

'Can any misfortune have happened at home?' thought Arkady, and running hurriedly up the stairs, he at once opened the door. The sight of Bazarov at once reassured him, though a more experienced eye might very probably have discerned signs of inward agitation in the sunken, though still energetic face of the unexpected visitor. With a dusty cloak over his shoulders, with a cap on his head, he was sitting at the window; he did not even get up when Arkady flung himself with noisy exclamations on his neck.

'This is unexpected! What good luck brought you?' he kept repeating, bustling about the room like one who both imagines himself and wishes to show himself delighted. 'I suppose everything's all right at home; everyone's well, eh?'

'Everything's all right, but not everyone's well,' said Bazarov. 'Don't be a chatterbox, but send for some kvass for me, sit down, and listen while I tell you all about it in a few, but, I hope, pretty vigorous sentences.'

Arkady was quiet while Bazarov described his duel with Pavel Petrovitch. Arkady was very much surprised, and even grieved, but he did not think it necessary to show this; he only asked whether his uncle's wound was really not serious; and on receiving the reply that it was most interesting, but not from a medical point of view, he gave a forced smile, but at heart he felt both wounded and as it were ashamed. Bazarov seemed to understand him.

'Yes, my dear fellow,' he commented, 'you see what comes of living with feudal personages. You turn a feudal personage yourself, and find yourself taking part in knightly tournaments. Well, so I set off for my father's,' Bazarov wound up, 'and I've turned in here on the way . . . to tell you all this, I should say, if I didn't think a useless lie a piece of foolery. No, I turned in here—the devil only knows why. You see, it's sometimes a good thing for a man to take himself by the scruff of the neck and pull himself up, like a radish out of its bed; that's what I've been doing of late. . . . But

I wanted to have one more look at what I'm giving up, at the bed where I've been planted.'

'I hope those words don't refer to me,' responded Arkady with some emotion; 'I hope you don't think of giving me up?'

Bazarov turned an intent, almost piercing look upon him.

'Would that be such a grief to you? It strikes me *you* have given me up already, you look so fresh and smart. . . . Your affair with Anna Sergyevna must be getting on successfully.'

'What do you mean by my affair with Anna Sergyevna?'

'Why, didn't you come here from the town on her account, chicken? By the way, how are those Sunday schools getting on? Do you mean to tell me you're not in love with her? Or have you already reached the stage of discretion?'

'Yevgeny, you know I have always been open with you; I can assure you, I will swear to you, you're making a mistake.'

'Hm! That's another story,' remarked Bazarov in an undertone. 'But you needn't be in a taking, it's a matter of absolute indifference to me. A sentimentalist would say, "I feel that our paths are beginning to part," but I will simply say that we're tired of each other.'

'Yevgeny . . .'

'My dear soul, there's no great harm in that. One gets tired of much more than that in this life. And now I suppose we'd better say good-bye, hadn't we? Ever since I've been here I've had such a loathsome feeling, just as if I'd been reading Gogol's effusions to the governor of Kalouga's wife. By the way, I didn't tell them to take the horses out.'

'Upon my word, this is too much!'

'Why?'

'I'll say nothing of myself; but that would be discourteous to the last degree to Anna Sergyevna, who will certainly wish to see you.'

'Oh, you're mistaken there.'

'On the contrary, I am certain I'm right,' retorted Arkady.

'And what are you pretending for? If it comes to that, haven't you come here on her account yourself?'

'That may be so, but you're mistaken anyway.'

But Arkady was right. Anna Sergyevna desired to see Bazarov, and sent a summons to him by a steward. Bazarov changed his clothes before going to her; it turned out that he had packed his new suit so as to be able to get it out easily.

Madame Odintsov received him not in the room where he had so unexpectedly declared his love to her, but in the drawing-room. She held her finger-tips out to him cordially, but her face betrayed an involuntary sense of tension.

'Anna Sergyevna,' Bazarov hastened to say, 'before everything else I must set your mind at rest. Before you is a poor mortal who has come to his senses long ago, and hopes other people too have forgotten his follies. I am going away for a long while; and though, as you will allow, I'm by no means a very soft creature, it would be anything but cheerful for me to carry away with me the idea that you remember me with repugnance.'

Anna Sergyevna gave a deep sigh like one who has just climbed up a high mountain, and her face was lighted up by a smile. She held out her hand a second time to Bazarov, and responded to his pressure.

'Let bygones be bygones,' she said. 'I am all the readier to do so because, speaking from my conscience, I was to blame then too for flirting or something. In a word, let us be friends as before. That was a dream, wasn't it? And who remembers dreams?'

'Who remembers them? And besides, love . . . you know, is a purely imaginary feeling.'

'Really? I am very glad to hear that.'

So Anna Sergyevna spoke, and so spoke Bazarov; they both supposed they were speaking the truth. Was the truth, the whole truth, to be found in their words? They could not themselves have said, and much less could the author. But a conversation followed between them precisely as though they completely believed one another.

Anna Sergyevna asked Bazarov, among other things, what he had been doing at the Kirsanovs'. He was on the point of telling her about his duel with Pavel Petrovitch, but he checked himself with the thought that she might imagine he was trying to make himself interesting, and answered that he had been at work all the time.

'And I,' observed Anna Sergyevna, 'had a fit of depression at first, goodness knows why; I even made plans for going abroad, fancy! . . . Then it passed off, your friend Arkady Nikolaitch came, and I fell back into my old routine, and took up my real part again.'

'What part is that, may I ask?'

'The character of aunt, guardian, mother—call it what you like. By the way, do you know I used not quite to understand your close friendship with Arkady Nikolaitch; I thought him rather insignificant. But now I have come to know him better, and to see that he is clever. . . . And he's young, he's young . . . that's the great thing . . . not like you and me, Yevgeny Vassilyitch.'

'Is he still as shy in your company?' queried Bazarov.

'Why, was he?' . . . Anna Sergyevna began, and after a brief pause she went on : 'He has grown more confiding now; he talks to me. He used to avoid me before. Though, indeed, I didn't seek his society either. He's more friends with Katya.'

Bazarov felt irritated. 'A woman can't help humbugging, of course!' he thought. 'You say he used to avoid you,' he said aloud, with a chilly smile; 'but it is probably no secret to you that he was in love with you?'

'What! he too?' fell from Anna Sergyevna's lips.

'He too,' repeated Bazarov, with a submissive bow. 'Can it be you didn't know it, and I've told you something new?'

Anna Sergyevna dropped her eyes. 'You are mistaken, Yevgeny Vassilyitch.'

'I don't think so. But perhaps I ought not to have mentioned it.' 'And don't you try telling me lies again for the future,' he added to himself.

'Why not? But I imagine that in this too you are

attributing too much importance to a passing impression. I begin to suspect you are inclined to exaggeration.'

'We had better not talk about it, Anna Sergyevna.'

'Oh, why?' she retorted; but she herself led the conversation into another channel. She was still ill at ease with Bazarov, though she had told him, and assured herself, that everything was forgotten. While she was exchanging the simplest sentences with him, even while she was jesting with him, she was conscious of a faint spasm of dread. So people on a steamer at sea talk and laugh carelessly, for all the world as though they were on dry land; but let only the slightest hitch occur, let the least sign be seen of anything out of the common, and at once on every face there comes out an expression of peculiar alarm, betraying the constant consciousness of constant danger.

Anna Sergyevna's conversation with Bazarov did not last long. She began to seem absorbed in thought, answered abstractedly, and suggested at last that they should go into the hall, where they found the princess and Katya. 'But where is Arkady Nikolaitch?' inquired the lady of the house; and on hearing that he had not shown himself for more than an hour, she sent for him. He was not very quickly found; he had hidden himself in the very thickest part of the garden, and with his chin propped on his folded hands, he was sitting lost in meditation. They were deep and serious meditations, but not mournful. He knew Anna Sergyevna was sitting alone with Bazarov, and he felt no jealousy, as once he had; on the contrary, his face slowly brightened; he seemed to be at once wondering and rejoicing, and resolving on something.

FATHERS AND CHILDREN

# 26

THE deceased Odintsov had not liked innovations, but he had tolerated 'the fine arts within a certain sphere', and had in consequence put up in his garden, between the hot-house and the lake, an erection after the fashion of a Greek temple, made of Russian brick. Along the dark wall at the back of this temple or gallery were placed six niches for statues, which Odintsov had proceeded to order from abroad. These statues were to represent Solitude, Silence, Meditation, Melancholy, Modesty, and Sensibility. One of them, the goddess of Silence, with her finger on her lip, had been sent and put up; but on the very same day some boys on the farm had broken her nose; and though a plasterer of the neighbourhood undertook to make her a new nose 'twice as good as the old one,' Odintsov ordered her to be taken away, and she was still to be seen in the corner of the threshing barn, where she had stood many long years, a source of superstitious terror to the peasant women. The front part of the temple had long ago been overgrown with thick bushes; only the pediments of the columns could be seen above the dense green. In the temple itself it was cool even at midday. Anna Sergyevna had not liked visiting this place ever since she had seen a snake there; but Katya often came and sat on the wide stone seat under one of the niches. Here, in the midst of the shade and coolness, she used to read and work, or to give herself up to that sensation of perfect peace, known, doubtless, to each of us, the charm of which consists in the half-unconscious, silent listening to the vast current of life that flows for ever both around us and within us.

The day after Bazarov's arrival Katya was sitting on her favourite stone seat, and beside her again was Arkady. He had besought her to come with him to the 'temple'.

There was about an hour still to lunch-time; the dewy morning had already given place to a sultry day. Arkady's face retained the expression of the preceding day; Katya had a preoccupied look. Her sister had, directly after their morning tea, called her into her room, and after some preliminary caresses, which always scared Katya a little, she had advised her to be more guarded in her behaviour with Arkady, and especially to avoid solitary talks with him, as likely to attract the notice of her aunt and all the household. Besides this, even the previous evening Anna Sergyevna had not been herself; and Katya herself had felt ill at ease, as though she were conscious of some fault in herself. As she yielded to Arkady's entreaties, she said to herself that it was for the last time.

'Katerina Sergyevna,' he began with a sort of bashful easiness, 'since I've had the happiness of living in the same house with you, I have discussed a great many things with you; but meanwhile there is one, very important . . . for me . . . one question, which I have not touched upon up till now. You remarked yesterday that I have been changed here,' he went on, at once catching and avoiding the questioning glance Katya was turning upon him. 'I have changed certainly a great deal, and you know that better than anyone else—you to whom I really owe this change.'

'I? . . . Me? . . .' said Katya.

'I am not now the conceited boy I was when I came here,' Arkady went on. 'I've not reached twenty-three for nothing; as before, I want to be useful, I want to devote all my powers to the truth; but I no longer look for my ideals where I did; they present themselves to me . . . much closer at hand. Up till now I did not understand myself; I set myself tasks which were beyond my powers. . . . My eyes have been opened lately, thanks to one feeling. . . . I'm not expressing myself quite clearly, but I hope you understand me.'

Katya made no reply, but she ceased looking at Arkady.

'I suppose,' he began again, this time in a more agitated voice, while above his head a chaffinch sang its song unheeding among the leaves of the birch—'I suppose it's the duty of everyone to be open with those . . . with those people who . . . in fact, with those who are near to him, and so I . . . I resolved . . .'

But here Arkady's eloquence deserted him; he lost the thread, stammered, and was forced to be silent for a moment. Katya still did not raise her eyes. She seemed not to understand what he was leading up to in all this, and to be waiting for something.

'I foresee I shall surprise you,' began Arkady, pulling himself together again with an effort, 'especially since this feeling relates in a way . . . in a way, notice . . . to you. You reproached me, if you remember, yesterday with a want of seriousness,' Arkady went on, with the air of a man who has got into a bog, feels that he is sinking farther and farther in at every step, and yet hurries onwards in the hope of crossing it as soon as possible; 'that reproach is often aimed . . . often falls . . . on young men even when they cease to deserve it; and if I had more self-confidence . . .' ('Come, help me, do help me!' Arkady was thinking, in desperation; but, as before, Katya did not turn her head.) 'If I could hope . . .'

'If I could feel sure of what you say,' was heard at that instant the clear voice of Anna Sergyevna.

Arkady was still at once, while Katya turned pale. Close by the bushes that screened the temple ran a little path. Anna Sergyevna was walking along it escorted by Bazarov. Katya and Arkady could not see them, but they heard every word, the rustle of their clothes, their very breathing. They walked on a few steps, and, as though on purpose, stood still just opposite the temple.

'You see,' pursued Anna Sergyevna, 'you and I made a mistake; we are both past our first youth, I especially so; we have seen life, we are tired; we are both—why affect not to know it?—clever; at first we interested each other, curiosity was aroused . . . and then . . .'

'And then I grew stale,' put in Bazarov.

'You know that was not the cause of our misunderstanding. But, however, it was to be, we had no need of one another, that's the chief point; there was too much . . . what shall I say? . . . that was alike in us. We did not realise it all at once. Now, Arkady . . .'

'Do you need him?' queried Bazarov.

'Hush, Yevgeny Vassilyitch. You tell me he is not indifferent to me, and it always seemed to me he liked me. I know that I might well be his aunt, but I don't wish to conceal

187

from you that I have come to think more often of him. In such youthful, fresh feeling there is a special charm . . .'

'The word *fascination* is most usual in such cases,' Bazarov interrupted; the effervescence of his spleen could be heard in his choked though steady voice. 'Arkady was mysterious over something with me yesterday, and didn't talk either of you or of your sister. . . . That's a serious symptom.'

'He is just like a brother with Katya,' commented Anna Sergyevna, 'and I like that in him, though, perhaps, I ought not to have allowed such intimacy between them.'

'That idea is prompted by . . . your feelings as a sister?' Bazarov brought out, drawling.

'Of course . . . but why are we standing still? Let us go on. What a strange talk we are having, aren't we? I could never have believed I should talk to you like this. You know, I am afraid of you . . . and at the same time I trust you, because in reality you are so good.'

'In the first place, I am not in the least good; and in the second place, I have lost all significance for you, and you tell me I am good. . . . It's like laying a wreath of flowers on the head of a corpse.'

'Yevgeny Vassilyitch, we are not responsible . . .' Anna Sergyevna began; but a gust of wind blew across, set the leaves rustling, and carried away her words. 'Of course, you are free . . .' Bazarov declared after a brief pause. Nothing more could be distinguished; the steps retreated . . . everything was still.

Arkady turned to Katya. She was sitting in the same position, but her head was bent still lower. 'Katerina Sergyevna,' he said with a shaking voice, and clasping his hands tightly together, 'I love you for ever and irrevocably, and I love no one but you. I wanted to tell you this, to find out your opinion of me, and to ask for your hand, since I am not rich, and I feel ready for any sacrifice. . . . You don't answer me? You don't believe me? Do you think I speak lightly? But remember these last days! Surely for a long time past you must have known that everything—understand me—everything else has vanished long ago and left no trace? Look at me, say one word to me . . . I love . . . I love you . . . believe me!'

Katya glanced at Arcady with a bright and serious look, and after long hesitation, with the faintest smile, she said, 'Yes.'

Arkady leapt up from the stone seat. 'Yes! You said Yes, Katerina Sergyevna! What does that word mean? Only that I do love you, that you believe me . . . or . . . or . . . I daren't go on . . .'

'Yes,' repeated Katya, and this time he understood her. He snatched her large beautiful hands, and, breathless with rapture, pressed them to his heart. He could scarcely stand on his feet, and could only repeat, 'Katya, Katya . . .' while she began weeping in a guileless way, smiling gently at her own tears. No one who has not seen those tears in the eyes of the beloved knows yet to what a point, faint with shame and gratitude, a man may be happy on earth.

The next day, early in the morning, Anna Sergyevna sent to summon Bazarov to her boudoir, and with a forced laugh handed him a folded sheet of notepaper. It was a letter from Arkady; in it he asked for her sister's hand.

Bazarov quickly scanned the letter, and made an effort to control himself, that he might not show the malignant feeling which was instantaneously aflame in his breast.

'So that's how it is,' he commented; 'and you, I fancy, only yesterday imagined he loved Katerina Sergyevna as a brother. What are you intending to do now?'

'What do you advise me?' asked Anna Sergyevna, still laughing.

'Well, I suppose,' answered Bazarov, also with a laugh, though he felt anything but cheerful, and had no more inclination to laugh than she had, 'I suppose you ought to give the young people your blessing. It's a good match in every respect; Kirsanov's position is passable, he's the only son, and his father's a good-natured fellow, he won't try to thwart him.'

Madame Odintsov walked up and down the room. By turns her face flushed and grew pale. 'You think so,' she said. 'Well, I see no obstacles . . . I am glad for Katya . . . and for Arkady Nikolaevitch too. Of course, I will wait for his father's answer. I will send him in person to him. But it turns out, you see, that I was right yesterday when I told you we were both old people. . . . How was it I saw nothing? That's what amazes me!' Anna Sergyevna laughed again, and quickly turned her head away.

'The younger generation have grown awfully sly,' remarked Bazarov, and he too laughed. 'Good-bye,' he began again after a short silence. 'I hope you will bring the matter to the most satisfactory conclusion; and I will rejoice from a distance.'

Madame Odintsov turned quickly to him. 'You are not going away? Why should you not stay *now?* Stay . . . it's exciting talking to you . . . one seems walking on the edge of a precipice. At first one feels timid, but one gains courage as one goes on. Do stay.'

'Thanks for the suggestion, Anna Sergyevna, and for your flattering opinion of my conversational talents. But I think I have already been moving too long in a sphere which is not my own. Flying fishes can hold out for a time in the air, but soon they must splash back into the water; allow me, too, to paddle in my own element.'

Madame Odintsov looked at Bazarov. His pale face was twitching with a bitter smile. 'This man did love me!' she thought, and she felt pity for him, and held out her hand to him with sympathy.

But he too understood her. 'No!' he said, stepping back a pace. 'I'm a poor man, but I've never taken charity so far. Good-bye, and good luck to you.'

'I am certain we are not seeing each other for the last time,' Anna Sergyevna declared with an unconscious gesture.

'Anything may happen!' answered Bazarov, and he bowed and went away.

'So you are thinking of making yourself a nest?' he said

the same day to Arkady, as he packed his box, crouching on the floor. 'Well, it's a capital thing. But you needn't have been such a humbug. I expected something from you in quite another quarter. Perhaps, though, it took you by surprise yourself?'

'I certainly didn't expect this when I parted from you,' answered Arkady; 'but why are you a humbug yourself, calling it "a capital thing", as though I didn't know your opinion of marriage.'

'Ah, my dear fellow,' said Bazarov, 'how you talk! You see what I'm doing; there seems to be an empty space in the box, and I am putting hay in; that's how it is in the box of our life; we would stuff it up with anything rather than have a void. Don't be offended, please; you remember, no doubt, the opinion I have always had of Katerina Sergyevna. Many a young lady's called clever simply because she can sigh cleverly; but yours can hold her own, and, indeed, she'll hold it so well that she'll have you under her thumb—to be sure, though, that's quite as it ought to be.' He slammed the lid to, and got up from the floor. 'And now, I say again, good-bye, for it's useless to deceive ourselves—we are parting for good, and you know that yourself . . . you have acted sensibly; you're not made for our bitter, rough, lonely existence. There's no dash, no hate in you, but you've the daring of youth and the fire of youth. Your sort, you gentry, can never get beyond refined submission or refined indignation, and that's no good. You won't fight—and yet you fancy yourselves gallant chaps— but we mean to fight. Oh well! Our dust would get into your eyes, our mud would bespatter you, but yet you're not up to our level, you're admiring yourselves unconsciously, you like to abuse yourselves; but we're sick of that—we want something else! we want to smash other people! You're a capital fellow; but you're a sugary, liberal snob for all that— *ay volla-too,* as my parent is fond of saying.'

'You are parting from me for ever, Yevgeny,' responded Arkady mournfully; 'and have you nothing else to say to me?'

Bazarov scratched the back of his head. 'Yes, Arkady, yes, I have other things to say to you, but I'm not going to say them, because that's sentimentalism—that means, mawkishness. And you get married as soon as you can; and build your nest, and get children to your heart's content. They'll have the wit to be born in a better time than you and me. Aha! I see the horses are ready. Time's up! I've said good-bye to everyone. . . . What now? embracing, eh?'

Arkady flung himself on the neck of his former leader and friend, and the tears fairly gushed from his eyes.

'That's what comes of being young!' Bazarov commented calmly. 'But I rest my hopes on Katerina Sergyevna. You'll see how quickly she'll console you! Good-bye, brother!' he said to Arkady when he had got into the light cart, and, pointing to a pair of jackdaws sitting side by side on the stable roof, he added, 'That's for you! follow that example.'

'What does that mean?' asked Arkady.

'What? Are you so weak in natural history, or have you forgotten that the jackdaw is a most respectable family bird? An example to you! . . . Good-bye!'

The cart creaked and rolled away.

Bazarov had spoken truly. In talking that evening with Katya, Arkady completely forgot about his former teacher. He already began to follow her lead, and Katya was conscious of this, and not surprised at it. He was to set off the next day for Maryino, to see Nikolai Petrovitch. Anna Sergyevna was not disposed to put any constraint on the young people, and only on account of the proprieties did not leave them by themselves for too long together. She magnanimously kept the princess out of their way; the latter had been reduced to a state of tearful frenzy by the news of the proposed marriage. At first Anna Sergyevna was afraid the sight of their happiness might prove rather trying to herself, but it turned out quite the other way; this sight not only did not distress her, it interested her, it even softened her at last. Anna Sergyevna felt both glad and sorry at this. 'It is clear that Bazarov was right,' she thought; 'it has been curiosity, nothing but curiosity, and love of ease, and egoism . . .'

'Children,' she said aloud, 'what do you say, is love a purely imaginary feeling?'

But neither Katya nor Arkady even understood her. They were shy with her; the fragment of conversation they had involuntarily overheard haunted their minds. But Anna Sergyevna soon set their minds at rest; and it was not difficult for her—she had set her own mind at rest.

# 27

BAZAROV'S old parents were all the more overjoyed at their son's arrival, as it was quite unexpected. Arina Vlasyevna was greatly excited, and kept running backwards and forwards in the house, so that Vassily Ivanovitch compared her to a 'hen partridge'; the short tail of her abbreviated jacket did, in fact, give her something of a bird-like appearance. He himself merely growled and gnawed the amber mouthpiece of his pipe, or, clutching his neck with his fingers, turned his head round, as though he were trying whether it were properly screwed on, then all at once he opened his wide mouth and went off into a perfectly noiseless chuckle.

'I've come to you for six whole weeks, governor,' Bazarov said to him. 'I want to work, so please don't hinder me now.'

'You shall forget my face completely, if you call that hindering you!' answered Vassily Ivanovitch.

He kept his promise. After installing his son as before in his study, he almost hid himself away from him, and he kept his wife from all superfluous demonstrations of tenderness. 'On Enyusha's first visit, my dear soul,' he said to her, 'we bothered him a little; we must be wiser this time.' Arina Vlasyevna agreed with her husband, but that was small com-

pensation since she saw her son only at meals, and was now
absolutely afraid to address him. 'Enyushenka,' she would say
sometimes—and before he had time to look round, she was
nervously fingering the tassels of her reticule and faltering,
'Never mind, never mind, I only——' and afterwards she
would go to Vassily Ivanovitch and, her cheek in her hand,
would consult him: 'If you could only find out, darling, which
Enyusha would like for dinner to-day—cabbage-broth or beetroot-soup?'—'But why didn't you ask him yourself?'—'Oh,
he will get sick of me!' Bazarov, however, soon ceased to
shut himself up; the fever of work fell away, and was replaced
by dreary boredom or vague restlessness. A strange weariness
began to show itself in all his movements; even his walk,
firm, bold and strenuous, was changed. He gave up walking
in solitude, and began to seek society; he drank tea in the
drawing-room, strolled about the kitchen-garden with Vassily
Ivanovitch, and smoked with him in silence; once even asked
after Father Alexey. Vassily Ivanovitch at first rejoiced at
this change, but his joy was not long-lived. 'Enyusha's breaking my heart,' he complained in secret to his wife: 'it's not
that he's discontented or angry—that would be nothing; he's
sad, he's sorrowful—that's what's so terrible. He's always
silent. If he'd only abuse us; he's growing thin, he's lost his
colour.'—'Mercy on us, mercy on us!' whispered the old
woman; 'I would put an amulet on his neck, but, of course,
he won't allow it.' Vassily Ivanovitch several times attempted
in the most circumspect manner to question Bazarov about his
work, about his health, and about Arkady. . . . But
Bazarov's replies were reluctant and casual; and, once
noticing that his father was trying gradually to lead up to
something in conversation, he said to him in a tone of vexation: 'Why do you always seem to be walking round me on
tiptoe? That way's worse than the old one.'—'There, there,
I meant nothing!' poor Vassily Ivanovitch answered hurriedly.
So his diplomatic hints remained fruitless. He hoped to
awaken his son's sympathy one day by beginning, *à propos* of
the approaching emancipation of the peasantry, to talk about

progress; but the latter responded indifferently: 'Yesterday I was walking under the fence, and I heard the peasant boys here, instead of some old ballad, bawling a street song. That's what progress is.'

Sometimes Bazarov went into the village and in his usual bantering tone entered into conversation with some peasant: 'Come,' he would say to him, 'expound your views on life to me, brother; you see, they say all the strength and future of Russia lies in your hands, a new epoch in history will be started by you—you give us our real language and our laws.'

The peasant either made no reply, or articulated a few words of this sort: 'Well, we'll try . . . because, you see, to be sure. . . .'

'You explain to me what your *mir* is,' Bazarov interrupted; 'and is it the same *mir* that is said to rest on three fishes?'

'That, little father, is the earth that rests on three fishes,' the peasant would declare soothingly, in a kind of patriarchal, simple-hearted sing-song; 'and over against ours, that's to say, the *mir*, we know there's the master's will; wherefore you are our fathers. And the stricter the master's rule, the better for the peasant.'

After listening to such a reply one day, Bazarov shrugged his shoulders contemptuously and turned away, while the peasant sauntered slowly homewards.

'What was he talking about?' inquired another peasant of middle age and surly aspect, who at a distance from the door of his hut had been following his conversation with Bazarov.— 'Arrears, eh?'

'Arrears, no indeed, mate!' answered the first peasant, and now there was no trace of patriarchal sing-song in his voice; on the contrary, there was a certain scornful gruffness to be heard in it: 'Oh, he clacked away about something or other; wanted to stretch his tongue a bit. Of course, he's a gentleman; what does he understand?'

'What should he understand!' answered the other peasant, and jerking back their caps and pushing down their belts, they proceeded to deliberate upon their work and their wants.

Alas! Bazarov, shrugging his shoulders contemptuously, Bazarov, who knew how to talk to peasants (as he had boasted in his dispute with Pavel Petrovitch), did not in his self-confidence even suspect that in their eyes he was all the while something of the nature of a buffooning clown.

He found employment for himself at last, however. One day Vassily Ivanovitch bound up a peasant's wounded leg before him, but the old man's hands trembled, and he could not manage the bandages; his son helped him, and from time to time began to take a share in his practice, though at the same time he was constantly sneering both at the remedies he himself advised and at his father, who hastened to make use of them. But Bazarov's jeers did not in the least perturb Vassily Ivanovitch; they were positively a comfort to him. Holding his greasy dressing-gown across his stomach with two fingers, and smoking his pipe, he used to listen with enjoyment to Bazarov; and the more malicious his sallies, the more good-humouredly did his delighted father chuckle, showing every one of his black teeth. He used even to repeat these sometimes flat or pointless retorts, and would, for instance, for several days constantly without rhyme or reason reiterate, 'Not a matter of the first importance!' simply because his son, on hearing he was going to matins, had made use of that expression. 'Thank God! he has got over his melancholy!' he whispered to his wife; 'how he gave it to me to-day, it was splendid!' Moreover, the idea of having such an assistant excited him to ecstasy, filled him with pride. 'Yes, yes,' he would say to some peasant woman in a man's cloak and a cap shaped like a horn, as he handed her a bottle of Goulard's extract or a box of white ointment, 'you ought to be thanking God, my good woman, every minute that my son is staying with me; you will be treated now by the most scientific, most modern method. Do you know what that means? The Emperor of the French, Napoleon, even, has no better doctor.' And the peasant woman, who had come to complain that she felt so sort of queer all over (the exact meaning of these words she was not able, however, herself to explain), merely bowed low and rummaged in her bosom, where four eggs lay tied up in the corner of a towel.

Bazarov once even pulled out a tooth for a passing pedlar of cloth; and though this tooth was an average specimen, Vassily Ivanovitch preserved it as a curiosity, and incessantly repeated, as he showed it to Father Alexey, 'Just look, what a fang! The force Yevgeny has! The pedlar seemed to leap into the air. If it had been an oak, he'd have rooted it up!'

'Most promising!' Father Alexey would comment at last, not knowing what answer to make, and how to get rid of the ecstatic old man.

One day a peasant from a neighbouring village brought his brother to Vassily Ivanovitch, ill with typhus. The unhappy man, lying flat on a truss of straw, was dying; his body was covered with dark patches, he had long ago lost consciousness. Vassily Ivanovitch expressed his regret that no one had taken steps to procure medical aid sooner, and declared there was no hope. And, in fact, the peasant did not get his brother home again; he died in the cart.

Three days later Bazarov came into his father's room and asked him if he had any caustic.

'Yes; what do you want it for?'

'I must have some . . . to burn a cut.'

'For whom?'

'For myself.'

'What, yourself? Why is that? What sort of a cut? Where is it?'

'Look here, on my finger. I went to-day to the village, you know, where they brought that peasant with typhus fever. They were just going to open the body for some reason or other, and I've had no practice of that sort for a long while.'

'Well?'

'Well, so I asked the district doctor about it; and so I dissected it.'

Vassily Ivanovitch all at once turned quite white, and, without uttering a word, rushed to his study, from which he returned at once with a bit of caustic in his hand. Bazarov was about to take it and go away.

'For mercy's sake,' said Vassily Ivanovitch, 'let me do it myself.'

Bazarov smiled. 'What a devoted practitioner!'

'Don't laugh, please. Show me your finger. The cut is not a large one. Do I hurt?'

'Press harder; don't be afraid.'

Vassily Ivanovitch stopped. 'What do you think, Yevgeny; wouldn't it be better to burn it with hot iron?'

'That ought to have been done sooner; the caustic even is useless, really, now. If I've taken the infection, it's too late now.'

'How . . . too late . . .' Vassily Ivanovitch could scarcely articulate the words.

'I should think so! It's more than four hours ago.'

Vassily Ivanovitch burnt the cut a little more. 'But had the district doctor no caustic?'

'No.'

'How was that, good Heavens? A doctor not have such an indispensable thing as that!'

'You should have seen his lancets,' observed Bazarov as he walked away.

Up till late that evening, and all the following day, Vassily Ivanovitch kept catching at every possible excuse to go into his son's room; and though far from referring to the cut—he even tried to talk about the most irrelevant subjects—he looked so persistently into his face, and watched him in such trepidation, that Bazarov lost patience and threatened to go away. Vassily Ivanovitch gave him a promise not to bother him, the more readily as Arina Vlasyevna, from whom, of course, he kept it all secret, was beginning to worry him as to why he did not sleep, and what had come over him. For two whole days he held himself in, though he did not at all like the look of his son, whom he kept watching stealthily . . . but on the third day, at dinner, he could bear it no longer. Bazarov sat with downcast looks, and had not touched a single dish.

'Why don't you eat, Yevgeny?' he inquired, putting on an expression of the most perfect carelessness. 'The food, I think, is very nicely cooked.'

'I don't want anything, so I don't eat.'

'Have you no appetite? And your head?' he added timidly; 'does it ache?'

'Yes. Of course it aches.'

Arina Vlasyevna sat up and was all alert.

'Don't be angry, please, Yevgeny,' continued Vassily Ivanovitch; 'won't you let me feel your pulse?'

Bazarov got up. 'I can tell you without feeling my pulse; I'm feverish.'

'Has there been any shivering?'

'Yes, there has been shivering too. I'll go and lie down, and you can send me some lime-flower tea. I must have caught cold.'

'To be sure, I heard you coughing last night,' observed Arina Vlasyevna.

'I've caught cold,' repeated Bazarov, and he went away.

Arina Vlasyevna busied herself about the preparation of the decoction of lime flowers, while Vassily Ivanovitch went into the next room and clutched at his hair in silent desperation.

Bazarov did not get up again that day, and passed the whole night in heavy, half-unconscious torpor. At one o'clock in the morning, opening his eyes with an effort, he saw by the light of a lamp his father's pale face bending over him, and told him to go away. The old man begged his pardon, but he quickly came back on tiptoe, and half-hidden by the cupboard door, he gazed persistently at his son. Arina Vlasyevna did not go to bed either, and leaving the study door just open a very little, she kept coming up to it to listen 'how Enyusha was breathing,' and to look at Vassily Ivanovitch. She could see nothing but his motionless bent back, but even that afforded her some faint consolation. In the morning Bazarov tried to get up; he was seized with giddiness, his nose began to bleed; he lay down again. Vassily

Ivanovitch waited on him in silence; Arina Vlasyevna went in to him and asked him how he was feeling. He answered, 'Better,' and turned to the wall. Vassily Ivanovitch gesticulated at his wife with both hands; she bit her lips so as not to cry, and went away. The whole house seemed suddenly darkened; everyone looked gloomy; there was a strange hush; a shrill cock was carried away from the yard to the village, unable to comprehend why he should be treated so. Bazarov still lay, turned to the wall. Vassily Ivanovitch tried to address him with various questions, but they fatigued Bazarov, and the old man sank into his arm-chair, motionless, only cracking his finger-joints now and then. He went for a few minutes into the garden, stood there like a statue, as though overwhelmed with unutterable bewilderment (the expression of amazement never left his face all through), and went back again to his son, trying to avoid his wife's questions. She caught him by the arm at last, and passionately, almost menacingly, said, 'What is wrong with him?' Then he came to himself, and forced himself to smile at her in reply; but to his own horror, instead of a smile, he found himself taken somehow by a fit of laughter. He had sent at daybreak for a doctor. He thought it necessary to inform his son of this, for fear he should be angry. Bazarov suddenly turned over on the sofa, bent a fixed dull look on his father, and asked for a drink.

Vassily Ivanovitch gave him some water, and as he did so felt his forehead. It seemed on fire.

'Governor,' began Bazarov, in a slow, drowsy voice; 'I'm in a bad way; I've got the infection, and in a few days you'll have to bury me.'

Vassily Ivanovitch staggered back, as though someone had aimed a blow at his legs.

'Yevgeny!' he faltered; 'what do you mean! . . . God have mercy on you! You've caught cold!'

'Hush!' Bazarov interposed deliberately. 'A doctor can't be allowed to talk like that. There's every symptom of infection; you know yourself.'

'Where are the symptoms . . . of infection, Yevgeny? . . . Good Heavens!'

'What's this?' said Bazarov, and, pulling up his shirt-sleeve, he showed his father the ominous red patches coming out on his arm.

Vassily Ivanovitch was shaking and chill with terror.

'Supposing,' he said at last, 'even supposing . . . if even there's something like . . . infection . . .'

'Pyæmia,' put in his son.

'Well, well . . . something of the epidemic . . .'

'Pyæmia,' Bazarov repeated sharply and distinctly; 'have you forgotten your text-books?'

'Well, well—as you like. . . . Anyway, we will cure you!'

'Come, that's humbug. But that's not the point. I didn't expect to die so soon; it's a most unpleasant incident, to tell the truth. You and mother ought to make the most of your strong religious belief; now's the time to put it to the test.' He drank off a little water. 'I want to ask you about one thing . . . while my head is still under my control. To-morrow or next day my brain, you know, will send in its resignation. I'm not quite certain even now whether I'm expressing myself clearly. While I've been lying here, I've kept fancying red dogs were running round me, while you were making them point at me, as if I were a woodcock. Just as if I were drunk. Do you understand me all right?'

'I assure you, Yevgeny, you are talking perfectly correctly.'

'All the better. You told me you'd sent for the doctor. You did that to comfort yourself . . . comfort me too; send a messenger . . .'

'To Arkady Nikolaitch?' put in the old man.

'Who's Arkady Nikolaitch?' said Bazarov, as though in doubt. . . . 'Oh, yes! that chicken! No, let him alone; he's turned jackdaw now. Don't be surprised; that's not delirium yet. You send a messenger to Madame Odintsov, Anna Sergyevna; she's a lady with an estate. . . . Do you know?' (Vassily Ivanovitch nodded.) 'Yevgeny Bazarov, say, sends his greetings, and sends word he is dying. Will you do that?'

'Yes, I will do it. . . . But is it a possible thing for you to die, Yevgeny? . . . Think only! Where would divine justice be after that?'

'I know nothing about that; only you send the messenger.'

'I'll send this minute, and I'll write a letter myself.'

'No, why? Say I sent greetings; nothing more is necessary. And now I'll go back to my dogs. Strange! I want to fix my thoughts on death, and nothing comes of it. I see a kind of blur . . . and nothing more.'

He turned painfully back to the wall again; while Vassily Ivanovitch went out of the study, and struggling as far as his wife's bedroom, simply dropped down on to his knees before the holy pictures.

'Pray, Arina, pray for us!' he moaned; 'our son is dying.'

The doctor, the same district doctor who had had no caustic, arrived, and after looking at the patient, advised them to persevere with a cooling treatment, and at that point said a few words of the chance of recovery.

'Have you ever chanced to see people in my state *not* set off for Elysium?' asked Bazarov, and suddenly snatching the leg of a heavy table that stood near his sofa, he swung it round, and pushed it away. 'There's strength, there's strength,' he murmured; 'everything's here still, and I must die! . . . An old man at least has time to be weaned from life, but I . . . Well, go and try to disprove death. Death will disprove you, and that's all! Who's crying there?' he added, after a short pause.—'Mother? Poor thing! Whom will she feed now with her exquisite beetroot-soup? You, Vassily Ivanovitch, whimpering too, I do believe! Why, if Christianity's no help to you, be a philosopher, a Stoic, or what not! Why, didn't you boast you were a philosopher?'

'Me a philosopher!' wailed Vassily Ivanovitch, while the tears fairly streamed down his cheeks.

Bazarov got worse every hour; the progress of the disease was rapid, as is usually the way in cases of surgical poisoning. He still had not lost consciousness, and understood what was said to him; he was still struggling. 'I don't want to lose my wits,' he muttered, clenching his fists; 'what rot it all is!' And at once he would say, 'Come, take ten from eight, what remains?' Vassily Ivanovitch wandered about like one possessed, proposed first one remedy, then another, and ended by doing nothing but cover up his son's feet. 'Try cold pack . . . emetic . . . mustard plasters on the stomach . . . bleeding,' he would murmur with an effort. The doctor, whom he had entreated to remain, agreed with him, ordered the patient lemonade to drink, and for himself asked for a pipe and something 'warming and strengthening'—that's to say, brandy. Arina Vlasyevna sat on a low stool near the door, and only went out from time to time to pray. A few days before, a looking-glass had slipped out of her hands and been broken, and this she had always considered an omen of evil; even Anfisushka could say nothing to her. Timofeitch had gone off to Madame Odintsov's.

The night passed badly for Bazarov. . . . He was in the agonies of high fever. Toward morning he was a little easier. He asked for Arina Vlasyevna to comb his hair, kissed her hand, and swallowed two gulps of tea. Vassily Ivanovitch revived a little.

'Thank God!' he kept declaring; 'the crisis is coming, the crisis is at hand!'

'There, to think now!' murmured Bazarov; 'what a word can do! He's found it; he's said "crisis", and is comforted. It's an astounding thing how man believes in words. If he's told he's a fool, for instance, though he's not thrashed, he'll be wretched; call him a clever fellow, and he'll be delighted if you go off without paying him.'

This little speech of Bazarov's, recalling his old retorts, moved Vassily Ivanovitch greatly.

'Bravo! well said, very good!' he cried, making as though he were clapping his hands.

Bazarov smiled mournfully.

'So what do you think,' he said; 'is the crisis over, or coming?'

'You are better, that's what I see, that's what rejoices me,' answered Vassily Ivanovitch.

'Well, that's good; rejoicings never come amiss. And to her, do you remember? did you send?'

'To be sure, I did.'

The change for the better did not last long. The disease resumed its onslaughts. Vassily Ivanovitch was sitting by Bazarov. It seemed as though the old man were tormented by some special anguish. He was several times on the point of speaking—and could not.

'Yevgeny!' he brought out at last; 'my son, my one, dear son!'

This unfamiliar mode of address produced an effect on Bazarov. He turned his head a little and, obviously trying to fight against the load of oblivion weighing upon him, he articulated: 'What is it, father?'

'Yevgeny,' Vassily Ivanovitch went on, and he fell on his knees before Bazarov, though the latter had closed his eyes and could not see him. 'Yevgeny, you are better now; please God, you will get well, but make use of this time, comfort your mother and me, perform the duty of a Christian! What it means for me to say this to you, it's awful . . . for ever and ever, Yevgeny . . . think a little, what . . .'

The old man's voice broke, and a strange look passed over his son's face, though he still lay with closed eyes.

'I won't refuse, if that can be any comfort to you,' he brought out at last; 'but it seems to me there's no need to be in a hurry. You say yourself I am better.'

'Oh, yes, Yevgeny, better certainly; but who knows, it is all in God's hands, and in doing the duty . . .'

'No, I will wait a bit,' broke in Bazarov. 'I agree with you that the crisis has come. And if we're mistaken, well! they give the sacrament to men who're unconscious, you know.'

'Yevgeny, I beg.'

'I'll wait a little. And now I want to go to sleep. Don't disturb me.' And he laid his head back on the pillow.

The old man rose from his knees, sat down in the arm-chair, and, clutching his beard, began biting his own fingers . . .

The sound of a light carriage on springs, that sound which is peculiarly impressive in the wilds of the country, suddenly struck upon his hearing. Nearer and nearer rolled the light wheels; now even the neighing of the horses could be heard. . . . Vassily Ivanovitch jumped up and ran to the little window. There drove into the courtyard of his little house a carriage with seats for two, with four horses harnessed abreast. Without stopping to consider what it could mean, with a rush of a sort of senseless joy, he ran out on to the steps. . . . A groom in livery was opening the carriage doors; a lady in a black veil and a black mantle was getting out of it. . . .

'I am Madame Odintsov,' she said. 'Yevgeny Vassilyitch is still living? You are his father? I have a doctor with me.'

'Benefactress!' cried Vassily Ivanovitch, and snatching her hand, he pressed it convulsively to his lips, while the doctor brought by Anna Sergyevna, a little man in spectacles, of German physiognomy, stepped very deliberately out of the carriage. 'Still living, my Yevgeny is living, and now he will be saved! Wife! wife! . . . An angel from heaven has come to us. . . .'

'What does it mean, good Lord!' faltered the old woman, running out of the drawing-room; and, comprehending nothing, she fell on the spot in the passage at Anna Sergyevna's feet, and began kissing her garments like a mad woman.

'What are you doing!' protested Anna Sergyevna; but Arina Vlasyevna did not heed her, while Vassily Ivanovitch could only repeat, 'An angel! an angel!'

'*Wo ist der Kranke?* and where is the patient?' said the doctor at last, with some impatience.

Vassily Ivanovitch recovered himself. 'Here, here, follow me, würdigster Herr Collega,' he added through old associations.

'Ah!' articulated the German, grinning sourly.

Vassily Ivanovitch led him into the study. 'The doctor from

Anna Sergyevna Odintsov,' he said, bending down quite to his son's ear, 'and she herself is here.'

Bazarov suddenly opened his eyes. 'What did you say?'

'I say that Anna Sergyevna is here, and has brought this gentleman, a doctor, to you.'

Bazarov moved his eyes about him. 'She is here. . . . I want to see her.'

'You shall see her, Yevgeny; but first we must have a little talk with the doctor. I will tell him the whole history of your illness since Sidor Sidoritch' (this was the name of the district doctor) 'has gone, and we will have a little consultation.'

Bazarov glanced at the German. 'Well, talk away quickly, only not in Latin; you see, I know the meaning of *jam moritur*.'

'*Der Herr scheint des Deutschen mächtig zu sein*,' began the new follower of Æsculapius, turning to Vassily Ivanovitch.

'*Ich . . . gabe . . .* We had better speak Russian,' said the old man.

'Ah, ah! so that's how it is. . . . To be sure . . .' And the consultation began.

Half an hour later Anna Sergyevna, conducted by Vassily Ivanovitch, came into the study. The doctor had had time to whisper to her that it was hopeless even to think of the patient's recovery.

She looked at Bazarov . . . and stood still in the doorway, so greatly was she impressed by the inflamed, and at the same time deathly face, with its dim eyes fastened upon her. She felt simply dismayed, with a sort of cold and suffocating dismay; the thought that she would not have felt like that if she had really loved him flashed instantaneously through her brain.

'Thanks,' he said painfully, 'I did not expect this. It's a deed of mercy. So we have seen each other again, as you promised.'

'Anna Sergyevna has been so kind,' began Vassily Ivanovitch . . .

'Father, leave us alone. Anna Sergyevna, you will allow it, I fancy, now?'

With a motion of his head, he indicated his prostrate, helpless frame.

Vassily Ivanovitch went out.

'Well, thanks,' repeated Bazarov. 'This is royally done. Monarchs, they say, visit the dying too.'

'Yevgeny Vassilyitch, I hope——'

'Ah, Anna Sergyevna, let us speak the truth. It's all over with me. I'm under the wheel. So it turns out that it was useless to think of the future. Death's an old joke, but it comes fresh to everyone. So far I'm not afraid . . . but there, senselessness is coming, and then it's all up!——' he waved his hand feebly. 'Well, what had I to say to you . . . I loved you! there was no sense in that even before, and less than ever now. Love is a form, and my own form is already breaking up. Better say how lovely you are! And now here you stand, so beautiful . . .'

Anna Sergyevna gave an involuntary shudder.

'Never mind, don't be uneasy. . . . Sit down there. . . . Don't come close to me; you know, my illness is catching.'

Anna Sergyevna swiftly crossed the room, and sat down in the armchair near the sofa on which Bazarov was lying.

'Noble-hearted!' he whispered. 'Oh, how near, and how young, and fresh, and pure . . . in this loathsome room! . . . Well, good-bye! live long, that's the best of all, and make the most of it while there is time. You see what a hideous spectacle; the worm half-crushed, but writhing still. And, you see, I thought too: I'd break down so many things, I wouldn't die, why should I! there were problems to solve, and I was a giant! And now all the problem for the giant is how to die decently, though that makes no difference to anyone either. . . . Never mind; I'm not going to turn tail.'

Bazarov was silent, and began feeling with his hand for the glass. Anna Sergyevna gave him some drink, not taking off her glove, and drawing her breath timorously.

'You will forget me,' he began again; 'the dead's no com-

207

panion for the living. My father will tell you what a man
Russia is losing. . . . That's nonsense, but don't contradict
the old man. Whatever toy will comfort the child . . . you
know. And be kind to mother. People like them aren't to
be found in your great world, if you look by daylight with a
candle. . . . I was needed by Russia. . . . No, it's clear, I
wasn't needed. And who is needed? The shoemaker's needed,
the tailor's needed, the butcher . . . gives us meat . . . the
butcher . . . wait, a little, I'm getting mixed. . . . There's
a forest here . . .'

Bazarov put his hand to his brow.

Anna Sergyevna bent down to him. 'Yevgeny Vassilyitch,
I am here . . .'

He at once took his hand away, and raised himself.

'Good-bye,' he said with sudden force, and his eyes gleamed
with their last light. 'Good-bye. . . . Listen . . . you know
I didn't kiss you then. . . . Breathe on the dying lamp, and
let it go out. . . .'

Anna Sergyevna put her lips to his forehead.

'Enough!' he murmured, and dropped back on to the pillow.
'Now . . . darkness . . .'

Anna Sergyevna went softly out. 'Well?' Vassily Ivanovitch
asked her in a whisper.

'He has fallen asleep,' she answered, hardly audibly.
Bazarov was not fated to awaken. Towards evening he sank
into complete unconsciousness, and the following day he died.
Father Alexey performed the last rites of religion over him.
When they anointed him with the last unction, when the holy
oil touched his breast, one eye opened, and it seemed as
though at the sight of the priest in his vestments, the smoking
censers, the light before the image, something like a shudder
of horror passed over the death-stricken face. When at last
he had breathed his last, and there arose a universal lamenta-
tion in the house, Vassily Ivanovitch was seized by a sudden
frenzy. 'I said I should rebel,' he shrieked hoarsely, with his
face inflamed and distorted, shaking his fist in the air, as
though threatening someone; 'and I rebel, I rebel!' But Arina

Vlasyevna, all in tears, hung upon his neck, and both fell on their faces together. 'Side by side,' Anfisushka related afterwards in the servants' room, 'they drooped their poor heads like lambs at noonday . . .'

But the heat of noonday passes, and evening comes and night, and then, too, the return to the kindly refuge, where sleep is sweet for the weary and heavy laden. . . .

# 28

SIX months had passed by. White winter had come with the cruel stillness of unclouded frosts, the thick-lying, crunching snow, the rosy rime on the trees, the pale emerald sky, the wreaths of smoke above the chimneys, the clouds of steam rushing out of the doors when they are opened for an instant, with the fresh faces, that look stung by the cold, and the hurrying trot of the chilled horses. A January day was drawing to its close; the cold of evening was more keen than ever in the motionless air, and a lurid sunset was rapidly dying away. There were lights burning in the windows of the house at Maryino; Prokofitch in a black frock-coat and white gloves, with a special solemnity, laid the table for seven. A week before in the small parish church two weddings had taken place quietly, and almost without witnesses—Arkady and Katya's, and Nikolai Petrovitch and Fenitchka's; and on this day Nikolai Petrovitch was giving a farewell dinner to his brother, who was going away to Moscow on business. Anna Sergyevna had gone there also directly after the ceremony was over, after making very handsome presents to the young people.

Precisely at three o'clock they all gathered about the table. Mitya was placed there too; with him appeared a nurse in a cap of glazed brocade. Pavel Petrovitch took his seat between Katya and Fenitchka; the 'husbands' took their places beside their wives. Our friends had changed of late; they all seemed to have grown stronger and better-looking; only Pavel Petrovitch was thinner, which gave even more of an elegant and 'grand seigneur' air to his expressive features. . . . And Fenitchka too was different. In a fresh silk gown, with a wide velvet head-dress on her hair, with a gold chain round her neck, she sat with deprecating immobility, respectful towards herself and everything surrounding her, and smiled as though she would say, 'I beg your pardon; I'm not to blame.' And not she alone—all the others smiled, and also seemed apologetic; they were all a little awkward, a little sorry, and in reality very happy. They all helped one another with humorous attentiveness, as though they had all agreed to rehearse a sort of artless farce. Katya was the most composed of all; she looked confidently about her, and it could be seen that Nikolai Petrovitch was already devotedly fond of her. At the end of dinner he got up, and, his glass in his hand, turned to Pavel Petrovitch.

'You are leaving us . . . you are leaving us, dear brother,' he began; 'not for long, to be sure; but still, I cannot help expressing what I . . . what we . . . how much I . . . how much we . . . There, the worst of it is, we don't know how to make speeches. Arkady, you speak.'

'No, daddy, I've not prepared anything.'

'As though I were so well prepared! Well, brother, I will simply say, let us embrace you, wish you all good luck, and come back to us as quick as you can!'

Pavel Petrovitch exchanged kisses with everyone, of course not excluding Mitya; in Fenitchka's case, he kissed also her hand, which she had not yet learned to offer properly, and drinking off the glass which had been filled again, he said with a deep sigh, 'May you be happy, my friends! *Farewell!*' This English finale passed unnoticed; but all were touched.

'To the memory of Bazarov,' Katya whispered in her husband's ear, as she clinked glasses with him. Arkady pressed her hand warmly in response, but he did not venture to propose this toast aloud.

The end, would it seem? But perhaps some one of our readers would care to know what each of the characters we have introduced is doing in the present, the actual present. We are ready to satisfy him.

Anna Sergyevna has recently made a marriage, not of love but of good sense, with one of the future leaders of Russia, a very clever man, a lawyer, possessed of vigorous practical sense, a strong will, and remarkable fluency—still young, good-natured, and cold as ice. They live in the greatest harmony together, and will live perhaps to attain complete happiness . . . perhaps love. The Princess K—— is dead, forgotten the day of her death. The Kirsanovs, father and son, live at Maryino; their fortunes are beginning to mend. Arkady has become zealous in the management of the estate, and the 'farm' now yields a fairly good income. Nikolai Petrovitch has been made one of the mediators appointed to carry out the emancipation reforms, and works with all his energies; he is for ever driving about over his district; delivers long speeches (he maintains the opinion that the peasants ought to be 'brought to comprehend things,' that is to say, they ought to be reduced to a state of quiescence by the constant repetition of the same words); and yet, to tell the truth, he does not give complete satisfaction either to the refined gentry, who talk with *chic* or depression of the *emancipation* (pronouncing it as though it were French), nor to the uncultivated gentry, who unceremoniously curse 'the damned *'mancipation.'* He is too soft-hearted for both sets. Katerina Sergyevna has a son, little Nikolai, while Mitya runs about merrily and talks fluently. Fenitchka, Fedosya Nikolaevna, after her husband and Mitya, adores no one so much as her daughter-in-law, and when the latter is at the piano, she would gladly spend the whole day at her side. A passing word of Piotr. He has grown perfectly rigid with stupidity and dignity, but he too is married, and received a respectable dowry with his bride, the daughter of a market-gardener of the town, who had refused two excellent suitors only because they had no watch; while Piotr had not only a watch—he had a pair of kid shoes.

In the Brühl Terrace in Dresden, between two and four o'clock—the most fashionable time for walking—you may meet a man about fifty, quite grey, and looking as though he suffered from gout, but still handsome, elegantly dressed, and with that special stamp which is only gained by moving a long time in the higher strata of society. That is Pavel Petrovitch. From Moscow he went abroad for the sake of his health, and has settled for good at Dresden, where he associates most with English and Russian visitors. With English people he behaves simply, almost modestly, but with dignity; they find him rather a bore, but respect him for being, as they say, 'a perfect gentleman.' With Russians he is more free and easy, gives vent to his spleen, and makes fun of himself and them, but that is done by him with great amiability, negligence, and propriety. He holds Slavophil views; it is well known that in the highest society this is regarded as *très distingué!* He reads nothing in Russian, but on his writing-table there is a silver ash-pan in the shape of a peasant's plaited shoe. He is much run after by our tourists. Matvy Ilyitch Kolyazin, happening to be in temporary opposition, paid him a majestic visit; while the natives, with whom, however, he is very little seen, positively grovel before him. No one can so readily and quickly obtain a ticket for the court chapel, for the theatre, and such things as *der Herr Baron von Kirsanoff.* He does everything good-naturedly that he can; he still makes some little noise in the world; it is not for nothing that he was once a great society lion; but life is a burden to him . . . a heavier burden than he suspects himself. One need but glance at him in the Russian church, when, leaning against the wall on one side, he sinks into thought, and remains long without stirring, bitterly compressing his lips, then suddenly recollects himself, and begins almost imperceptibly crossing himself. . . .

Madame Kukshin, too, went abroad. She is in Heidelberg, and is now studying not natural science, but architecture, in which, according to her own account, she has discovered new laws. She still fraternises with students, especially with the